Change Your Career: Teaching As Your New Profession

Lauren Starkey, M.A.

KAPLAN

PUBLISHING

New York • Chicago

This publication is designed to provide accurate and authoritative information in regard to the subject matter covered. It is sold with the understanding that the publisher is not engaged in rendering legal, accounting, or other professional service. If legal advice or other expert assistance is required, the services of a competent professional should be sought.

Editorial Director: Jennifer Farthing
Project Editor: Cynthia Ierardo
Senior Managing Editor, Production: Jack Kiburz
Production Artist: Joseph Budenholzer
Cover Designer: Carly Schnur

© 2007 by Kaplan, Inc.
Published by Kaplan Publishing,
a division of Kaplan, Inc.
888 Seventh Ave.
New York, NY 10106

"Transferable Skills" (DWSJ-8961-P) from the Wisconsin Job Center Publication, *www.wisconsinjobcenter.org/publications*. Used with permission.

"Educational Technology Standards and Performance Indicators for All Teachers." Reprinted with permission from *National Educational Technology Standards for Teachers: Preparing Teachers to Use Technology*, © 2002, ISTE ® (International Society for Technology in Education), iste@iste.org, *www.iste.org*. All rights reserved.

"Parsippany Hills High 2004-05 School Report Card" reprinted with permission from the New Jersey Department of Education website *http://education.state.nj.us*

"Birchwood Elementary 2004-05 School Report Card" reprinted with permission from the Washington State Office of the Superintendent for Public Instruction, *http://reportcard.ospi.k12.wa.us*

"Average Teacher Salary in 2003-2004, State Rankings" and "Actual Average Beginning Teacher Salaries, 2002-03, Estimated 2004" from Annual Salary & Analysis of Teacher Salary Trends. American Federation of Teachers, Washington, DC 2004. Retrieved July 28, 2006, from *http://www.aft.org/salary/2004/download/2004AFTSalarySurvey.pdf* and *http://www.aft.org/research/downloads/2004beginning.pdf*.

"State Departments of Education" and "Key to Alternative Licensure Programs" reprinted with permission from Recruiting New Teachers, Inc. *http://www.recruitingteachers.org/channels/clearinghouse/*

"Alternative Route Certification" reprinted with permission from The National Comprehensive Center for Teacher Quality, *http://www.tqsource.org*

"Complete State by State List of Accredited Institutions" reprinted with permission from National Council for Accreditation of Teacher Education, *http://www.ncate.org*

Printed in the United States of America

January 2007
10 9 8 7 6 5 4 3 2 1

ISBN 13: 978-1-4195-9152-5
ISBN 10: 1-4195-9152-5

Library of Congress Cataloging-in-Publication Data

Starkey, Lauren B., 1962–
  Change your career : teaching as your new profession / Lauren Starkey
    p. cm.
  Includes index.
  ISBN-13: 978-1-4195-9152-5
  ISBN: 10: 1-4195-9152-5
  1. Teaching—Vocational guidance—United States. I. Title.
  LB1775.2.S73 2006
  371.10023 73
                                          2006031610

Kaplan Publishing books are available at special quantity discounts to use for sales promotions, employee premiums, or educational purposes. Please call our Special Sales Department to order or for more information at 800-621-9621, ext. 4444, e-mail kaplanpubsales@kaplan.com, or write to Kaplan Publishing, 30 South Wacker Drive, Suite 2500, Chicago, IL 60606-7481.

Contents

ABOUT THE AUTHOR

Lauren Starkey, M.A., is the author of more than a dozen books. A freelance writer and editor for the past 15 years, she specializes in educational and reference works. Before beginning her writing career, Lauren worked on the editorial staff of the *Oxford English Dictionary*. She lives in Vermont with her husband and three children.

Why Teaching?

Career changer and student teacher Karen Kirkland remembers, "My teaching origins trace back 40 or so years ago to when my little sister and I were each teachers in our own classrooms (our bedrooms). We had badly behaved students who responded best to 'NOW CLASS!' screeched in our harshest voices, and we diligently dealt out as many Fs as As. I pity our poor students! Thankfully, my desire to teach remained, but with real students my tactics changed."

Perhaps your desire to become an educator has been discovered more recently. But most people who choose to teach make their decision at least in part because of their past—in particular, a teacher who made a strong, positive, lasting impression on them. They want to "give back" to society what that teacher gave to them.

What are some of the other often-cited reasons for choosing a career in the classroom?

- A love for children and the desire to help them reach their potential
- A passion for teaching that fulfills a sense of mission
- A passion for a particular subject and interest in sharing that knowledge
- A desire to put real-life experience to use (lessons learned on the job, as a parent, and in everyday life)
- A background with successful educators (parents, grandparents, siblings)

WHAT'S NEW? WHAT'S NOT?

Much has changed in the field of education since you graduated from high school. Theories of learning and of teaching, the amount of standardized testing, and compliance with the federal No Child Left Behind law have all left their mark in the classroom. There is also more collaboration among teachers, less homogeneous grouping of students, and an increasing need to deal with students with special needs. These changes are explained and discussed at length in the next few chapters.

But much has remained the same—for example, the skills needed to teach successfully (although now, in addition, is the need to use and embrace a variety of technologies). The best teachers are the ones who are passionate about what they do. They are extremely satisfied working with children and making a positive difference in their lives. They're organized and results-oriented, and they form positive relationships with their students, parents, fellow teachers, and administrators. They're willing to continue to learn and grow in their profession. Good teachers themselves haven't changed—they've just stayed flexible enough to embrace the changes around them.

A NATIONAL SHORTAGE

You are considering the profession at an opportune time: the U.S. Bureau of Labor Statistics reports that there will be a shortage of qualified teachers through the next decade, even though overall student enrollments are expected to remain level or rise more slowly than they have in the past. The shortage is primarily due to two factors: the number of teachers who will be retiring and the high turnover rate, especially in urban schools with economically disadvantaged students. In fact, turnover numbers are startling. The U.S. Department of Education reports that one in every five teachers leaves after the first year; that number doubles within the first three years.

The shortage means that job opportunities for teachers range from good to excellent. Location, subject taught, and grade level are the major determining factors. For example, many Western states are experiencing population booms, and their enrollments are growing rapidly. In the Northeast and Midwest, enrollments are projected to be stagnant.

There is an urgent need for teachers in almost every subject and every grade in large urban districts. The seriousness of the shortage has resulted in those districts competing with one another for qualified applicants. Some have developed programs to lure teachers from other states and districts with bonuses and higher pay. They use job fairs and websites to reach thousands of applicants and have simplified the process of applying for and getting employment.

Because of teacher shortages and problems with retention, schools and districts are making it easier for career changers to enter the education field. Almost every state has an alternative route to certification that allows people from other professions who already have a bachelor's degree to get a teaching license without having to go back to school full-time or earn another degree.

SALARIES AND BENEFITS

Another response to the need for qualified educators is an improvement in salaries and other benefits. The National Education Association (NEA), the nation's largest teachers' union, launched a Professional Pay Campaign in 2005 that calls for a $40,000 minimum salary. While compensation hasn't risen across the country, there are many states and districts that are heeding the call. In 2006, every metropolitan district in Texas increased its starting teacher salary to meet or exceed the NEA's minimum.

As many industries do away with pension plans and other nonsalary benefits, school districts continue to offer them. Most teachers have health, life, and disability insurance plans; retirement and other savings programs; pensions; and job security. The tenure system, in which teachers who reach a specified level of experience and/or education receive immunity from firing (except in extreme circumstances), is alive and well.

Another benefit of the teaching profession is the school schedule. Although every teacher we interviewed warned that prospective educators should not make their decision based on the schedule, it is a substantial perk. Time spent out of the school environment can add up to at least three months for most teachers. For those with school-aged children, they enjoy the same vacations, including summers. Some choose to use their breaks to pursue professional development opportunities or work at another job. Others use the time to travel, develop hobbies, or just relax.

Perhaps the most oft-cited benefit, however, is job satisfaction. Teachers affect an average of 3,000 children during their careers. That means 3,000 chances to make a positive difference in students' emotional, intellectual, and social development. An effective teacher not only imparts knowledge of course content, but also builds the self-confidence and enthusiasm that can lead to a lifetime of learning.

IS IT TOO LATE TO CHANGE CAREERS?

More schools are hiring career changers than ever before, due in part to the fact that they've purposely made it easier for those who want to enter the field of education as a second career with the introduction of alternative certification programs. If you're worried that it's too late to change, or that you'll have difficulty finding a job, read on.

The shortage of teachers we've described is one reason you should not be discouraged. If you're interested in teaching math or science, and your previous experience means you are particularly strong in one of those subjects, you're in an even better position. Most career changers who become teachers become licensed in one of those two high-demand subjects.

In addition, the Age Discrimination in Employment Act of 1967 makes it a crime to discriminate against any job seeker who is 40 years of age or older. You have the law on your side when you apply for a teaching position. But there are also some proactive steps you can take to make yourself a more desirable job candidate. The first is to embrace technology, learn as much as you can about its applications in the classroom, and be prepared to use it to its fullest advantage. Second, keep up-to-date with your subject. Even the field of mathematics has changed and continues to change. (Do you know how to use a graphing calculator?) Stay current, and indulge your lifelong curiosity and love for learning. Third, be adaptable. The nation's schools have undergone enormous changes since you were in school, which are described in detail in the next few chapters. Don't be stuck in the "old ways are the best ways" mentality. Understand how education has evolved, and be prepared to join in, in the 21st century. No matter your age or previous experience, the teaching profession can offer you countless benefits, increased job satisfaction, and a sense of purpose and fulfillment not found in most other careers.

PART ONE

Making a Decision

CHAPTER 1

Should You Change Your Career?

If you're contemplating a career change, you're not alone. The average American changes careers between five and seven times during a working lifetime. Some make a change because they must; they might be working in an industry that is downsizing or get laid off due to economic factors and are unable to find similar work in the same field. If you're thinking about changing careers, you have a distinct advantage. You're not forced by outside circumstances to look for employment, which gives you the time and resources to think carefully through such a decision. Do you really want to leave your field? Is the timing right? What profession would you rather be in? These types of questions are best answered thoughtfully, without the pressures of time and finances.

What are the factors that cause most people to want to leave one career for another? Job satisfaction ranks high on the list. Perhaps you've decided you want to do something you love, rather than simply get up every morning and get work over with. Loss of interest is another key factor. When you started in your current position, it may have been exciting, challenging, or both. But now you're bored, and you dream of finding different work that can take you across town, across state lines, or even across the ocean while making a living. A change in circumstances can trigger a career change, too. For example, high-powered executives might find their jobs incompatible with raising a family, and empty nesters might have the financial freedom to move to a lower-paying, but more satisfying, profession.

What are your factors? To determine whether to change careers—and what career to choose—you need to know what's important to you, what your attitude toward your current position is, and where you might see yourself in the future. Self-assessment tools are used widely by career counselors when they begin working with clients. These tests are not meant to provide definitive answers, but rather to get you thinking in new ways and give suggestions worth taking.

DO YOU WANT TO MAKE A CHANGE?

Are you simply bored with your job, or do you dream about more fulfilling work in another field? The first step in deciding to change your career is determining that you have solid reasons for doing so. The following questions will help you think through your current situation and examine why you are contemplating a change.

1. I can honestly say at the end of each workday that I have learned one new skill or item of practical information.
   - Completely agree
   - Mostly agree
   - Somewhat agree
   - Mostly disagree
   - Completely disagree

2. When I picture myself at work five years from now, I have a sense that the intervening years were productive and made me happy.
   - Completely agree
   - Mostly agree
   - Somewhat agree
   - Mostly disagree
   - Completely disagree

3. I am able to make important decisions at work.
   - Completely agree
   - Mostly agree
   - Somewhat agree
   - Mostly disagree
   - Completely disagree

4. I would be good at working with people who are in crisis.
   - Completely agree
   - Mostly agree
   - Somewhat agree
   - Mostly disagree
   - Completely disagree

5. I feel like I want my job to make a difference.
   - Completely agree
   - Mostly agree
   - Somewhat agree
   - Mostly disagree
   - Completely disagree

6. I am willing to persevere if it means that I will achieve my goal eventually.
   - Completely agree
   - Mostly agree
   - Somewhat agree
   - Mostly disagree
   - Completely disagree

7. I feel ready to take on new challenges.
   - Completely agree
   - Mostly agree
   - Somewhat agree
   - Mostly disagree
   - Completely disagree

9. My last performance evaluation showed that my supervisor and I are on the same wavelength.
   - Completely agree
   - Mostly agree
   - Somewhat agree
   - Mostly disagree
   - Completely disagree

10. When I read or hear about someone changing careers, I envy them.
    - Completely agree
    - Mostly agree
    - Somewhat agree
    - Mostly disagree
    - Completely disagree

11. I don't think I have reached my full potential yet.
    - Completely agree
    - Mostly agree
    - Somewhat agree
    - Mostly disagree
    - Completely disagree

12. I find myself taking new routes to work and making changes in my daily routine to ensure variety.
    - Completely agree
    - Mostly agree
    - Somewhat agree
    - Mostly disagree
    - Completely disagree

13. When I have made my mind up to get something done, I usually can accomplish the task.
    - Completely agree
    - Mostly agree
    - Somewhat agree
    - Mostly disagree
    - Completely disagree

14. Brainstorming practical solutions to real problems makes me feel valued.
    - Completely agree
    - Mostly agree
    - Somewhat agree
    - Mostly disagree
    - Completely disagree

15. I feel I could do my job in my sleep, because I am still doing what I was trained to do many years ago.
    - Completely agree
    - Mostly agree
    - Somewhat agree
    - Mostly disagree
    - Completely disagree

Choose the option that best describes your current career.

16. If I had a free ticket to go back to school, I would
    - Take it with no regrets
    - Take it with some anxiety
    - Make a list of pros and cons
    - Postpone acceptance
    - Decline it with thanks

17. You read a newspaper article about a colleague. That person has been recognized for their unique contribution to the profession. Which of the following describes your reaction most accurately?
    - It inspires you to give a little more energy and thought at work.
    - You think about the differences between you and your colleague.
    - You think about the differences between your work situation and that of your colleague.
    - It affirms your idea that politics at work is not worth playing.
    - You feel that you could never measure up to their level.

18. If you were to you open a textbook for a course that you have not taken, do you think you would feel
    - Elated that you will be able to learn new material
    - Happy to know that the content is summarized
    - Anxious about whether you can understand it
    - Ambivalent about whether it is important to know
    - Uninterested

19. If you fast forward to five years from now, and picture yourself in the same career that you are in now, how would you feel?
    - I would wonder what would have happened had I taken another career path.
    - I would have felt secure that I did the best I could with what I was given.
    - I would think that everyone has good days and bad days at work, and they can't control the proportion.
    - I would be hoping for a promotion or change of administration that would make my job better.
    - I would be happy, because I have a job and a steady income.

20. If you had a choice to start over again from an entry-level position in a challenging field, would you
    - Feel like you could (and wanted to) rise to the challenge
    - Worry about whether you could produce results effectively
    - Keep comparing it with the comfort level you now enjoy, questioning whether it is a viable decision
    - Talk about it with someone close to you, to see what they think you should do
    - Decline the opportunity because you don't want the added stress

21. If your local newspaper asked to interview you for a Career Day article, would you
    - Tell them the pros and cons of your job
    - Make it sound like your job has been an easy road to success
    - Have a noncommittal response
    - Give them the name of a colleagues that they could interview instead of you
    - Decline the invitation

21 Is job security important to you?
    - Very important
    - Moderately important
    - Can take it or leave it
    - Sometimes
    - No longer

22. If you were invited to be a speaker at a Career Day event at your neighborhood school, would you want to talk about
    - The financial rewards of your job
    - The self-esteem-raising aspects of doing a good job
    - The feeling of being needed by the organization
    - The sense that everyone can find their own niche, and you have found yours
    - The meaningfulness of your current position

For each question, rate how important it is that your career has this characteristic.

23. Different challenges
    - Very important
    - An added bonus, but not very important
    - Not important

24. New skills
    - Very important
    - An added bonus, but not very important
    - Not important

25. Career advancement potential
    - Very important
    - An added bonus, but not very important
    - Not important

26. Sense of powerful influence
    - ◉ Very important
    - ◉ An added bonus, but not very important
    - ◉ Not important

To what degree would you be willing to accept the following changes in order to have a new career?

27. More stress
    - ◉ I'm willing to accept it.
    - ◉ I could accept it, but only to a certain extent.
    - ◉ I could not accept it at all.

28. A new work environment and team
    - ◉ I'm willing to accept it.
    - ◉ I could accept it, but only to a certain extent.
    - ◉ I could not accept it at all.

29. A leadership role
    - ◉ I'm willing to accept it.
    - ◉ I could accept it, but only to a certain extent.
    - ◉ I could not accept it at all.

30. Decision-making authority
    - ◉ I'm willing to accept it.
    - ◉ I could accept it, but only to a certain extent.
    - ◉ I could not accept it at all.

Evaluate your answers. Circle negative responses, and look for links among them. For example, if you would decline an invitation to speak at a Career Day, why? Could it be because you feel you can do your job in your sleep, or because you can't make important decisions at work? Your negative answers will give you a better picture of why you are contemplating a career change.

Then, check those answers that are positive. What do they have in common? A willingness to accept a leadership role, learn new skills, and reach your full potential show that you are ready to enter a profession that causes you to grow. Teaching could be a great match, offering all three. To find out more about the qualities needed by teachers, check Chapter 2.

Career-Changer Mistakes

These are the three biggest mistakes made by those changing professions:

1. *Making a move before doing your homework.* Congratulations—by reading this book, you are avoiding the number one mistake! Before making a career break, you need to know what you're getting into, and why. Understand what's lacking from your current job, and do enough research, including visiting or even working in schools, to know that teaching is right for you.

2. *Expecting the change to be quick.* Becoming a teacher takes time. Even alternative routes to certification involve a year or more of controlled experience and study. You may need to conduct a lengthy job search once you're certified. The more you understand about the process and how long it can take, the less likely you are to become discouraged.

3. *Changing for the wrong reasons.* Many career changers are looking for more money. That's not the case for those thinking about teaching, but changing for a summer vacation is. Months of vacation won't make up for a job you don't like. Become a teacher because you love kids, you're passionate about your subject, and you want to make a difference. The vacations are a bonus, not a solid reason to choose a career.

IS THE TIMING RIGHT?

Changing your career will affect many aspects of your life and will likely require some sacrifices, so you need to examine some personal factors as you make the decision to find a new work identity. Sometimes, the decision to make a change is a sound one, but you need to wait for the timing to be right.

Here are several factors you will need to consider as you make your decision. Take a moment to consider each question and answer each thoughtfully.

Health

Are you in good physical condition?

_____

_____

Do you have any mental or emotional issues that should be resolved before you make a major life change?

_____

_____

Do you have an acceptable and affordable medical insurance coverage plan if you do not continue in your present job?

_____

_____

Stress

How would you rate your current level of stress?

_____

_____

Have you discovered successful methods of managing stress?

_____

_____

Can you handle additional stress?

_____

_____

Support System

Do you have relationships with people who can help you when you encounter obstacles during your transition?

_____

_____

Do you have people who encourage you?

_____

_____

Do you have individuals close to you who are willing to listen to your frustrations, questions, and concerns?

_____

_____

Finances

Can you afford to change your current income level?

_____

_____

Could you live on less money in the near future if you knew you were going to make a reasonably comfortable salary in the long run?

_____

_____

Do you know the cost of enrolling in an education program? If so, can you calculate the amount of financial assistance you would need to supplement your contribution?

_____

_____

Do you have other sources of income or sufficient savings to support yourself while going to school?

_____

_____

Time

Do you have family obligations that could interfere with an education program?

_____

_____

Where could you find help meeting those obligations if you go back to school?

_____

_____

Can you meet the enrollment deadline for your education program?

_____

_____

Have you researched education options and alternatives?

_____

_____

Will you have enough time to spend to attend classes and do homework?

_____

_____

Focus

Do you have other life situations right now that demand your attention?

_____

_____

Are you contemplating making other major changes in your life?

_____

_____

Access

Is there a suitable educational facility or an alternate certification program in your area?

_____

_____

Do you have a sense of the commute time and options for how to make the commute?

_____

_____

Are classes available online?

_____

_____

Are you able or willing to relocate to pursue an education?

_____

_____

Motivation

Can you visualize yourself in a different career?

_____

_____

Do you know how you would like to be fulfilled in a new work setting? How does this compare with the fulfillment you experience in your current job?

_____

_____

Have you tried sampling the new career or talking to people who have experience in the field you would like to enter?

_____

_____

If the timing is right for changing careers, you will have the resources, both financial and personal, to go ahead with your plans. If your answers to any of the questions flag a problem area, such as health insurance or family obligations, you might want to enlist the help of a career counselor to work through your options. Colleges and universities have Career Services offices that offer guidance; if you're not enrolled, they may charge a small fee for their services. Career counseling professionals can help you find solutions that you weren't aware of.

Profile of a Career Changer

Nancy Kenyon has been teaching middle school science, social studies, and math for five years. She left a 13-year career as an engineering technician at IBM to run a decorating business. Three years later, when her daughter entered middle school, she heard about the difficulty finding good substitute teachers. She interviewed with the assistant principal and was hired.

Kenyon says, "I eventually got a reputation as being a hard worker who had good rapport with the students. My sub assignments began to get longer and longer. I took one long-term assignment that ended up lasting a whole school year. I loved it. I was teaching math and reading to sixth- and seventh-graders with learning disabilities. That is when I decided to go and get a teaching certification."

But that didn't happen overnight. "Because I only had an associate's degree in applied science, I had to enroll as an undergraduate student. I completed a bachelor's degree in biology and also took classes to become certified as a teacher. I studied subjects such as philosophy, religion, history, French, art, statistics, and various biology disciplines ranging from evolution to developmental biology (all with labs). I also had to take educational instruction courses in adolescent psychology, reading, language, and learning across the curriculum as well as senior seminars for both biology and teaching."

She offers this advice to those contemplating a career in teaching: "The best preparation for teaching, aside from being a substitute, was raising my own children. Watching them

(continued)

Profile of a Career Changer *(continued)*

navigate the academic and social aspects of the world was quite an eye opener for me. Teaching is a lot of work. Do not enter the profession thinking you get summers off in addition to free time during the school breaks. It just doesn't work that way, and that's not a good reason to enter the profession. You also need to be realistic about the salary. I left a great paying job because I was very unhappy in the path my career was taking. I'm not in teaching for the money. If I was working for a business, I would be paid more. To learn more about the realities of teaching, I recommend Frank McCourt's *Teacher Man* (Scribner, 2005) and Parker Palmer's *The Courage to Teach* (Jossey-Bass, 1997).

I have found my dream job, and I love it. If you are passionate about sharing your skills and knowledge with kids, then teaching is a great vocation. You must be creative, hard working, and a little bit crazy!"

FIGURE 1.1–The Career Decision Pyramid

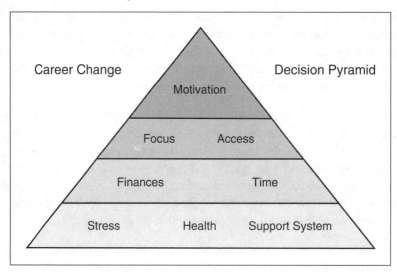

TIMING: A VISUAL TOOL

The career decision pyramid shown in Figure 1.1 is a visual representation of the factors you need to consider. It begins with the most practical concerns and moves toward more intellectual and emotional ones. At its base are the categories health, stress, and support system. Think of these three as your base: Make sure all of them are in place before moving further up the pyramid

Next, consider your finite resources: money and time. Although finite, they can be flexible. Use the budget planning worksheet in Figure 1.2 to get a picture of where your money is going now and where you might be able to cut expenses if you need to go back to school or take a lower-paying position. Check the "Time Management" section in Chapter 8 for ideas about where to find extra time for studying, homework, and attending classes.

You also need to examine how much energy you are willing to commit to a career change. Are you focused on your goal and willing to access an education program, even if it involves travel or online work? Finally, if you are highly motivated, you'll be willing to do what it takes, including making some sacrifices, to get the career you want.

IDENTIFYING YOUR TRANSFERABLE SKILLS

In the career counseling field, the term *transferable skills* refers to the strengths you developed in one job (or through life experience) that are assets in another. If you're contemplating leaving a career in marketing, for example, you would take with you valuable experience dealing with people, selling ideas, and managing many tasks at once. Those skills are needed in many different careers.

A strong understanding of your transferable skills will be important when you need to convince a future employer that although you don't have experience, you have what it takes to be a teacher. You can highlight them on your résumé, applications, cover letters, and interviews. When used to your best advantage, transferable skills can even make you a more desirable job candidate than someone with a classroom track record.

Read the list of transferable skills in Figure 1.3 and check the ones you have developed. Check the Education column if you acquired that skill during your education or through a training program. Check the Life column if you acquired the skill anywhere else, which would include paid employment, volunteer activities, and general life experience. Check the third column, Next Job, if you feel you will need that skill in your next job.

FIGURE 1.2–Budget Planning Worksheet

Estimated Income	Monthly Amount	Estimated Expenses	Monthly Amount
Income Sources		**Housing**	
• Net Salary		• Rent/Mortgage	
• Interest Income		• Gas/Electricity	
• Investment Income		• Water	
• Family		• Telephone/cell phone	
• *Other*		***Food***	
Non-Taxable Income		• Buying lunch at work	
• Child Support		***Transportation***	
• Veterans Benefits		• Car Payment	
• Social Security		• Car Insurance	
• Other		• Car Repair	
		• Bus	
		• Subway	
		• Other	
		Health	
		• Doctors	
		• Insurance	
		• Prescriptions	
		• Other	
		Dependent Care	
		• Child care	
		• Elder care	
		Personal/Miscellaneous	
		• Clothing	
		• Laundry	
		• Dry Cleaning	
		• Personal items (shampoo, etc.)	
		• Other	
		Entertainment	
		• Movies	
		• Concerts	
		• Eating out	
		• Other	
		Debt Obligations	
		• Student Loans	
		• Credit Cards	
		• Other	
		Emergencies	
Total Income		***Total Expenses***	

Career Change Success

Karen Nee held several positions at department and off-price stores for almost 20 years. She was a store manager, buyer, and vice president of merchandising. Her decision to become a teacher began during those years. "Part of my job was training and recruiting college students to work for my company. Through that I realized I enjoyed the teaching and training aspects of my job. My initial plan was to become a child psychologist. I was side-tracked because I started subbing and found I really liked it."

A math teacher for two years, Nee had to go back to school because there was no alternate route to certification in her state, and her college degree was in marketing and more than 25 years old. She majored in education and minored in mathematics. "I loved being a student again. I was much more motivated as an adult than as an undergraduate, probably because I hadn't been in school for a while. It wasn't difficult to juggle my schedule as I was used to a much more difficult lifestyle. For several years I traveled every week; trying to balance that with a husband and two kids was very difficult. I learned that you really can't have it all and not make a lot of personal sacrifices. Going back to school was actually quite liberating and helped me regain some of my youthful idealism!"

She adds, "My life and work experiences are an enormous asset in this profession. Having kids the age I teach has also been a big help. The work ethic and skills I acquired along the way in my career have helped me step in at a higher level than most students coming right out of college. I think I relate better to parents and can deal with kids more effectively having had 'practice' with my own. I'm also more tolerant and wiser than I was when I was younger; maturity is helpful as a teacher.

"Working in the schools as a substitute and as a student teacher was the best preparation for 'how' to teach. I was able to observe some of the best teachers out there from many different schools. I still draw on those lessons and when I have questions, I call upon those teachers I think are the best. I was able to practice many of the teaching techniques I saw, and this has helped me to work on developing my own style.

"I had a professor tell me that unless I loved math I shouldn't become a teacher. I didn't agree with her and I'm glad I didn't listen to her. I love *teaching* math—if I loved math I would have become a mathematician. I think you have to like the age group of kids you are working with first, then you should like the subject you are teaching."

(continued)

Career Change Success *(continued)*

Nee's advice for those thinking of becoming a teacher? "I get up most mornings looking forward to going to work. I love working with kids—all kinds of kids. My reward is knowing I helped a young person learn something they need to know, or helping them figure something out about themselves that makes them more successful. My advice is, do it—if it's what you really want to do. It's not about the summer vacations, or the perceived short hours—teaching is more about the giving of yourself without a whole lot of tangible reward. But, the intangible rewards are so much more meaningful!"

Once you've identified your transferable skills, you can begin to think of them in terms of your anticipated career change. List your skills, looking for patterns. Link those skills that are similar. For example, "prepare," "plan," and "organize" all have to do with spending time before an activity to ensure success in that activity.

Then choose at least three skills that you enjoy. After the skills you have selected, write a phrase about how you visualize using that skill in a teaching career. Don't worry if you are not completely familiar with the work environment of teachers; think about what you do know about their tasks. Here are some examples:

- Prepare/plan/organize: Good at writing lesson plans and coming to class every day knowing what I'm going to do.
- Resolve problems/help people: Able to manage a classroom and deal well with behavioral issues.
- Communicate: Keep parents in the loop by contacting them when there are positives and negatives to report.

This list will be useful in several settings. When you conduct informational interviews with teachers about their work, you can ask specific questions about how they think you could use these skills. If you checked "tolerate interruptions," you might ask about the day-to-day interruptions that teachers experience on the job.

The list will also be helpful when you apply to a college or alternative certification program. Highlighting your transferable skills will make your application stand out; other applicants may not have acquired the same skills you have.

Finally, during a job search, your list of transferable skills will be a vital tool to market yourself. Cover letters and résumés are great places to list or describe the skills you can bring to the job.

Figure 1.3—Transferable Skills

Education	Life	Next Job		Education	Life	Next Job		Education	Life	Next Job	
❑	❑	❑	act/perform	❑	❑	❑	do precision work	❑	❑	❑	lift (moderate)
❑	❑	❑	adapt to situations	❑	❑	❑	do public relations work	❑	❑	❑	listen
❑	❑	❑	advise people	❑	❑	❑	draft	❑	❑	❑	locate information
❑	❑	❑	analyze data	❑	❑	❑	drive	❑	❑	❑	log information
❑	❑	❑	anticipate problems	❑	❑	❑	edit	❑	❑	❑	make/create
❑	❑	❑	appraise service	❑	❑	❑	encourage	❑	❑	❑	make decisions
❑	❑	❑	arrange functions	❑	❑	❑	endure long hours	❑	❑	❑	make policy
❑	❑	❑	assemble products	❑	❑	❑	enforce	❑	❑	❑	manage a business
❑	❑	❑	assess situations	❑	❑	❑	entertain	❑	❑	❑	manage people
❑	❑	❑	audit records	❑	❑	❑	establish	❑	❑	❑	measure boundaries
❑	❑	❑	bargain/barter	❑	❑	❑	estimate	❑	❑	❑	mediate problems
❑	❑	❑	be cost conscious	❑	❑	❑	evaluate	❑	❑	❑	meet the public
❑	❑	❑	be responsible for	❑	❑	❑	examine	❑	❑	❑	memorize information
❑	❑	❑	budget money	❑	❑	❑	exchange	❑	❑	❑	mentor others
❑	❑	❑	build	❑	❑	❑	exhibit	❑	❑	❑	monitor progress
❑	❑	❑	buy products/services	❑	❑	❑	expand	❑	❑	❑	motivate others
❑	❑	❑	calculate numbers	❑	❑	❑	expedite	❑	❑	❑	move materials
❑	❑	❑	chart information	❑	❑	❑	explain	❑	❑	❑	negotiate
❑	❑	❑	check for accuracy	❑	❑	❑	explore	❑	❑	❑	nurse
❑	❑	❑	classify information	❑	❑	❑	file records	❑	❑	❑	nurture
❑	❑	❑	collect money	❑	❑	❑	find information	❑	❑	❑	observe
❑	❑	❑	communicate	❑	❑	❑	fix/repair	❑	❑	❑	obtain
❑	❑	❑	compare data	❑	❑	❑	follow directions	❑	❑	❑	operate equipment
❑	❑	❑	compile statistics	❑	❑	❑	follow through	❑	❑	❑	order goods/supplies
❑	❑	❑	compute data	❑	❑	❑	gather information	❑	❑	❑	organize data
❑	❑	❑	conceptualize	❑	❑	❑	gather materials	❑	❑	❑	organize people
❑	❑	❑	conduct	❑	❑	❑	generate	❑	❑	❑	organize tasks
❑	❑	❑	confront others	❑	❑	❑	guide/lead	❑	❑	❑	own/operate business
❑	❑	❑	construct buildings	❑	❑	❑	handle complaints	❑	❑	❑	paint
❑	❑	❑	consult w/ others	❑	❑	❑	handle equipment	❑	❑	❑	perceive needs
❑	❑	❑	contact others	❑	❑	❑	handle money	❑	❑	❑	perform routine work
❑	❑	❑	contact w/ others	❑	❑	❑	help people	❑	❑	❑	persuade others
❑	❑	❑	control costs	❑	❑	❑	illustrate	❑	❑	❑	plan
❑	❑	❑	control people	❑	❑	❑	imagine solutions	❑	❑	❑	plant
❑	❑	❑	control situations	❑	❑	❑	implement	❑	❑	❑	prepare materials
❑	❑	❑	converse w/ others	❑	❑	❑	improve	❑	❑	❑	print
❑	❑	❑	coordinate activities	❑	❑	❑	improvise	❑	❑	❑	process information
❑	❑	❑	cope w/ deadlines	❑	❑	❑	inform people	❑	❑	❑	process materials
❑	❑	❑	copy information	❑	❑	❑	initiate actions	❑	❑	❑	produce
❑	❑	❑	correspond w/ others	❑	❑	❑	inspect products	❑	❑	❑	program
❑	❑	❑	create	❑	❑	❑	install	❑	❑	❑	promote
❑	❑	❑	delegate	❑	❑	❑	instruct	❑	❑	❑	protect property
❑	❑	❑	deliver	❑	❑	❑	interpret data	❑	❑	❑	provide maintenance
❑	❑	❑	demonstrate	❑	❑	❑	interview people	❑	❑	❑	question others
❑	❑	❑	design	❑	❑	❑	invent	❑	❑	❑	raise money
❑	❑	❑	detail	❑	❑	❑	inventory	❑	❑	❑	read reference books
❑	❑	❑	detect	❑	❑	❑	investigate	❑	❑	❑	recommend
❑	❑	❑	determine	❑	❑	❑	lead people	❑	❑	❑	record data
❑	❑	❑	develop	❑	❑	❑	learn	❑	❑	❑	recruit people
❑	❑	❑	direct others	❑	❑	❑	learn quickly	❑	❑	❑	rectify
❑	❑	❑	dispense information	❑	❑	❑	liaise	❑	❑	❑	reduce costs
❑	❑	❑	distribute	❑	❑	❑	lift (heavy)	❑	❑	❑	refer people

Figure 1.3—Transferable Skills, continued

Education	Life	Next Job		Education	Life	Next Job		Education	Life	Next Job	
❑	❑	❑	rehabilitate people	❑	❑	❑	shape	❑	❑	❑	transfer
❑	❑	❑	remember information	❑	❑	❑	signal	❑	❑	❑	translate
❑	❑	❑	remove	❑	❑	❑	size up situations	❑	❑	❑	travel
❑	❑	❑	repair	❑	❑	❑	sketch	❑	❑	❑	treat
❑	❑	❑	replace	❑	❑	❑	socialize	❑	❑	❑	troubleshoot
❑	❑	❑	report information	❑	❑	❑	solve problems	❑	❑	❑	tutor
❑	❑	❑	research	❑	❑	❑	sort	❑	❑	❑	type
❑	❑	❑	resolve problems	❑	❑	❑	speak in public	❑	❑	❑	understand
❑	❑	❑	restore	❑	❑	❑	study	❑	❑	❑	unite people
❑	❑	❑	retrieve information	❑	❑	❑	supervise	❑	❑	❑	update information
❑	❑	❑	review	❑	❑	❑	supply	❑	❑	❑	upgrade
❑	❑	❑	run meetings	❑	❑	❑	support	❑	❑	❑	use hand/eye coord.
❑	❑	❑	schedule	❑	❑	❑	survey	❑	❑	❑	use words correctly
❑	❑	❑	seek out	❑	❑	❑	synthesize	❑	❑	❑	verify
❑	❑	❑	select	❑	❑	❑	tabulate	❑	❑	❑	visit
❑	❑	❑	sell	❑	❑	❑	take instructions	❑	❑	❑	visualize
❑	❑	❑	separate	❑	❑	❑	tend equipment	❑	❑	❑	volunteer
❑	❑	❑	sequence	❑	❑	❑	test	❑	❑	❑	weigh
❑	❑	❑	service customers	❑	❑	❑	think ahead	❑	❑	❑	work quickly
❑	❑	❑	service equipment	❑	❑	❑	think logically	❑	❑	❑	write procedures
❑	❑	❑	set goals/objectives	❑	❑	❑	tolerate interruptions	❑	❑	❑	write promo material
❑	❑	❑	set up equipment	❑	❑	❑	track	❑	❑	❑	write proposals
❑	❑	❑	set up systems	❑	❑	❑	train/teach	❑	❑	❑	write reports
❑	❑	❑	sew	❑	❑	❑	transcribe	❑	❑	❑	write technical work

Source: Wisconsin Job Center Publication, "Transferable Skills" (DWSJ-8961-P); www.wisconsinjobcenter.org/publications. Used with permission.

SHOULD YOU HIRE A CAREER COUNSELOR?

This chapter includes three types of the most important tool used by career counselors: self-assessment tests. So why might you choose to consult a professional counselor? Career counselors (also known as career coaches or career consultants) offer personalized services that go beyond traditional assessments. Many have an advanced degree in counseling, psychology, or human resources. They typically charge at least $75 an hour, but many charge more or use a service fee rather than an hourly rate.

Career counselors provide various services based on the needs of their clients, but you can expect them to offer:

- A counseling session to understand your life and career goals
- An objective voice

- Counseling to provide emotional support during transition
- Tests and inventories to assess your needs, strengths, interests, and suitability for various careers
- Help exploring careers you are interested in (including, but not limited to, arranging shadow days with teachers, scheduling informational interviews with teachers and administrators, and suggesting readings)
- Instruction in how to improve key skills, such as conflict management and decision making
- Assistance with a job search (locating openings, developing résumés, cover letters, and portfolios)
- Help in setting and meeting deadlines

HOW CAN YOU FIND A CAREER COUNSELOR?

Begin with your local phone book or an Internet site that allows you to search by location. Try the National Board for Certified Counselors (*www.nbcc.org*), which offers searches by state, or search the Web with the terms "find career counselor." The National Career Development Association provides a list of Master Career Counselors and Master Career Development Professionals on their website (*www. ncda.org*). Check with local colleges and universities; the counselors at their Career Services offices may offer their services to the public for a fee.

When you have a list of counselors in your area, contact them and ask for information. Look for credentials such as degrees and certifications. Groups such as the Council for Accreditation of Counseling and Related Educational Programs (*www.cacrep.org*) and the National Board for Certified Counselors and Affiliates offer career counseling certifications. Ask them about their experience with career changes; some counselors specialize in one industry or work only with recent graduates.

Finally, like any other kind of counseling, you are looking for someone with whom you feel comfortable and who will offer the services you're looking for. Ask questions, and get the names of some of their former clients to contact as references. If the counselor is too busy to field your questions, or charges more than a nominal amount for an initial quick interview, you should probably keep looking.

CHAPTER 2

Is Teaching the Right Profession for You?

If you're thinking of entering the teaching profession, you have an interesting advantage over those in other fields: you've spent years in schools and around educators. That is, you will begin teaching with some knowledge of the environment and the job. But that knowledge, drawn from a student's perspective, isn't everything. Students don't necessarily see the preparation teachers must do, the staff meetings, the continuing education classes, the dealings with parents and administrators. In other words, there is much more to the job than meets the student's eye.

Once you've decided that conditions are right for a change in careers, how can you get a more complete picture to find out if teaching is what you want to do? In this chapter, you'll get an overview not only of the profession, but of the process you'll need to go through in order to get into the classroom.

THE GRADE-LEVEL CHOICE

Your experience as a teacher will depend in large part on the age or grade of your students and how much you enjoy that age. Some teachers are energized and motivated by the challenge of working with very young children, and others are only interested in teaching a specialized subject to young adults. One of the teachers we interviewed put it well: "You have to like the age group of kids you are working with first, then you should like the subject you are teaching. If you think middle school kids are funny and interesting to work with, then be a middle school teacher. If you think high school kids are cool, be a high school teacher. Then, once you've made your decision, choose a subject you really like and study it."

Career Change Profile

Anna Goodnow is an elementary school teacher and former product manager in the publishing industry. She earned a degree in elementary education and worked as a teacher for two years after college. "I honestly felt it was a calling. I was very good at working with children, and I especially wanted to work with emergent readers." But after a few years, Goodnow decided to try something different, and she got a job in publishing. Three years later, she couldn't resist the calling, and went back to teaching.

"Working as a camp counselor and part-time in schools during college were great experiences. But the best preparation, and the experience that helped me choose my career, was growing up the oldest of five. My younger sister is 15 years my junior. I always felt very comfortable around children."

What about the compensation? Goodnow took a pay cut to return to teaching. "I think I should be paid more, frankly. I am compensated very fairly compared with other teachers in Chicago, but I work 50 to 60 hours a week, and when I am at work, I am working nonstop. But I would much rather work extremely hard while I am at work for a greater purpose, and then have more free time at the end. The end of the school year is a wonderful time, when I can see the results of my and the students' work and know that a break is coming up, that our work for the time being is done."

Goodnow emphasizes that a lower salary is a trade-off for doing a job she finds rewarding. "I love the joy of helping a child to progress. I love teaching writing and helping students to be able to express themselves on the written page. It is such a wonderful gift to give to someone, to help him or her gain proficiency in this vital life skill."

Her advice to career changers? "I recommend that they spend time in the classroom first. You can't take a class that will really tell you how to teach. You can get great curriculum ideas and learn about pedagogy in the classroom, but to understand what teaching is really like, you have to actually do it."

The decision about which grade to teach is a critical one, not only for your future enjoyment of your career, but for the path you need to take to get there. Understanding how a 5-year-old learns, and what they need from a kindergarten teacher, is very different from understanding the needs and learning styles of a 16-year-old. Chapter 4 deals with the different education programs required to get licensed to teach various grades. Here, we'll look at the three major groups of students (elementary, middle, and high school) and what it takes to teach them.

Elementary Schools

In a standard elementary school, the teachers have degrees in elementary education and are licensed to teach the entire curriculum to any student within the grade range. They have one class of students, and they instruct that class in math, reading, writing, science, and other subjects. Teachers bring students to separate areas for classes in music, art, physical education, and sometimes foreign languages. Weekly trips to the library or media center are also part of the schedule.

Elementary school teachers enjoy very young children and the positive role a teacher plays in a child's most formative years. They inspire their students' curiosity, engaging them in lessons and building their self-esteem. They instruct children in basic skills, including getting along with each other, learning self-control, and sharing resources.

Students at elementary schools range in age from 5 to 11 or 12, when they may be in the first stages of adolescence. They require patience, flexibility, and stamina of their teachers. There is very little "down time" at elementary schools—teachers may be with their classes without breaks for hours at a time, and the young students are demanding of attention and assistance throughout. Many schools without cafeteria facilities even require teachers to eat lunch in the classroom with their students.

Teachers must understand child development and be able to support children in each stage of development in the classroom. Increasingly, they must be able to recognize and assess educational, emotional, and behavioral problems and work with specialists, parents, and students to deal with these problems.

According to the U.S. Department of Labor, these tasks are required of elementary school teachers:

- Teach basic skills such as color, shape, number and letter recognition, personal hygiene, and social skills
- Establish and enforce rules for behavior and policies and procedures to maintain order among students
- Observe and evaluate children's performance, behavior, social development, and physical health
- Instruct students individually and in groups, adapting teaching methods to meet students' varying needs and interests
- Read books to entire classes or to small groups

- Demonstrate activities to children
- Provide a variety of materials and resources for children to explore, manipulate, and use, both in learning activities and in imaginative play
- Plan and conduct activities for a balanced program of instruction, demonstration, and work time that provides students with opportunities to observe, question, and investigate
- Confer with parents or guardians, other teachers, counselors, and administrators to resolve students' behavioral and academic problems
- Prepare children for later grades by encouraging them to explore learning opportunities and to persevere with challenging tasks

Middle Schools

Middle school teachers guide adolescent students from the early stages of learning to a deeper understanding of many of the subjects they were introduced to in elementary school. Their training involves both specialization (courses or a degree in a subject such as English or math) and general education courses that cover, for example, teaching methods, adolescent development, and methods of learning. Some states have licenses specifically for middle school, with a specialization in the subject to be taught. Others require that middle school teachers attain the same type of license secondary school teachers must have (subject specific).

Most middle schools hire single or dual subject teachers who see many classes during the day for instruction. A science teacher, for example, may have five or more different classes of students at varying levels of ability. Some schools use a team approach, in which a larger group of students form a team and are taught all subjects (other than art, music, foreign languages, and physical education) by two or three teachers.

Middle school students are considered by many teachers to be among the most challenging to teach. Adolescence is a time of rapid change, both physically and emotionally, and students are more likely to act out during this stage than their younger or older counterparts. However, successful middle school teachers enjoy the challenges they are presented with, and most choose to stay with this level throughout their careers.

The U.S. Department of Labor summarizes the tasks of a middle school teacher:

- Establish and enforce rules for behavior and procedures for maintaining order among the students for whom they are responsible

- Adapt teaching methods and instructional materials to meet students' varying needs and interests
- Instruct through lectures, discussions, and demonstrations in one or more subjects such as English, mathematics, or social studies
- Prepare, administer, and grade tests and assignments to evaluate students' progress
- Establish clear objectives for all lessons, units, and projects, and communicate these objectives to students
- Plan and conduct activities for a balanced program of instruction, demonstration, and work time that provides students with opportunities to observe, question, and investigate
- Maintain accurate, complete, and correct student records as required by laws, district policies, and administrative regulations
- Observe and evaluate students' performance, behavior, social development, and physical health
- Prepare materials and classrooms for class activities
- Assign lessons and correct homework

High Schools

Secondary or high school teachers instruct students in grades 9 to 12. The goal of teachers at this level is to teach skills that students will need in college or the job market. Subjects become even more specialized than in middle school. For example, instead of teaching a general science class, you might teach biology, chemistry, physics, or earth science. General English classes give way to composition; American, British, and world literature; expository writing; and even creative writing.

High school students are generally more mature than middle school students, but that doesn't mean there won't be discipline issues. Teachers need strong classroom management techniques to engage their students and elicit positive behavior.

The U.S. Department of Labor lists these as the most important tasks performed by secondary school teachers:

- Establish and enforce rules for behavior and procedures for maintaining order among the students for whom they are responsible
- Instruct through lectures, discussions, and demonstrations in one or more subjects such as English, mathematics, or social studies
- Establish clear objectives for all lessons, units, and projects, and communicate those objectives to students
- Prepare, administer, and grade tests and assignments to evaluate students' progress

- Prepare materials and classrooms for class activities
- Adapt teaching methods and instructional materials to meet students' varying needs and interests
- Maintain accurate and complete student records as required by laws, district policies, and administrative regulations
- Assign and grade class work and homework
- Observe and evaluate students' performance, behavior, social development, and physical health
- Enforce all administration policies and rules governing students

Back to Work: Choosing to Teach

Karen Kirkland worked in the technical industry for 15 years as a programming consultant, customer education specialist (systems engineer), internal education specialist, tools developer, program manager, and marketing materials project manager.

After her daughter was born, she tried being a mother and working at IBM but found the two to be incompatible. Kirkland spent six years at home, making money with her sewing skills and thinking about her next career.

She says her entry into the teaching profession has been "an evolution. I knew I didn't want to return to the corporate world. But I taught adult learners in my other career and knew that I enjoyed that part of my job. When I started substitute teaching a few years ago, I realized I had developed a love for children that I was unaware of earlier in my life when I didn't know any kids. It is very satisfying working with the kids, helping them learn, grow, and have confidence in their abilities. I also spent time watching other teachers in action. The more teachers I've seen, the more I can pick and choose what I like that reflects me and my style. It's a great learning experience to see teachers deal with difficult situations.

"I have a B.A. in humanities (areas of emphasis: music, philosophy and logic, and business), and a M.S. in computer science. When I decided to become a teacher, I looked into pursuing alternative certification. My state's program is 20 weeks long, including 13 full-day seminars on education topics, 20 weeks of student teaching

(continued)

Back to Work: Choosing to Teach *(continued)*

with teacher mentors, and a continuing development of a portfolio to be presented to the Peer Review panel."

Her advice to others considering a career change? "Observe classes, and substitute teach if you can. Get a good feel for what it's really like. See many teachers in action because they all have their own style. Choosing your content area is slightly less important than making sure you love kids and can inspire them."

TECHNOLOGY IN THE CLASSROOM

You can't get away from it: emailing, cell phones, text messaging, the Internet—even the most technologically challenged among us have begun to accept that it's part of our daily lives. Technology has entered the classroom, too. More than 75 percent of students have access to at least one computer in their classroom. Even kindergartners spend time on the computer—the National Center for Educational Statistics (NCES, *www.nces.ed.gov*) reports that elementary teachers were more likely than middle or secondary school teachers to say that their students used computers at school.

What does this mean for teachers? They're expected to be, if not already tech savvy, very open to learning. That's good news for new teachers, who are learning through their education programs how to use and integrate technology at work. Districts and their principals are providing an increasing number of seminars and workshops for their staffs as they purchase new types of equipment and move some of the equipment they have from learning centers directly to the classroom. Teachers note that independent learning also prepares them to use technology on the job.

Teachers use technology in a number of ways. According to the NCES, they create instructional materials, gather information for planning lessons, access model lesson plans, access research and best practices for teaching, create multimedia presentations for the classroom, and perform administrative record keeping. They also communicate via email with colleagues, parents, and students outside the classroom, as well as post homework or project information on websites.

Although no national standards are currently in place, the International Society for Technology in Education (ISTE, *www.iste.org*) is conducting a project to determine such standards. Funded by the U.S. Department of Education's (DOE's) Preparing Tomorrow's Teachers to Use Technology (*www.pt3.org*) grant program, the

National Educational Technology Standards for Teachers (NETS-T, *http://cnets.iste. org/Teachers/t_stands.html*) is a project that has developed six standard areas with performance indicators that indicate specific outcomes to be assessed:

1. *Technology operations and concepts.* Teachers demonstrate a sound understanding of technology operations and concepts. Teachers:
   a. Demonstrate introductory knowledge, skills, and understanding of concepts related to technology.
   b. Demonstrate continual growth in technology knowledge and skills to stay abreast of current and emerging technologies.

2. *Planning and designing learning environments and experiences.* Teachers plan and design effective learning environments and experiences supported by technology. Teachers:
   a. Design developmentally appropriate learning opportunities that apply technology-enhanced instructional strategies to support the diverse needs of learners.
   b. Apply current research on teaching and learning with technology when planning learning environments and experiences.
   c. Identify and locate technology resources and evaluate them for accuracy and suitability.
   d. Plan for the management of technology resources within the context of learning activities.
   e. Plan strategies to manage student learning in a technology-enhanced environment.

3. *Teaching, learning, and the curriculum.* Teachers implement curriculum plans that include methods and strategies for applying technology to maximize student learning. Teachers:
   a. Facilitate technology-enhanced experiences that address content standards and student technology standards.
   b. Use technology to support learner-centered strategies that address the diverse needs of students.
   c. Apply technology to develop students' higher order skills and creativity.
   d. Manage student-learning activities in a technology-enhanced environment.

4. *Assessment and evaluation.* Teachers apply technology to facilitate a variety of effective assessment and evaluation strategies. Teachers:
   a. Apply technology in assessing student learning of subject matter using a variety of assessment techniques.

    b. Use technology resources to collect and analyze data, interpret results, and communicate findings to improve instructional practice and maximize student learning.

    c. Apply multiple methods of evaluation to determine students' appropriate use of technology resources for learning, communication, and productivity.

5. *Productivity and professional practice.* Teachers use technology to enhance their productivity and professional practice. Teachers:
   a. Use technology resources to engage in ongoing professional development and lifelong learning.
   b. Continually evaluate and reflect on professional practice to make informed decisions regarding the use of technology in support of student learning.
   c. Apply technology to increase productivity.
   d. Use technology to communicate and collaborate with peers, parents, and the larger community in order to nurture student learning.

6. *Social, ethical, legal, and human issues.* Teachers understand the social, ethical, legal, and human issues surrounding the use of technology in PK–12 schools and apply those principles in practice. Teachers:
   a. Model and teach legal and ethical practice related to technology use.
   b. Apply technology resources to enable and empower learners with diverse backgrounds, characteristics, and abilities.
   c. Identify and use technology resources that affirm diversity.
   d. Promote safe and healthy use of technology resources.
   e. Facilitate equitable access to technology resources for all students.

In addition, curriculum standards are being developed for individual courses such as mathematics, science, social studies, English, and foreign languages. Many states have already developed their own technology standards, some using NETS as a base model. For example, the Louisiana K–12 State Educational Technology Standards are based on NETS and the Louisiana State Content Standards. Their technology standards are designed to support the state educational technology goal: "All educators and learners will have access to technologies that are effective in improving student achievement."

STANDARDIZED TESTING

Public school teachers have always dealt with tests—not only the ones they devise to assess whether their students are learning the curriculum, but tests designed by companies hired by state and federal governments to compare schools with one another. The number and frequency of standardized tests has increased over the past few years for a variety of reasons, and not everyone is pleased.

What are the arguments against so much standardized testing? The first involves the tests themselves. Opponents argue that they are poorly constructed and largely irrelevant, focusing almost exclusively on math and reading. Others say they are biased in favor of nonminority students. They also cite the pressure felt by individual schools to have their students attain high scores—pressure that ends up in the classroom, where "teaching to the test" is becoming a greater part of the curriculum. Teaching to the test means other valuable units and lessons can't be taught due to time constraints, and teachers' creativity can be stifled.

States are directed by the federal government to set high academic standards and then assess how well their students are meeting those standards through testing. The outmoded phrase "teaching to the test," with all of its negative connotations, is being replaced with "curriculum alignment." Simply put, curriculum alignment means teaching knowledge and skills that are assessed by tests written around the state's academic standards. The new buzzword means, on a basic level, teaching to the test.

It doesn't appear that this system of increased, higher-stakes standardized testing is going to change any time soon. Public school teachers need to teach in alignment with state standards or face consequences for themselves and their schools. What's at stake? In Texas, for example, principals can be fired if their schools' test scores aren't high enough. On a district level, poor scores can cost superintendents their jobs and force school boards to be dissolved. In Maryland, schools that perform poorly on tests forfeit thousands of dollars in reward money. And in an increasing number of states, including Florida, teachers' evaluations are based in part on standardized test scores.

With such high stakes, schools can't afford to stop with simply aligning curriculum with test content. They need to spend time teaching students how to take tests, too. Standardized test scores are higher for students who are familiar with the format of the tests and know a variety of test-taking strategies to apply. Armed with this knowledge, many teachers find themselves required to teach those strategies, taking more time away from course content. Proponents of curriculum alignment argue that students will be taking tests for the rest of their lives and that knowing how to approach them and "beat" them is important information. Although test designers

No Child Left Behind (NCLB)

This federal law was signed in 2002 to reform the American public school system. It is based, according to a government website, on "greater accountability for results, more freedom for states and communities, encouraging proven education methods, and providing more choices for parents."

NCLB requires states to increase the scope and frequency of student testing, set deadlines, meet teacher qualification standards, and target results. The controversial law is being challenged in courts by a handful of states and the National Education Association (NEA). Opponents cite the law as a mandate that doesn't provide the funding needed to comply. The cost, say lawyers for the plaintiffs, of state testing is increasingly being borne by the states whose budgets are already strained, and funds are being diverted from important educational programs in order to do so.

The DOE has shown a willingness to ease some standards, however NCLB still stands—and is expected to do so in the future. As with all standardized testing, the challenge rests primarily with teachers, who must creatively determine how best to prepare their students for those tests, while continuing to cover mandated curriculum.

say their creations are not "teachable" (in other words, learning the format of the test and practicing taking the test will not improve scoring), school districts that focus on test-taking skills earn higher scores.

SALARIES AND BENEFITS

It's no secret that teachers are not paid as well as those with similar levels of education and training in other fields. But teachers rarely cite salary as a factor in their decision to become educators. They know they won't become rich working in the classroom, but they also know they will enjoy compensation that goes beyond a weekly paycheck.

Public school teachers typically have the following benefits:

- Health insurance
- Disability insurance
- Leave programs, including sick and/or personal days, and holidays (most teachers do not get annual vacation time because their positions are for 9 or 10 months)

- Retirement plans
- Life insurance
- Savings plans
- Career development opportunities
- Tuition reimbursement
- Long-term care benefits
- Employee assistance programs (EAPs) and mental health benefits
- Meal plans and subsidized or free housing (at some independent schools)

PREPARATION

A common misconception is that great teachers are born, not made; that there are people who simply—by instinct—can stand in front of a class and convey a successful lesson because of natural talent. Educators know how wrong this is. Great teaching can involve some instinctual skills; for example, some people are able to discipline well without having to study theories of classroom management (although even experienced, successful teachers believe in professional development and are still learning new ways of doing things).

The misconception not only underestimates how hard teachers work, but it diminishes the idea of teacher education. What would you need to study, other than the subject content of the field you are going to teach, if teaching is instinctual? To give you an idea of the kind of curriculum you'd encounter in a teacher education program, below is a "lesson" on three theories of learning. In this lesson, students explore a few ways in which educational theorists explain how students learn.

THREE THEORIES OF LEARNING

Constructivism

The theory of constructivism is based on the premise that students construct an understanding of the world they live in through their experiences. They develop their own "rules" and "mental models" to make sense of their experiences. When a student learns something, she has to adjust her rules and mental models to accommodate that new experience. To teach well, there must be an understanding of those mental models.

Constructivists want to eliminate standardized curricula, grades, and standardized testing. They instead favor curricula that are customized to students' prior knowledge. They call for hands-on problem solving, use open-ended questions, and promote dialogue among their students. Students assess their own progress because such assessment is considered part of the learning process.

Behaviorism

Behaviorism is a theory of learning that focuses on objectively observable behaviors and discounts mental activities. Learning is therefore defined as simply the acquisition of new behaviors. Behaviorists describe the learning process as conditioning: Classic conditioning is a natural reflexive response to a stimulus, and operant conditioning is a reinforced response to a stimulus (as in a reward system). Because positive and negative reinforcement techniques are so effective, they are frequently used by teachers.

Piaget

This theory was developed by Swiss biologist and psychologist Jean Piaget (1896–1980) and is based on the premise that children build "mental maps" or schemes as they develop in order to understand and respond to their environment. These maps or schemes become more sophisticated as development moves forward. Piaget identified four key developmental stages:

1. *Sensorimotor (birth–2 years).* Children create concepts about reality based on their physical interaction with their environment; the knowledge of object permanence is not yet developed.
2. *Preoperational stage (ages 2–7).* Children need concrete physical situations to understand reality; abstract thinking is not yet developed.
3. *Concrete operations (ages 7–11).* Children begin to conceptualize as their physical experiences accumulate; they create logical structures and use abstract problem solving to explain those experiences.
4. *Formal operations (begins by ages 11–15).* Children have developed adult cognitive skills and can use conceptual reasoning.

Proponents of this theory call for a curriculum that is developmentally appropriate and that takes into account the critical role that interactions with the environment play in student learning.

NEW PATHS TO THE CLASSROOM

Every state has requirements that public (and some private) school teachers must fulfill before they can work in a classroom. Upon fulfillment of those requirements, a certificate or license is granted, and employment may begin. Years ago, the only way to get a license was to go through a traditional teacher training program. Based in colleges and universities, these programs consisted of courses in your subject field (elementary education if you planned to teach the youngest grades, and individual subjects—e.g., English, history, art—if you planned to teach older students). The curriculum included

On His Way

Roger Hurwitz left a 23-year career in book publishing to become a teacher. He has completed his preservice program as a New York Teaching Fellow (the program is one of New York state's alternative routes to certification) and currently has his first classroom.

"Teaching has been a passion and a goal since high school. A variety of college and career decisions led me into publishing—a decision I've never regretted. However, last year the time felt absolutely right to go back and fulfill a dream I've had for a long time. I have many years of experience in NYC classrooms as a reading volunteer, plus I introduced—and then ran for a number of years—the Junior Great Books program in an elementary school. In addition, I am a parent of two children who graduated from that same school. As a parent, and a lover of books and learning, I feel confident that my goal to teach in high-need schools has a sound foundation."

Hurwitz offers these words of advice: "Everyone I've met in the Teaching Fellow program has a tremendous sense of joy and passion. No one is second-guessing his or her career switch, despite a very intense program taking up more than 12 hours each day. Anyone considering leaving his career for teaching must feel a true calling, be willing to work very hard, be prepared to re-examine who you are, what you know, and where you are going."

plenty of pedagogy, that is, the study of theories on how students learn and how to teach. Before graduation, education majors got practical experience from student teaching in a local classroom with some supervision from the regular teacher.

What's different today? Education programs themselves haven't changed much. They still include pedagogy, student teaching, and coursework in a chosen field. However, in response to a shortage of teachers, and recognition of the value and expertise of career changers, a number of alternatives have been created to lure qualified people into education. Perhaps you have a bachelor's degree and a dozen years of experience in another industry. Today, you don't necessarily need to go back to school for a degree in education.

Alternative routes to certification are available in almost every state that prepare you for the classroom by placing you in one and providing a shorter course of study to supplement your practical experience. For example, Connecticut developed the

Alternate Route to Teacher Certification (ARC) specifically for mid-career professionals. ARC is a two-part program: first, applicants attend a rigorous 8- or 24-week period of full- or part-time intensive instruction. Second, applicants spend two years teaching with close supervision in a middle or secondary school. In Idaho, an applicant must find a teaching position with a school that has an urgent need first and then apply for an alternative route license. The hiring school must attest to the fact that the applicant is qualified to fill the position (including having a bachelor's degree in the subject to be taught) and that urgent need exists. The Appendix lists contact information for you to check the type(s) of program(s) available in your state.

MOST WANTED

While there are serious teacher shortages across the country, these shortages do not exist in every state for every type of teacher. Demand varies by state and region; some regions have shortages of every type of teacher and others have few shortages. However, nationwide, these are the types of teachers in highest demand:

- *Mathematics and science teachers.* The timing of this shortage makes it more urgent to solve. Students need to know more math and science than ever before, as Americans must compete in a global economy in which those areas are not only valued highly, but in which American students lag behind their international counterparts.

  The NCES assessed math literacy in 15-year-old students from around the world for its Program for International Student Assessment (PISA). Here are their results:

Country	Average Math Literacy Score
1. Finland	544
2. South Korea	542
3. Netherlands	538
4. Japan	534
5. Canada	532
6. Belgium	529
7. Switzerland	527
8. Australia	524
9. New Zealand	523
10. Czech Republic	516
11. Iceland	515

12.	Denmark	514
13.	France	511
14.	Sweden	509
15.	Austria	506
16.	Germany	503
17.	Ireland	503
18.	Slovak Republic	498
19.	Norway	495
20.	Luxembourg	493
21.	Poland	490
22.	Hungary	490
23.	Spain	485
24.	United States	483
25.	Portugal	466
26.	Italy	466
27.	Greece	445
28.	Turkey	423
29.	Mexico	385

Source: NCES, Program for International Student Assessment.

For more information, check the National Science Foundation Math and Science Partnership (MSP) Program *(www.nsta.org/mspnsf)*, which supports projects to improve K–12 student achievement in math and science. The National Council for Teachers of Mathematics *(www.nctm.org)* and the National Science Teachers' Association *(www.nsta.org)* are also good sources of information.

■ *Bilingual teachers.* The number of students with limited English proficiency (LEP) has grown substantially over the past decade. But the number of qualified teachers ready to work with them has remained relatively constant; it has been estimated that the nation needs more than 300,000 additional bilingual teachers who are trained to teach English to non-native speakers. To find out more about this specialization, check the National Association for Bilingual Education *(www.nabe.org)*.

- *Special education teachers.* Special education teachers work with students who have mental, behavioral, sensory, physical, and/or learning disabilities. Almost every large urban school district across the country reports severe shortages of these teachers. Check the National Association of Special Education Teachers *(www.naset.org)* for more information.
- *Teachers of color.* As America's classrooms become more multicultural and multi-ethnic, its teachers remain mostly white. Ideally, the demographics of a student population should be closely matched with the teaching population, but that is becoming increasingly more difficult as fewer minorities choose to enter the profession. A National Commission on Teaching and America's Future report from 2003 reveals that just 14 percent of K–12 teachers are African American, Hispanic and Latino, Asian, and Native American, while 36 percent of the nation's students are from such backgrounds.
- *Male teachers.* More than 80 percent of urban school districts report a shortage of male teachers, and the need is especially acute at the elementary level. Across the nation, the number of male teachers is at a 40-year low.

SAMPLE THE ENVIRONMENT

You can read every book and visit every website on the subject, but the best way to find out what teaching is really like is to spend time in a school with teachers, students, and administrators. Fortunately, that's not hard to do—public schools are easy to access. Here are four ideas to help you sample the work environment of a teacher.

Become a Substitute

Most school districts around the country need substitute teachers. Some are needed for daily assignments, but there are often longer-term substitute positions to fill in for a teacher who may be on leave for medical or other personal reasons. Substitutes do not have to be certified or have any previous teaching experience. They can choose which grade level they want to teach and can turn down assignments they don't want (or turn them down when they need time off).

Substitutes are paid an average of $40 to $150 for a six- or seven-hour workday. They typically do not write lesson plans or grade homework. In exchange, they can sample various grade levels and subjects and try out different teaching methods. They gain valuable work experience that will enhance a résumé when looking for a full-time teaching position and make contacts within a school or district that can lead to future employment.

How can you become a substitute? Call the district office where you would like to work (you can apply to more than one district) and ask what their job requirements are. Most ask you to fill out an application, get fingerprinted, and provide proof of a bachelor's degree (in any subject). You will be notified of a decision—most applicants are placed on a list used by administrators to fill daily vacancies—and be given a copy of a contract (substitutes are unionized like regular teachers). Your rights and benefits, including pay, should be clearly communicated. Then, you wait for a call either the night before or the morning of an assignment, which you can accept or reject.

If you choose to become a substitute, the check the following resources for more information and assistance:

- Substitute teachers' message board (*http://teachers.net/mentors/substitute_teaching/*)
- Tips for Substitutes (*http://geocities.com/Athens/8020/subtips.html*)
- *The Substitute Teaching Survival Guide: Emergency Lesson Plans and Essential Advice* (Grades K–5 and 6–12) by John Dellinger (Jossey-Bass, 2006)

Become a Paraeducator

Like their counterparts in the legal and medical fields (paralegal and paramedic), paraeducators work alongside licensed professionals providing support services. More specifically, they are nonlicensed school employees who work under the supervision of a licensed teacher. They are known by many titles, such as teacher aide, teacher assistant, classroom assistant, educational aide, educational assistant, instructional aide, instructional assistant, and paraprofessional.

The approximately 750,000 paraeducators working in the United States provide support to licensed teachers and their students in a number of ways: one-on-one tutoring; assistance with classroom management; instructional assistance in computer labs, libraries, and media centers; parental involvement activities; translator; and/or other instructional support services. This work provides the paraeducator with an intimate bird's-eye view of the school environment and the teaching profession. A year or more working in this capacity should be sufficient for any career changer to determine whether education is the right field.

Many states previously required only a high school diploma to become a paraeducator, and there were no limits on the duties of paraeducators once they were hired. Today, there are stricter requirements concerning both qualifications and duties. The No Child Left Behind law mandates that all paraeducators have an associate's degree (or higher), complete 60 semester units of study at a recognized college or university, or pass the hiring district's proficiency and instructional assistance tests.

What kinds of testing are required for paraeducators? States and districts have varying assessment programs. In Kentucky, for example, paraeducators must pass the KPA (Kentucky Paraeducators' Assessment). The untimed test consists of 40 questions, 10 in each of four sections: reading, mathematics, writing, and instructional strategies. All questions are multiple-choice or true/false. The instructional strategies section may question the test-taker's knowledge of Kentucky's System of Education; the instructional support parts of reading, mathematics, and writing; paraeducator roles and responsibilities; and instructional interventions. To pass the KPA, 28 questions must be answered correctly.

Thirty-five states, as well as districts in four additional states, accept the ParaPro Assessment given by the Educational Testing Service. The test was developed to meet the requirements of No Child Left Behind and measures skills and knowledge in three areas: reading, writing, and math. It also assesses a prospective paraeducator's ability to apply those skills and knowledge in the classroom. Test takers have two and one-half hours to answer 90 multiple-choice questions. For more information on ParaPro, including participating states and their score requirements, check *www.ets.org*.

Resources for paraeducators include the following:

- The Paraeducator's Learning Network (*www.paraeducator.net/*)
- National Clearinghouse for Paraeducator Resources (*www.usc.edu/dept/education/CMMR/Clearinghouse.html*)
- The Para Center at the University of Colorado *(www.paracenter.org/PARACenter/)*

Arrange an Informational Interview

You don't need to know where you want to teach to ask for an interview. Informational interviews are conducted for the purpose to gain knowledge about the teaching profession from the "inside"; you're the interviewer, gathering information, and the teacher or administrator is the interviewee, providing information. Most are happy to talk with prospective teachers, sharing their insights and a real picture of what working in a school is like. Arranging an informational interview isn't difficult, even if you don't have leads. Follow these steps to get the most out of any interview you schedule:

- *Make a list of contacts.* Who do you know who already works in a school? Even if they're not teachers, they'll have good leads for you. Relatives, friends, and acquaintances are all possible contacts.
- *Make the appointment.* Get the names of teachers and administrators who may be willing to talk with you from your contact list. When you call a teacher, identify

yourself and mention the contact who gave you her name. Briefly explain your decision to change careers and your interest in teaching. Then, ask for a 15- to 30-minute interview. Don't be discouraged if the first few calls don't result in an appointment—call the next contact. If you exhaust your list of contacts, try the education department at a local college or university.

- *Write an agenda for your interview.* Come up with a list of questions for the teacher(s) and administrator(s). If you're not prepared, all you'll learn is the information they offer. Possible questions include: How did you decide on your career? How did you choose the grade level at which you teach? What is the biggest challenge you face on the job?
- *Be professional.* Your manner, dress, and body language (handshake, eye contact, etc.) should convey your seriousness and interest in the field. Although you're still in the information-gathering stage, the person you're interviewing could one day be a job lead or the person who hires you. A positive impression is crucial.
- *Ask for another contact or contacts.* Your interviewee knows other teachers and administrators who may be willing to speak with you.
- *Arrange a shadow day or period.* See the following section.
- *Send a thank-you note.* Check Chapter 11 for an example. This often overlooked step is an important part of your professional image. Mention a specific example of something the interviewee said that was particularly helpful.
- *Evaluate the interview.* What did you learn? Even though you're not yet looking for a job, did the school seem like a pleasant place to work? Did the teachers seem to be good potential colleagues? If you found the school, teacher, or administrator not to your liking, what can you learn about the kind of environment and people you would like to work with?
- *Begin the process again with new contacts.* The more teachers you speak with, the better idea you'll get of what the field is like. After one or two interviews, you'll probably have better, more refined questions to ask, too.

Shadow a Teacher

You can arrange a "shadow day" during an informational interview or directly through a teacher contact. Choose someone whose skills impress you, and ask him if you can schedule a time in which you observe him teaching. Shadow days are common, and most teachers are flattered to be asked.

If you haven't already interviewed the teacher, come prepared with questions. During the observation, take notes and formulate more questions. Why does the teacher use a certain method of teaching? How do his classroom management techniques work? Reading the rest of this book will give you more ideas of the kinds of concerns you should be interested in.

CHAPTER 3

Private Schools versus Public Schools

Most teachers work in public schools—that is, schools funded by tax dollars, run by local school boards, and governed by state and federal laws. But more than 10 percent of the nation's educators are employed by private schools. What are these schools like to work in, and how do they differ from public schools? In this chapter, we'll explore those questions and give you reasons to consider working in this unique learning environment.

There are more than 30,000 private schools in the United States that enroll 6.5 million students. Private, or independent, schools can be day, boarding, or a blend of day/boarding schools; elementary, secondary, or both; boys', girls', or coeducational; military; or religious. They are governed by a board of trustees, meaning each school is autonomous. They choose the board members and have to answer to no one else but the board. They receive most of their financial support from tuitions, charitable giving, and endowment income. Private schools may be found in cities, rural settings, and suburbs, and they range from small (fewer than 100 students) to large (more than 3,000 students).

Private school teachers report a higher level of job satisfaction than their public school counterparts. Greater autonomy, fewer discipline problems, and smaller class sizes are just a few of the reasons they cite. These findings, as well as other studies and statistics in this chapter, are from the U.S. Department of Education, National Center for Education Statistics, including Private Schools: A Brief Portrait, NCES 2002–013, by Martha Naomi Alt and Katharin Peter (Washington, DC: 2002), and Schools and Staffing Survey (SASS), "Public, Public Charter, and Private School Teacher Surveys," 1999–2000.

ENVIRONMENT

What is it like to work in an independent school? Many factors, from types of students to class size and professional environment are different than public schools. If you haven't visited or attended a private school, the facts and figures here will give you an idea of what to expect.

School Size

Public school size is determined by the local population's size and its age distribution of its children. Private school size, too, is dependent on the size and age of the population, but it is also determined by other factors. Some parents are willing to drive longer distances to private schools, making the area from which a school draws its pupils larger. The size of a private school can also be determined by the wealth of an area: How many people are able to afford the tuition? School philosophy also plays a part; different schools appeal to different segments of the population. Religious schools, military academies, and single-sex schools are examples of institutions that appeal to a smaller group of their area's population.

In 1999–2000, the average private school had 193 students. The average public school that year had 535 students. Eighty percent of private schools had fewer than 300 students, while only 29 percent of public schools were that size.

Budgets

Public schools are supported primarily by local property taxes, making their budgets fixed (and often hotly debated political issues). Wealthy communities have larger budgets, and poor communities, or those with large populations of fixed-income residents, tend to have smaller (sometimes inadequate) budgets. Some schools supplement their budgets with grants from foundations and businesses and federal aid. Parent-teacher organizations can also add to the budget through fundraising activities.

Private schools depend on tuition and donations. Large donations become investments (known as endowment funds) that provide interest income. These schools have more flexibility with their budgets because they are able to increase tuition, and they also can raise significant amounts of money from a variety of development activities, including annual appeals, cultivation of alumni, and solicitation of grants from foundations and corporations. The strong ties of alumni to their private schools means many of them give generously to their alma maters throughout their lives.

Facilities

The size and quality of private school facilities varies as much as it does for public schools. In wealthier public school districts, you'll find facilities that are modern and well designed. Computer labs, state-of-the-art learning centers, and music performance and practice spaces are common. However, in poorer districts, buildings can be in a dangerous state of disrepair. Because public schools must educate every student in their geographical area, and because the numbers of students fluctuates, overcrowding can occur. Buildings erected decades ago, when enrollments were lower, are used for student populations that have, in some cases, doubled. Some schools resort to holding classes in gymnasiums, closets, and other spaces not designed to be classrooms.

Large private schools, especially those with long histories, look like college campuses, with impressive buildings and manicured lawns. Small private schools with few students may rent space from a church or civic group or hold classes in a converted home or other space. Most independent schools fall somewhere in between. But whether large or small, the income needed to maintain and improve facilities can fluctuate. Independent schools rely financially on tuition, endowment fund income, and donations. Factors such as the economy, headmaster or principal, development office staff, and even sports team performance can affect income. On an "off" year, or during a string of "off" years, even large, well-established schools can forego maintenance and facilities upgrades. It's important to visit the school(s) you are interested in working for; only in person will you be able to judge the facilities and their condition.

Student Body

The student body at a private school is typically less diverse than at a public school. A higher percentage of students are white, and according to the DOE, about 14 percent of private schools had no minority students, compared with only 4 percent of public schools. Private schools also have significantly fewer LEP students. While these students help introduce different cultures and languages to their schools, they also present challenges for teachers and administrators. Few independent school teachers must adapt their lessons and instruction techniques to reach LEP students.

Socioeconomically, students are also less diverse in private schools. Almost every public school in the country has students who are eligible for free or reduced-price lunches. (According the DOE, the eligibility rate for the National School Lunch Program is a measure of school poverty.) Less than half of all private schools had any students eligible for the program.

Selectivity is another factor that determines the makeup of a student body. First, parents select an independent school, rather than simply having their children attend the public school their district has assigned them to. This selection is based primarily on perceived quality and ability to afford the tuition. When their child applies, the school then sets the parameters for the selection process: Most private schools receive more applications than they have vacancies and, therefore, do not have to accept every student who applies. Enrollment decisions are based on the child's ability (most private schools require an admissions test such as the Secondary School Aptitude Test or Independent School Entrance Examination); parental ability to pay tuition (a limited number of scholarships are usually available); and other qualities such as athletics, musicianship, and leadership qualities.

Admissions Tests

Most private schools have a testing requirement for admission. Although the most common test is the SSAT, five other tests are also used. Testing is typically conducted onsite; once a student applies, they are given a testing date on which all applicants come to the school and take the test.

- *COOP (Catholic High School Entrance Practice Exam).* Required for eighth graders by Catholic schools primarily in the dioceses of New Jersey. The two-and-one-half-hour exam consists of seven sections: sequences (20 multiple-choice questions regarding recognition of patterns or sequences), analogies (20 multiple-choice questions regarding relationships between pairs), quantitative reasoning (20 multiple-choice questions on number relationships, visual problems, and symbol relationships), verbal reasoning—words (20 multiple-choice questions regarding deductive reasoning, category analysis, and relationship/pattern identification), verbal reasoning—context (20 multiple-choice questions concerning deductive reasoning), reading and language arts (40 multiple-choice questions covering reading passages, sentence and paragraph structure, and grammar), and mathematics (40 multiple-choice questions on number relations and patterns, computation and operations, geometry and spatial sense, data analysis and probability, functions, and measurement).
- *HSPT (High School Placement Test).* For Catholic schools in the dioceses of Baltimore, Boston, Buffalo, Charleston, Chicago, Kansas City–St. Joseph, Los Angeles, Miami, and Trenton. Many other private schools also use the HSPT. The two-and-one-half-hour test has five multiple-choice segments: verbal (60 questions including synonyms, antonyms, analogies, logic, and verbal classification problems), quantitative (52 questions covering geometric comparisons, nongeometric comparisons, and number manipulations), reading comprehension (62 questions about several short reading passages), mathematics

(64 questions on arithmetic, elementary algebra, and basic geometry), and language (60 questions covering capitalization, punctuation, usage, spelling, and composition).

- *ISEE (The Independent School Entrance Examination).* This three-hour test has three levels: lower (for students currently in grades 4 and 5), middle (for students in grades 6 and 7), and upper (for students in grades 8 through 11). There are five sections in each test, which vary in number of questions and time limits depending on the level: essay, mathematics achievement, reading comprehension, quantitative reasoning, and verbal reasoning.
- *SHSAT (Specialized Science High Schools Admissions Test).* Offered to all eighth- and ninth-graders in New York. A qualifying score allows a student entry into the Bronx High School of Science; Brooklyn Technical High School; Stuyvesant High School; the High School for Math, Science, and Engineering at City College; the High School of American Studies at Lehman College; or Queens High School for the Sciences at York College. The two-and-one-half-hour test has two sections: verbal (45 questions on scrambled paragraphs, logical reasoning, and reading comprehension) and mathematics (50 questions on quantitative comparisons and problem solving).
- *SSAT (Secondary School Admission Test).* Taken by approximately 55,000 students a year, two levels of the test are administered: grades 5 through 7 and grades 8 through 11. The two-hour-and-25-minute test is divided into five sections: an essay (support or argue a topic statement, using specific examples from personal experience, current events, history, or literature), two math segments (25 questions each), two verbal portions (30 synonym and 30 and analogy questions), and a reading comprehension section (40 questions based on seven reading passages).
- *TACHS (Test for Admission to Catholic High Schools).* For eighth-graders applying for admission to Catholic high schools in the Diocese of Brooklyn/Queens and Archdiocese of New York. Approximately two hours long, the TACHS has four sections: reading (vocabulary and reading comprehension), language (spelling, capitalization, punctuation, and usage), mathematics (skills, number properties and operations, measurement, probability, statistics, estimation skills, and data analysis), and ability (evaluates a student's ability to generalize a principle and apply it to a new situation).

Because most private schools are selective when it comes to a student's ability to learn, classes are typically more intellectually homogeneous, and teachers are not as likely to have to modify curriculum and instruction techniques for varying student abilities. As a result, more private high school seniors than public school seniors take and pass Advanced Placement (AP) tests and attend college.

Public schools, in contrast, typically accept every student assigned to them by their school districts. This system is beginning to change, however, especially in urban areas. School choice options including magnet and charter schools and open enrollment, and publicly funded vouchers are slowly becoming available. The DOE reports that in 1999, 16 percent of public school students in grades 1 through 12 attended a school the family had chosen, up from 12 percent in 1993.

Diversity in schools presents challenges to teachers and administrators who may need to become proficient in another language, adapt lessons for students of different abilities, and hire more specialists. However, and more important, diversity can improve the academic and social environment and help students learn to function well in a heterogeneous community (which mirrors the ones they will become a part of in society). Student body diversity can also improve the academic achievement of low-income and minority students, lower dropout rates, and improve tolerance and critical thinking skills. Therefore, teachers looking for diversity typically apply for jobs in public schools.

Class Size

Independent schools have smaller average class sizes and lower student-teacher ratios than public schools. They have approximately two fewer students per teacher, but that number shrinks when overcrowded inner-city schools are taken into account. Some public schools have classes of up to 40 students, while private schools average 12.

Why is class size important? Individual attention is infrequent in large classes; one teacher does not have the time to address many separate concerns. Therefore, students who don't understand a lesson or who need extra help may suffer. Managing a large class is also more difficult; think of 40 different personalities, attention spans, and intellectual abilities versus 12. Behavior problems are more common in larger classes; it's much easier not only to teach to a smaller group, but also to maintain order.

Many teachers prefer smaller classes for an additional reason: They are less work. Lesson plans remain the same no matter how many students you teach, but the number of tests to grade, papers to read, and conferences to hold is obviously smaller.

Supplies

Private school budgets and spending per pupil amounts are typically higher than those of public schools. That means you're likely to find newer textbooks, more technology, and more basic supplies in private schools. In Chapter 12, we report that many public school teachers spend their own money on supplies such as science lab materials, calculators, and even writing utensils. Private school teachers are less likely to have to shop for their classroom needs.

Curriculum

Because private schools do not have to teach a local, state, or federally mandated curriculum, and they do not have to give standardized tests designed to measure how well students learned that curriculum, they have greater autonomy over the content of their classes. Private school teachers cite this autonomy as an important factor in measuring job satisfaction.

Administrative Support

The bureaucracy in public schools is two-tiered: (1) There is a principal, and typically an assistant principal, in each school. (2) At the district level, there is a superintendent, and depending on the size of the district, other staff such as a curriculum director. These levels mean that it can be slower and more difficult to get things done. For teachers, this translates to waiting for requests to be fulfilled and often to feeling like change can't happen.

Principals in public schools are accountable to their local, state, and federal governments. If standardized test scores are lower than expected, for example, they might lose funding or receive some other form of reprimand, and they must then plan changes to improve instruction (if only to raise the scores). They can pressure individual teachers to raise scores through more attention to test content.

Diverse student bodies mean working with learning consultants, counselors, linguists, and other specialists. In addition, principals must address the concerns of parents, teachers, and students. What does that mean for teachers? Typically, less guidance and support. Although professional development (workshops, lectures, tuition reimbursement) is stronger in public schools, day-to-day administrative aid is weaker.

Private school teachers, in contrast, give their principals high marks when it comes to supporting them, enforcing rules, and communicating expectations and goals. That support means that teachers count on getting help when they need it—a real concern of new, inexperienced teachers.

Figure 3.1—Percentage of teachers who thought they had a lot of control over various teaching practices, by sector and private school type, 1999–2000

Sector and type	Selecting teaching techniques	Evaluating and grading students	Determining homework quality	Disciplining students	Choosing content and skills to teach	Selecting textbook, materials
Public	87.4	89.1	87.9	73.3	56.7	54.1
Private	92.5	92.4	87.3	85.5	75.0	70.6
Private school type						
Catholic	93.8	93.7	89.7	85.8	73.1	69.4
Other religions	91.5	91.5	84.8	85.8	70.4	64.5
Nonsectarian	92.3	91.7	87.5	83.0	85.0	81.8

Source: U.S. Department of Education, NCES. Schools and Staffing Survey (SASS), "Public, Public Charter, and Private School Teacher Surveys," 1999–2000.

Professional Climate

Teachers interact and work not only with their students, but also with administrators, fellow teachers, and parents. The quality of those interactions, especially those with their peers, has an enormous effect on the school environment. Teachers who have positive relationships with other teachers report higher rates of job satisfaction and contribute to the positive climate of the school.

Private school teachers report that they collaborate more with other teachers and that their principals encourage such collaboration and collegiality. Collaboration with other teachers helps create a beneficial environment and also increases the quality of instruction. When teachers are willing to share their best lessons and techniques, especially with less experienced teachers, the standards of the school rise.

High Standards

Private school students' academic achievements are above-average, due in part to the selection process described earlier and also to the high standards set for them. Those standards are an integral part of an independent school's reputation: When parents have a choice of schools, academic standards are an important measure of quality and count heavily in the decision-making process.

One measure of those standards is graduation requirements. Private schools demand more; for example, their students must take and pass higher levels of math, science,

The Goals of Private Schools

Whether in independent or public institutions, principals share many of the same visions for their schools. A 1999–2000 U.S. Department of Education survey found that private school principals' top goals for their schools (in order of popularity) were academic excellence, fostering religious/spiritual development, literacy skills, and developing self-discipline. What are the top goals of public school principals? Building basic literacy skills in core areas (reading, writing, and mathematics), encouraging academic excellence, and developing self-discipline and good work habits.

and foreign language courses. But how do teachers communicate those standards? In every classroom, they set clear, high expectations. Most students respond positively to those expectations and work to meet or exceed them. Teachers who want to demand and receive excellent results (and want support from administrators and other faculty) do well in private schools.

Standardized Testing

You already know something about the amount of standardized testing federal and state governments require in public schools. Teachers note that as testing increases, they feel more pressure to cover curriculum because of the amount of time testing takes away from instruction. And parents complain about "teaching to the test." Educators have to skip some lessons to adequately prepare their students, and there is no guarantee that the test content is as valuable as the material they don't have time to cover.

School districts are forced to spend money on testing, often necessitating the making of tough decisions to cut other items, such as arts and music, from their budgets. And there are other monetary concerns: Some federal funding can be denied to schools if scores aren't high enough, and some states "reward" teachers whose students score well, creating animosity and competition between colleagues.

Here's an example: In New Jersey, standardized tests are administered at grades 3, 4, 8, and 11. Third-graders take a test of language arts literacy and math (NJ ASK 3). Fourth-graders take NJ ASK 4, which covers language arts literacy, mathematics, and science. The Grade Eight Proficiency Assessment (GEPA) also covers language arts literacy, mathematics, and science. In grade 11, students take the High School Proficiency Assessment (HSPA) of language arts literacy and mathematics. They cannot graduate from high school without passing all sections of the HSPA (three chances are given). In addition, New Jersey is developing more tests to comply fully with No Child Left Behind (refer to Chapter 2 for an explanation of NCLB standards).

Where can you find respite from the standardized testing frenzy? Private schools. Because they don't have to answer to federal or state governments, they do significantly less standardized testing. Teachers don't have to tailor lessons to test content, and they

---

Dispelling Myths about Independent Schools

1. *The students are snobs.* Years ago, private schools were in the business of educating the elite. While it is still true that many children from wealthy families attend private schools, these schools know the value of a diverse student body. They seek to attract students of different socioeconomic backgrounds, races, and religions. The student bodies of private schools are therefore much less homogeneous than they were a few decades ago.

2. *Teachers get paid less to do more.* Many private schools expect their teachers to participate in extracurricular activities such as coaching. Some boarding schools require teachers to live on campus and supervise dorms. But public school teachers have to deal with more student behavioral issues, administer more standardized tests, and accumulate continuing education credits. In general, salaries at private schools are lower, but the workload is not necessarily greater, and many teachers make as much as, or almost as much as, their public school counterparts.

3. *Private schools don't have certified teachers.* While many private schools hire teachers with no certification or experience, they often expect those teachers to earn certification within their first few years of teaching. In addition, some states, such as Pennsylvania, require certification of all teachers in independent schools that are licensed by the state department of education.

---

don't have to spend time on drills and other exercises designed to help kids improve test-taking skills.

Discipline

Student behavior at private schools is often better than at public schools, and teachers report that safety is much less of a concern at private schools. There are a number of reasons for these differences. First, let's return to the issue of choice. When a parent chooses and enrolls her child in a private school, a commitment is made. That parent agrees to abide by the rules of the school, and understands that the student must also do so. Communication of clear expectations and consequences are a part of the enrollment process.

Second, private schools get to choose whom to enroll. Think of the application process as a screening tool: the school uses many sources to find out as much about the student as it can. Students with a history of behavior issues might have a more difficult time making the cut.

Third, private schools don't have to make extraordinary, government-mandated efforts to retain students who don't follow school rules or who pose a safety threat to others in the school. There is no lengthy legal process for expulsion, and there is no one to answer to except the student and his parents. If a student violates a school rule, and the clear consequence for that violation is expulsion, the school can expel the student without having to go through layers of bureaucracy.

Special Programs

Younger students in independent schools are offered more special programs than their older counterparts. More than 65 percent of private elementary schools offer extended, before-school, or after-school day care programs, while less than 47 percent of public elementary schools do. And more private schools offer language instruction to elementary-age students.

A greater number of public secondary schools offer Advanced Placement courses. These courses provide college-level instruction and are typically followed by AP exams. Students who pass these exams are awarded college credit by most colleges and universities. More than 84 percent of public schools offer AP courses, as opposed to fewer than 36 percent of private schools. Other courses and programs offered predominantly in public schools include gifted and talented programs, vocational courses, and career academies.

SALARIES AND BENEFITS

More than half of all public school teachers belong to a union (the American Federation of Teachers or the National Education Association) that works to negotiate with school districts for higher salaries and better benefits. As a result, educators in public schools are paid, on average, more than their private school counterparts, and they receive benefits from their employers such as pensions and medical and life insurance. Their union membership allows them to take advantage of other benefits, such as discounts on loans, insurance, and travel expenses.

Public school districts typically use a salary schedule to calculate base salaries for teachers. The schedule also details the experience and qualifications needed for raises, which includes years of experience and advanced degrees and/or coursework. In contrast, private school teachers do not have a union. Benefits, such as pension plans, vary from school to school. Some private schools offer room and board or subsidized housing as a benefit to their teachers, and others pay teachers for involvement in activities such as coaching.

According to the U.S. Bureau of Labor Statistics, new public school teachers earned an average of $31,704 in the 2003–2004 school year. The average salary of all public teachers in that year was $46,597. New teachers at private schools earned an average of $29,484. The average salary for all private school teachers was $41,470. Independent school teachers' salaries are based on the number of years of teaching experience, number of years employed at the current school, degrees and credits, and, unlike public schools, merit and performance and teaching load.

However, it is important to consider the relevance of salary to the level of job satisfaction. Public school districts, especially those with severe shortages, offer increased compensation packages to lure new teachers. But that technique has not been very successful. Why? New teachers report that they certainly need to make a living, but they aren't changing (or beginning) careers for the money. They are more interested in working with well-behaved students, involved parents, smaller classes, and supportive administrators—all benefits of working in a private school.

> ## Trying Out Private Schools
>
> The National Association of Independent Schools (NAIS) offers internship programs for those considering becoming a private school teacher. These programs vary by location; they range from mentored first-year experiences for recent college graduates to master's degree programs (in conjunction with local colleges or universities). In some cases, interns can apply for a full-time position once the internship is complete. Check *www.nais.org* for more information.

BECOMING A PRIVATE SCHOOL TEACHER

Career changers may find it easier, and possibly more desirable, to become a private rather than a public school teacher. The absence of some requirements, such as certification and traditional teacher training programs, means you can get hired and have your own classroom, without going through months or years of study. A recent report by NCES concluded that even with less stringent requirements, private schools were better at attracting the most qualified job candidates, including those with previous job experience (career changers). The study found that SAT and ACT scores of private school teachers were higher than those of their public school counterparts, concluding that private schools, even while offering lower pay, were more successful in recruiting better teachers. If they're not looking for certification or an education degree, what kind of job candidates are private schools most likely to hire? Strength in three areas is usually required:

1. Education. A bachelor's degree in the subject you want to teach is necessary. A high GPA and a minor in another subject you are willing to teach are plusses. Degrees with the most demand include physics, chemistry, computer science, math, biology, Spanish, Latin, and French. Other high-demand positions include elementary teachers (with certification), music (vocal and instrumental), fine arts, and physical education.

   There are very few, if any, positions available for teachers with a degree in psychology, economics, anthropology, political science, philosophy, or nontraditional foreign languages. If you have one of these degrees, emphasize study (e.g., a number of courses in history, or a minor in physics) in a traditional subject and be willing to teach at the middle school level or lower.

2. Activities. Your abilities and willingness to get involved in extracurriculars should be strong. Coaching, advising the yearbook or newspaper staff, leading community service projects, and running clubs such as photography and drama are all necessary, and your interest in such activities can set you apart from the competition.

3. Experience. Demonstrate your love for children by highlighting your experience working with them. Paid positions such as camp counseling and tutoring, volunteer work (youth groups, community service, etc.), or experience through an education program (supervised student teaching, college teaching assistant) should be on your résumé.

While it's true that most schools don't require certification at the time of hiring, the trend is for more private schools to add licensing requirements. In fact, some states regulate private schools; the U.S. Department of Education (*www.ed.gov*) maintains a list of these regulations. Maine, for example, requires independent schools to hire certified teachers and teach mandated curriculum. Some schools not bound by such regulations require their teachers to earn certification within a few years of hiring. In addition, private schools may require other types of certification such as the NAPCIS Teacher Certification Program for Catholic Educators, or the ACSI (Association of Christian Schools International) certification.

While much of the advice in Chapter 11 regarding job searches is pertinent to private schools, the timing of hiring decisions is somewhat earlier. Most fill their vacancies between February and May, meaning you should contact them in the fall rather than waiting until spring.

PRIVATE SCHOOL TEACHING RESOURCES

If you are considering seeking employment at an independent school, check out some of these resources for more information.

- *National Association of Independent Schools (www.nais.org).* Represents nearly 1,200 U.S. independent schools. Publishes *Independent School* magazine; website has a career center with articles on job searching, posted jobs, and résumé posting.
- *The California Association of Independent Schools (caisca.org).* An example of a state organization that offers information about member schools and a career center. Search the Internet for a similar organization in your state or region, or try a general search using the terms "independent school association."
- *Independent Teacher (www.independentteacher.org).* Free electronic journal for private school teachers that publishes articles on curriculum, testing, and pedagogy.
- *Private School Review (www.privateschoolreview.com).* Profiles of elementary and high school day schools, articles on finding a job in a private school, differences between public and private schools, and other topics.
- *All Else Equal: Are Public and Private Schools Different?* Luis Benveniste (RoutledgeFalmer, 2002).
- *The Handbook of Private Schools: An Annual Descriptive Survey of Independent Education.* Sargent Porter (Porter Sargent Publishers, 2006).

PART TWO

Learning More about the Teaching Profession

CHAPTER 4

Credentials: Certification and Education Programs

Teachers are educated professionals; they know their subject, handle classroom and curriculum, and keep up with the latest research and trends. They begin with a bachelor's degree, and often earn a master's or doctoral degree; therefore, changing careers to become a teacher usually involves a strong commitment to furthering your education.

Once you're certified and working in a school, you may decide to specialize (see Chapters 5 and 6), or continue in the classroom. Continuing education is vital to both choices—specializing requires coursework or another degree, and teaching requires instruction in new techniques, new ways of getting through to children dealing with learning disabilities and other issues, and new curriculum.

In this chapter, you'll learn about the education of teachers, from certification to advanced degrees.

STATE CERTIFICATION

To teach in a public school, you need to be certified by your state Department of Education. Licensing requirements differ, but most include:

- Completing an accredited program (including student teaching)
- Meeting testing requirements
- Passing background checks

Quick Check!

The University of Kentucky's College of Education website has links to every state's certification requirements. Check out *www.uky. edu/Education/TEP/usacert.html*.

Teaching certificates (called licenses in some states) are typically awarded in the following areas: elementary, middle grades, secondary, special education, and early childhood. Most states also offer endorsements, which are acknowledgments of specializations attached to teaching certificates. Endorsements approved by the Arizona Department of Education, for example, include art, bilingual education, computer science, cooperative education, dance, dramatic arts, driver education, early childhood, elementary foreign language, English as a second language (ESL), gifted, library media specialist, mathematics specialist, middle grade, music, physical education, reading specialist, and structured English immersion.

There are a number of ways to fulfill the accredited program requirement, all of which are described in detail in this chapter. If you already have a bachelor's degree, you can enroll in a master's program that includes education courses, licensing requirements, and practice teaching. Most states also have alternative certification programs in place, which give credit for life experiences, such as another career. These programs require a bachelor's degree, but many allow you to bypass an advanced degree.

Some educational programs are offered online and are typically accepted for alternative route certification. Obviously, though, the student teaching component must be done separately. Some states allow you to secure a teaching position while working on certification, and provide a teacher mentor for your first year (sometimes called a "teacher in residence" program). Check your state's requirements to determine whether online study is accepted.

To receive a license, you must probably (depending on where you live) also pass one or more tests. Some states use their own tests; Colorado, for example, requires a passing grade on a PLACE test (Program for Licensing Assessments for Colorado Educators), and California gives the CBEST test (California Basic Educational Skills Test). Others use nationally administered tests such as PRAXIS, which is currently required by 44 states, or a combination of national and state tests.

Background checks must be completed before a teaching license is granted in every state. They include fingerprinting and checks of state and federal criminal records. Many education programs perform these checks on their students before or immediately after accepting them.

ALTERNATIVE CERTIFICATION PROGRAMS

In the 1980s, the U.S. Department of Education began forecasting the teacher shortages our schools are currently experiencing. In response to this projection, states began devising routes to certification other than the traditional teacher training programs. New Jersey was the first, implementing a program in 1984 that recruited liberal arts graduates for a school-based licensing route. Candidates taught while gaining instruction in a university as well as from a mentor teacher. Today, New Jersey's Provisional Teacher Program is expanded to include special education and ESL. It produces approximately one-fourth of all new teachers hired in the state.

Currently, 47 states plus the District of Columbia have more than 120 different forms of alternative certification (Alaska, Indiana, and Nevada are the exceptions) that have already placed more than 250,000 teachers in the classroom. Alternative certification programs vary widely. Some, like New Jersey, put you in the classroom immediately after evaluating your credentials (college transcript, résumé, etc.). Others require coursework before a license is awarded, followed by a one-year internship and more coursework.

Some states offer a number of different alternative routes to traditional licensure. In Texas, for example, there are 67 state programs, including 21 based in community colleges and 8 conducted by private entities; 41 school districts also have their own programs. Some such programs involve online coursework, and most place candidates in the classroom upon acceptance to the program. More than half of all teachers hired in Texas each year are certified through an alternative route.

Alternative licenses often have restrictions. For example, some states allow them only for secondary schools, and others allow them only for certain subjects (typically math and/or science). Recently, more states have expanded their programs, loosening restrictions and allowing licenses to be obtained in more areas; technology and vocational education, special education, and bilingual education have been added in dozens of programs.

To find out about alternative certification routes in your state, including a listing of local programs, visit the website of the National Center for Alternative Certification (*www.teach-now.org*).

Example

The American Board for Certification of Teacher Excellence (ABCTE) offers a certification program called Passport to Teaching. It is designed for career-changing professionals and is currently recognized by Florida, Idaho, New Hampshire,

Pennsylvania, and Utah (check *www.abcte.org* for a complete and up-to-date listing). Passport to Teaching certifications are earned in elementary education (K–6), English (6–12), mathematics (6–12), general science (6–12), biology (6–12) or special education (K–6). ABCTE is currently developing, but does not yet offer, certifications in reading, physics, chemistry, and history.

To be eligible, a candidate must have a bachelor's degree, pass a federal background check, and perform well on exams in both the subject area and professional teaching knowledge. Passport to Teaching is highly individualized; candidates are assigned a Learning Plan Advisor who helps her evaluate her learning needs and develops an Individual Learning Plan. Resources such as books, websites, and online courses are used to fulfill the requirements of the Plan. Once a candidate completes the Learning Plan and state licensure requirements are met, she can take the exams. To learn more about this program, log onto *www.abcte.org/passport*.

THE BACHELOR'S DEGREE

Almost all public school teaching jobs require a bachelor's degree; if you don't already have one, you'll need to go back to school before beginning your new career. A significant advantage to this choice is that most programs integrate degree coursework with certification requirements and an internship or student teaching component. You can therefore complete your degree as you get a teaching certificate, making it possible to start working as a teacher as soon as you graduate.

Bachelor's degree programs typically take four years to complete; however, there are a number of methods that can be used to accelerate a program. Many schools accept scores from tests such as CLEP (College Level Examination Program) to exempt students from certain required courses. Others evaluate life and professional experiences for possible credit. Chapter 7 describes these and many other programs in detail.

The cost of a bachelor's degree varies greatly (and can depend, in part, on whether the program can be accelerated). State universities offer the lowest prices: Some schools in Florida, California, and Nevada cost less than $3,000 a year, including tuition and fees. At the other end of the spectrum, private colleges can cost more than 10 times that amount. Columbia University, which has a renowned Teachers College, costs more than $31,000 a year.

Prospective teachers enter a program to earn a bachelor of science degree in education. Most colleges and universities that offer this degree have three available programs: elementary or early childhood education major, middle school education minor, and secondary school education minor. Middle and secondary school minors major in a subject area, such as English, math, or science. Some schools also offer other education majors such as special education, deaf education, and athletic coaching.

A program leading to teacher certification typically involves three types of courses:

1. General liberal arts courses
2. Required courses in the major (e.g., elementary education or biology)
3. Professional education courses, including student teaching

Example

This is a course of study that would lead to a bachelor of science degree in elementary education:

First Year, First Semester

Number	Credits	Course Title
EDUC 131	3	Foundation Models of Education
ENG 150	3	English Composition, Written
GEOG	3	Geography
COMM	3	Communications
NUTR 100	3	Nutrition
Total, first year, first semester	15	

First Year, Second Semester

Number	Credits	Course Title
EDPS 250	3	Fundamentals of Child Development
TEAC 297A	2	Topics in Elementary Education
ARTS	3	Art
CONCEN	3	Concentration
SCI	3	Biological Science/Lab
Total, first year, second semester	14	

Second Year, First Semester

ENGL	3	English Composition, Written
NUTR 380	2	Physical Education for Elementary Schools
SCI	3	Science
CONCEN	3	Concentration
POLS 100	3	Power and Politics in America
Total, second year, first semester	12	

Second Year, Second Semester

SCI	4	Physical Science/Lab
HIST	3	History 201 or 202
TEAC 330	3	Multicultural Education
MATH 203	3	Contemporary Math
CONCEN	3	Concentration
Total, second year, second semester	17	

Second Year, Summer Semester

HIST	3	History 100 or 101
PHIL 101	3	Philosophy 101 or 106
EDPS 362	3	Learning in the Classroom
MATH 201	3	Geometry for Elementary Teachers
Total, second year, summer semester	12	

Third Year, First Semester

TEAC 351	3	Learner-Centered Classroom
TEAC 308	3	Teaching Math, Elementary School
TEAC 297b	3	Practicum: Elementary School
MATH 300	3	Mathematics Matters
TEAC 302	3	Children's Literature
MUED 370	3	Elementary School Music
Total, third year, first semester	18	

Third Year, Second Semester

ENG LIT	3	Race and Ethnicity
TEAC 259	3	Instructional Technology
HUM ELEC	3	Humanities
CONCEN	3	Concentration
TEAC 306	3	Teaching Art, Elementary School
TEAC 315	3	Teaching Science, Elementary School
Total, third year, first semester	18	

Fourth Year, First Semester

TEAC 311	3	Teaching Reading, Elementary School
TEAC 313	3	Teaching Reading II, Elementary School
TEAC 397A	3	Practicum 2: Elementary School
SPED 401A	3	Exceptional Learners in the Elementary Classroom
TEAC 307	3	Teaching Social Studies
Total, fourth year, first semester	15	

Fourth Year, Second Semester

TEAC 497A	10	Student Teaching, Elementary K–6
TEAC 497Y	1	Student Teaching, Mainstream
TEAC 497Z	1	Student Teaching, Multicultural
Total, fourth year, second semester	12	

THE MASTER'S DEGREE

If you already have a bachelor's degree in a field other than education, you may need to earn a master's degree before you can begin teaching (the section on Alternative Certification explains how, in some states, you can become certified without additional coursework). Many master's programs can be completed in less than two years and also include licensure requirements. The major for a master of science in education degree is typically elementary or secondary education. Secondary education majors must have a bachelor's degree or required coursework in their subject (biology, French, art, etc.).

Example

Master's degree requirements (31 semester hours minimum) would include the following courses:

Professional Core Courses (also meets licensure requirements)
(9 semester hours minimum)

Humanistic Dimensions of Education (Foundations) (3 semester hours), *choice of one*

EDUC 305	Advanced Social and Philosophical Aspects of Education (3)
EDUC 3030	Sociology of the Classroom (3)

Behavioral Studies (6 semester hours)

EDUC 3110	Psychological Foundations of Education (3)
SPED 3000	Educational Psychology of Exceptional Learners (3)

Teaching Related Coursework (also meets licensure requirements)
(9 semester hours)

EDUC 3500	Foundations of Education (3)
EDUC 3510	Advanced Teaching in Schools (3)
EDUC 2320	Teaching for Understanding and Academic Literacy (2)
EDUC 2360	Practicum in Secondary Schools III (1)

Subject Matter Methods (3 semester hours), *one of the following*

MTED 3370	Advanced Teaching of Mathematics in Secondary Schools (3)
SCED 3370	Advanced Teaching of Science in Secondary Schools (3)
SSED 3370	Advanced Teaching of Social Studies in Secondary Schools (3)
ENED 3370	English Education Theories and Practices (3)
FLED 2370	Teaching Foreign Language in Secondary Schools (3)

Student Teaching / Internship (7–9 semester hours)

EDUC 3002	Internship in Teaching: Secondary (6)
EDUC 3007	Internship Seminar: Secondary (1) English students take ENED 2400 (3 hours) in place of EDUC 3007

Electives (3 semester hours)

ONLINE EDUCATION OPTIONS

With the number of online courses and degrees offered today, you may be able to fulfill educational requirements without ever stepping into a classroom (other than the one in which you student teach!). Whether you need a few education courses or a master's degree, there is an option available on the Internet. Distance education programs allow you to learn material when you have the time, submit assignments electronically, and even take tests online. Professors are available to answer questions via email. Some courses run for a period of weeks or months, with specific dates for assignments and tests. Others are open-ended, so you can take as long as you like to complete them.

Most schools with distance programs in education offer a limited number of courses and majors. Because you are working to fulfill your state's licensing requirements, it is vital that you check that your state's department of education will recognize your work before beginning any program.

Example

An ESL certificate may be earned online from a large state university. It includes five graduate courses (which may be applied to a master's degree at a later date), three of which are required.

Core Courses

L540	Current Approaches in Instruction and Assessment in EFL/ENL Classrooms	
L500	Current Approaches in Instruction and Assessment in EFL/ENL Classrooms	
L530	Computer Assisted Language Learning	

Courses 4 and 5 *(select two)*

L541	Teaching Writing to Non-Native Speakers of English
L506	Teaching Writing to Non-Native Speakers of English
L630	Strategies and Styles in Language Learning

CERTIFICATE PROGRAMS

An alternative to a master's degree program, certificate programs accept students with bachelor's degrees in the subject in which they will teach and provide the additional coursework and teaching practice needed to earn a state teaching certificate. Certificate programs are typically completed in a year and may include some online instruction.

Example

The Post-Bachelor's Teaching Certificate Program requires seven courses in education after a transcript review of undergraduate content courses. Completion of the program, plus passing scores on necessary PRAXIS tests, satisfies the requirements for a teaching certificate. The Practicum is a 12-week student teaching experience with a licensed teacher.

Course Title	Number	Credits
Professional Instruction Studies	EDU 520	3
Diagnostic Teaching	EDU 521	4
Instruction Evaluation	EDU 522	4
Curriculum Trends and Research	EDU 523	3
Technology in the Classroom	EDU 524	3
Language Arts Instruction	EDU 525	3
Practicum	EDU 530	3

CONTINUING EDUCATION

Most states require licensed teachers to complete a number of continuing education units each year. Requirements vary, and some may be met through school-sponsored workshops, in-service day events, or online study. Other teachers choose to continue their education to advance their careers—the more education they have, the higher their salary, and in many cases, the more jobs that are available to them.

For example, an elementary school teacher might decide to become a reading specialist. An advanced degree is not required in most states for this specialist endorsement, but rather requirements may be fulfilled through a certification program.

Example

Reading Specialist Certification Program

The Reading Specialist Certification program confers a certificate only, although coursework may be applied to a future degree. Applicants must have a current state teaching certificate and a bachelor's degree with a 3.0 grade-point average, and they must have taken the following courses (or equivalent):

- Developmental psychology
- Adolescence

■ Methods in teaching beginning (or intermediate or advanced) readers

The program consists of 29 to 35 credits and prepares current educators for employment as:

■ A developmental reading teacher (K–12)
■ A reading teacher for special needs learners (K–12) who uses corrective, remedial, or advanced instruction
■ A reading resource teacher who assists other educators in his school or district

Required Courses

Course Title	Number	Credits
Literature for Children and Adolescents	EDU 378	3
Literacy Assessment	EDU 380	3
The Teaching of Writing	EDU 391	3
Best Practices in Literacy	EDU 420	3
Case Studies of Reading Difficulties	EDU 431	3
Administration and Supervision of Reading Program	EDU 460	3

NATIONAL BOARD CERTIFICATION

Another credential option for experienced teachers is National Board Certification. This voluntary certificate is offered through the National Board for Professional Teaching Standards and does not replace a state license, but rather enhances it. National Board Certification measures teachers' performance against a set of advanced standards, examining students' work, teaching portfolios, videos, and written tests. Candidates for certification must have a bachelor's degree and at least three years of teaching experience.

The process of attaining this certification is a rigorous one. Teachers who have completed it note that candidates should expect to spend approximately 500 hours total, including time spent creating portfolios, writing essays, videotaping lessons, and studying for and taking the six-hour exam. In addition, many teachers end up with a large bill; some school districts reimburse the $2,500 fee, but many do not. (The cost for those who won't be reimbursed can be offset by scholarships from the NBPTS and by companies and organizations such as State Farm Insurance, Boeing, and the William Randolph Hearst Foundation.)

However, teachers with National Board Certification report that the benefits far outweigh the costs. Those who relocate to another state often find it easier to find employment; although the national certification can't replace a state license, many states waive license requirements (except for a criminal background check) for teachers with the certification. There are financial incentives, too. Stipends or bonuses are awarded to teachers with the certification in many states. Arkansas and Alabama, for example, offer $5,000 annually. Illinois raises a nationally certified teacher's salary by $3,000.

Currently, there are 24 certifications available in 14 subject areas:

Generalist: early childhood, middle childhood, early adolescence

Art: early and middle childhood, early adolescence through young adulthood

Career and Technical Education: early adolescence through young adulthood

English as a New Language: early and middle childhood, early adolescence through young adulthood

English Language Arts: early adolescence, adolescence through young adulthood

Exceptional Needs Specialist: early childhood through young adulthood

Library Media: early childhood through young adulthood

Literacy (Reading, Language Arts): early and middle childhood

Mathematics: early adolescence; adolescence through young adulthood

Music: early and middle childhood; early adolescence through young adulthood

Physical Education: early and middle childhood; early adolescence through young adulthood

School Counseling: early childhood through young adulthood

Science: early adolescence, adolescence through young adulthood

Social Studies/History: early adolescence; adolescence through young adulthood

World Languages Other Than English: early adolescence through young adulthood

The NBPTS website lists standards for each certification, including portfolio work and testing. For example, an early adolescence social studies teacher must include samples of students' work, a video or DVD showing himself teaching, and evidence of his use of "whole-class lessons" to foster "civic competence." The assessment for this certification tests knowledge of "historical documents, population movements, political and economic systems, social movements, natural resources, and conflict in society." For more information on National Board Certification, contact the NBPTS through their website (*www.nbpts.org*) or **1-800-22TEACH** (1-800-228-3224).

CHAPTER 5

Teaching Specializations

Once you decide to embark on a career in teaching, you'll need to focus on the type of teaching you'd like to do. State certifications are specialized, with most states offering endorsements in dozens of areas. Tennessee, for example, offers 70 endorsements. Some of the most common are art, elementary or early childhood education, English, English as a second language (ESL), world languages (Chinese, French, Latin, German, Japanese, Spanish, etc.), mathematics, music, physical education and health, sciences (biology, chemistry, earth science, etc.), social studies, and special education.

But before you choose an area in which to specialize, you will need to decide on a setting. Almost every school district in the country divides its students among elementary, middle, and high schools. These schools offer unique teaching opportunities, as the abilities and needs of their students vary greatly. Most entry-level teachers have a clear idea about the setting they prefer—some enjoy small children, while others look forward to the challenge of introducing Shakespeare to a group of 11th-graders. If you're undecided, read the brief setting descriptions in this chapter, and check out the resources at the end of each section for more information.

ELEMENTARY SCHOOL

Kindergarten and elementary school teachers introduce their students not only to subjects such as language, math, and science, but they help them learn how to learn and provide them with their first experience of education. Educators of young children are familiar with and use many tools of teaching, such as books, music, artwork, computers, and games.

Most elementary teachers have one classroom in which they instruct one class of children in many subjects. Some schools have multi-age classes of two or more grades, and others use teams of two or three teachers for each class. Many elementary schools hire teachers to teach one specialized subject (typically art, music, or physical education).

Resources

1. National Association for the Education of Young Children *(www.naeyc.org)*: provides elementary school teachers with opportunities for professional development; publishes *Young Children* magazine, holds annual conferences for members.
2. National Science Teachers Association's Elementary Science Classroom Web pages *(www.nsta.org/elementaryschool)*: discussion board, lesson plans, research, and links.
3. Kentucky Educational Television's resources for Elementary school teachers *(www.ket.org/Education/IN/elem.html)*: comprehensive list of links to lesson plans, curriculum ideas, networking, etc.

MIDDLE SCHOOL

Middle school teachers instruct grades 5 or 6–8, and often consider these grades a highly challenging and highly rewarding group to teach. Students in these grades experience rapid growth and change physically, emotionally, socially, and intellectually, and adjustment to those changes can be difficult. Successful middle school teachers understand and work well with this group, acknowledging that their needs are very different from elementary and high school students.

Teachers typically offer instruction in one or two subjects, such as social studies, science, math, or language arts. They are certified to teach their subject(s) specifically to those grades. As with elementary schools, most middle schools hire additional teachers to instruct many classes in single subjects, such as art, physical education, and technology. Music classes in middle schools often involve instruction in instruments, and a music teacher may conduct the school band and/or chorus.

Resources

1. National Middle School Association *(www.nmsa.org)*: publishers of the periodicals *Middle Ground* and *Middle School Journal;* provides opportunities for professional development, research, and information on professional preparation.
2. *www.middleweb.com*: "Exploring Middle School Reform"; free newsletter with news and resources, teacher blogs and listserv, and articles.
3. *What Every Middle School Teacher Should Know,* by Trudy Knowles, Dave F. Brown (Heinemann, 2000).

THIRD-GRADE TEACHER

Job Location: Fernwood Elementary School, Rutland, Massachusetts

Job Summary: The Classroom Teacher shall assist students to learn subject matter and develop skills that will contribute to their development as mature, able, and responsible citizens. To meet this responsibility, the Teacher shall:

1. Plan a program of study that meets the individual needs, interests, and abilities of students.
2. Create a classroom environment that is conducive to learning and appropriate to the maturity and interests of students.
3. Guide the learning process toward the achievement of curriculum goals and establish, in harmony with the goals, clear objectives for all lessons, units, projects, and the like to communicate these objectives to students.
4. Employ instructional methods and materials that are most appropriate for meeting stated objectives.
5. Assess the accomplishment of students on a regular basis and provide progress reports as provided.

6. Diagnose the learning disabilities of students on a regular basis, seeking the assistance of district specialists as required.
7. Counsel with colleagues, students, and parents on a regular basis.
8. Assist the administration in implementing all policies and rules governing student life and conduct, and, for the classroom, develop reasonable rules of classroom behavior and procedure, and maintain order in the classroom in a fair and just manner.
9. Assist the administration in implementing District goals and policies related to the educational and operational needs of the District.
10. Attend staff or team meetings and serve on staff committees as required.
11. Maintain and improve professional competence.
12. Perform any other related task or duty at the direction of the building principal or designee.

■ **Qualifications**

Bachelor's degree from an accredited college or university

Valid Massachusetts Elementary teaching license

SEVENTH/EIGHTH-GRADE SCIENCE TEACHER

Job Location: Hopkins Middle School, Williston, Vermont

Job Summary: The Classroom Teacher is directly responsible to the principal of the school to which she/he is assigned, and will be held accountable for the performance responsibilities listed below.

1. Instruct and guide students according to their developmental needs and in accordance with district curricula.

2. Create a classroom environment and climate that is open, flexible, and conducive to learning.

3. Understand and demonstrate best practices in teaching and learning as well as current subject matter expertise.

4. Maintain appropriate student records and program documentation.

5. Communicate effectively with parents, students, and peers.

6. Implement District policies; follow school practices/procedures.

7. Assume supervisory responsibilities as assigned.

8. Demonstrate a commitment to continuing professional development.

9. Model professional behavior at all times.

10. Collaborate with other school and District staff members to achieve the District's mission and school's annual goals.

11. Perform other responsibilities as assigned by the building principal or designee.

■ **Qualifications**

Current Vermont teacher license with appropriate subject area endorsement(s)

Demonstrated understanding and applications of best practices in teaching and learning

Skills in collaborative problem solving, critical thinking, and teamwork

Knowledge of Vermont Framework of Standards and the ability to create interdisciplinary lessons/units

Commitment to District's mission and strategic plan

HIGH SCHOOL

High school teachers expand on the curricula taught to middle school students and almost always specialize in one subject. Lessons, homework, and exams are more sophisticated and are geared toward the maturing student population. Many high schools also offer courses in career and technical areas, and the teachers hired for those courses may also be in charge of assisting with career counseling and/or job placement.

High school teachers may be required to perform duties outside the classroom as well. Some teachers may assist with or lead an extracurricular activity, such as the school newspaper, a sports team, or a club involved with community outreach. Music teachers may form various bands or choral groups, conduct those groups, and travel with them to perform. Language teachers may travel with groups of students to foreign countries where they can practice their skills and observe the culture.

Resources

1. Discovery School *(http://school.discovery.com)*: includes teaching tools (quiz makers, lesson plan templates, etc.), Kathy Schrock's Guide for Educators, curriculum center, and teacher store.
2. "101 Things You Can Do the First Three Weeks of Class" (guide for high school teachers from the University of Nebraska, Lincoln): *ss.uno.edu/SS/TeachDevel/FirstDay/101Things.html*
3. *Your First Year as a High School Teacher,* by Lynne Marie Rominger and Suzanne Packard Laughrea (Three Rivers Press, 2001).

SECONDARY ENGLISH TEACHER

Job Location: Logan High School, Clark County, Nevada

Job Summary: As a Secondary English Teacher in the Clark County School District,

you will be instrumental in the development of the future workforce of this dynamic community. You will have access to the best technologies to facilitate development and management of your course work. To assist your success in the classroom, mentors will be assigned to share their best teaching practices.

■ Qualifications

To be hired for a position as a secondary English teacher, you must hold or be able to obtain a clear Nevada secondary teaching license, which includes:

A bachelor's degree from an accredited college/university

Completing an approved program of preparation for teaching in the secondary grades (grades 7–12)

Earning a comprehensive major in English consisting of at least 36 semester hours of college/university credit in a course of study in English

Passing the Pre-Professional Skills Test (PPST), the Principles of Learning and Teaching (PLT) test, and the English Content Knowledge and the English Language, Literature and Composition: Pedagogy specialty area tests.

CORE SUBJECTS

For middle and high school students, four subjects form the "core" of their studies: English, mathematics, science, and social studies. Teachers who specialize in them can teach in a variety of areas within these subjects. For example, a science teacher might have a certificate in biology, chemistry, or physics. Social studies teachers might be certified to teach geography, politics, or world history, among other areas.

Typically core teachers are certified to work in either middle school or high school (see earlier sections for brief descriptions of each). Most states require a minimum of a bachelor's degree in the area of specialization.

Resources

1. National Council of Teachers of English *(www.ncte.org)*: provides newsletter, conferences, and professional development for its members.
2. Purdue University's Online Writing Lab Internet resources for English Teachers page *(http://owl.english.purdue.edu/internet/Resources/teachers. html)*: premier site for grammar and mechanics lessons; offers many links for English teachers.
3. National Council of Teachers of Mathematics *(www.nctm.org)*: provides newsletter, conferences, and professional development for its members.
4. Terri Husted's New Math Teacher Homepage *(http://people.clarityconnect. com/webpages/terri/terri.html)*: advice on classroom management, lesson planning, and professional suggestions; links to other new math teacher resources.
5. National Science Teachers Association *(www.nsta.org)*: provides newsletter, conferences, and professional development for its members.
6. Science Teachers Resource Center *(http://chem.lapeer.org)*: forum in which science teachers share ideas; areas include AP Chemistry, AP Biology, Chemistry, Life Science, and Physics.
7. National Council for the Social Studies *(www.socialstudies.org)*: provides newsletter, conferences, and professional development for its members.
8. Dwayne Voegeli's Social Studies Teacher's Page *(www.jarviscomputer.com/ voegeli)*: links and other resources for secondary school teachers.

HIGH SCHOOL MATH TEACHER

Job Location: Phoenix High School, Oakland, California

Job Summary: Phoenix seeks a Math Instructor who is committed to working with traditionally underserved high school students. The successful candidate must be able to work in a startup environment and will have experience, energy, and enthusiasm. Phoenix is looking for candidates with at least two years of teaching experience who have developed and delivered curriculum that engages students in learning that builds their academic skills through the exploration of self, community, and culture. Phoenix curriculum is aligned with California state standards.

The Math Instructor will be responsible for:

1. Teaching two classes of 18–24 students, grades 9–12, which include students with widely varying skill levels

2. Advising 12–15 students, which requires monitoring overall participation in school and maintaining regular contact with parents

3. Assisting with the development and implementation of schoolwide practices, policies, and procedures

4. Helping coordinate extracurricular and curricular community resources

■ **Qualifications:**

Valid California single-subject teaching credential in math.

Experience in the following:

1. Diverse population of young people

2. Bringing community issues and resources into the classroom and taking students into the community

3. Developing curriculum that includes individual and group projects, portfolios, and/or final exhibitions or presentations of learning

4. Developing projects and lessons plans for a wide range of skill level; managing classes of 20—25 students

5. Collaborating with others in the design of curriculum and school policies

SEVENTH-GRADE SOCIAL STUDIES TEACHER

Job Location: Sheridan High School, Sheridan, Wyoming

Job Summary: Candidate must demonstrate the professional and personal qualities necessary to be successful as a teacher at the high school level. Coaching endorsements in conjunction with subject matter certification will receive extra consideration. Successful candidate will be involved in teaching students to read, write, problem solve, compute, find information, think, and work cooperatively with others. Candidate will be helping students meet all district requirements and curriculum objectives.

■ **Qualifications**

Must hold or be eligible for a Wyoming Teaching Certificate with endorsements in General Social Studies, Geography, Political Science or Government, and U.S. History.

GIFTED EDUCATION

The teaching of gifted children has changed dramatically over the past century. It began with an acceleration-only method, in which students whose IQs were above a set standard (and who could demonstrate that intelligence) were simply moved up through grades until an appropriately challenging level was reached. While that method is still in use (especially in single subjects such as math or science), gifted education has expanded to include separate curriculum, "tiered curriculum" (the same lesson is taught at different levels within one classroom to challenge students at each level), and specially trained teachers.

Teachers of gifted (often called "gifted and talented") students work in elementary and middle schools and typically do not have their own class. Instead, they provide enrichment and support for students in addition to their regular classroom experience. Their responsibilities may include organizing enrichment activities; presenting information to other teachers about new teaching practices, materials, resources, and opportunities for their gifted students; modifying regular curriculum for gifted students; meeting with students, parents, and teachers to offer advice and support regarding issues and problems associated with giftedness; and encouraging their students to achieve at the levels they are capable of.

Resources

1. The National Research Center on the Gifted and Talented (*www.gifted.uconn. edu/nrcgt.html*): newsletter, research reports, and online resources.
2. National Association for Gifted Children *(www.nagc.org)*: publishers of Teaching for High Potential, a resource for teachers; searchable online articles.
3. Hoagies' Gifted Education Page *(www.nagc.org)*: includes lists, boards, and blogs for teachers; extensive annotated bibliography of books about gifted education; and employment listings.

GIFTED AND TALENTED—ELEMENTARY

Job Location: Johnson Elementary School, Boise, Idaho

Job Summary: Seeking highly motivated, creative teacher who is a resourceful thinker and self-starter, and who has an appreciation/understanding of the gifter learner. Successful candidate will teach a multi-age class of older elementary students.

■ **Qualifications**

Must hold or be eligible for Idaho State Standard Elementary Teaching Certificate with Gifted and Talented Endorsement.

B.A. minimum in approved field

SPECIAL EDUCATION

Most special education teachers work in elementary, middle, or high schools with students who have mild to moderate disabilities, including specific learning disabilities, speech or language impairment, mental retardation, emotional disturbance, hearing or visual impairment (or both), orthopedic impairment, and autism. They help to develop Individualized Education Programs (IEPs) for their students, which include goals for each student based on the student's needs and abilities.

Special education teachers may have their own classrooms, or share a classroom with a general education teacher in schools where inclusiveness is stressed. They develop curricula appropriate for their student's needs and abilities, and teach it using a wide variety of techniques. In addition to academics, special education teachers focus on their students' emotional, behavioral, and social development. They also work closely with parents, social workers, school psychologists, therapists, and school administrators.

Every state requires licensure for special education teachers. Some grant general licenses that allow teaching of students with all disabilities, from kindergarten through high school. Others acknowledge specialties such as learning disabilities or hearing impairment.

Resources

1. The Office of Special Education Programs of the U.S. Department of Education *(www.ed.gov/about/offices/list/osers/osep/index.html?src=mr)*: information on the Individuals with Disabilities Education Improvement Act, teacher workshops, research, and newsletter.
2. Council for Exceptional Children *(www.cec.sped.org//AM/Template .cfm?Section=Home)*: organization for special education teachers, with information on professional development, licensure, and teacher support.
3. *Exceptional Children: An Introduction to Special Education,* 8th ed., by William L. Heward (Prentice Hall, 1999).

SPECIAL EDUCATION TEACHER

Job Location: Denver, Colorado

Job Summary: Seeking experienced teacher responsible for providing curriculum instruction to groups of school-aged students in a self-contained classroom. Will provide educational and treatment programming and the supervision of two classroom assistants. This position works collaboratively on a multidisciplinary team model and reports to the Director of Education.

■ **Qualifications**

Must have a valid Colorado Teaching Certificate with a Teacher II (Severe Effective) or Special Education Generalist endorsement (or willing to obtain)

Must have a current Colorado driver's license.

Previous Special Education experience required.

MUSIC

Music teachers who work in elementary schools often teach a general music class to all the students in their school. They develop a curriculum based on guidelines set by a school music department head, district music supervisors, state music education supervisor, and/or national standards. General classes introduce students to song, simple instruments, and reading music (in higher grades).

Middle and secondary school music teachers typically do not teach general classes, but rather are hired to work with instrumental or choral groups. They may teach students how to play instruments and may specialize in one instrument or group of instruments (such as wind or brass). They may lead a band, orchestra, or choir, which involves rehearsing, conducting, and putting on concerts. Most states require music teachers to have a bachelor's degree in music or art, even for those seeking licensure through an alternative route.

Resources

1. K–12 resources for Music Educators *(www.isd77.k12.mn.us/music/k-12music/)*: comprehensive set of links for band, choral, orchestra, and classroom.
2. "Why Teach? Why Music? Why Me?" *(www.menc.org/guides/whyteach/whymusic.html)*: article from the National Association for Music Education website.
3. *The Music Teacher's Survival Guide: Practical Techniques and Materials for the Elementary Music Teacher,* by Rosalie Haritun (Parker Publishing Company, 1994).

ELEMENTARY MUSIC TEACHER

Job Location: Sullivan Elementary School, Cambria, California

Job Summary: Sullivan Elementary School is seeking an enthusiastic teacher who loves working with children for our K–4 music program. This is a full-time, ten-month position with benefits. Our small district has dedicated itself to offering a full music and arts program to all students grades K–8.

■ **Qualifications**

The successful candidate must:

Love music and children!

Hold a California Teaching Credential in Music

Have knowledge of Orff-Schulwerk methodology

ART

Art teachers, whether hired by elementary, middle, or high schools, are hired to teach one subject. All states require certification that typically covers grades K–12; requirements include a bachelor's degree (or comparable work experience in some cases). Elementary art teachers work with their young students in various mediums, both two and three dimensional, and may introduce them to artists and their work. In middle school, art instruction and projects are more sophisticated as students' abilities increase. Some middle schools include art history in their art curriculum, while others maintain general studio classes. High school art teachers may specialize in one area, such as pottery, photography, or textile design, or they may be required to offer instruction in more than one area.

Resources

1. National Art Education Association *(www.naea-reston.org)*: "Why Art Education?" page, membership, and bimonthly journal.
2. National Gallery of Art Teaching Resources (*www.nga.gov/education/ classroom*): comprehensive search engine for artists, topics, and curriculum.
3. The Art Teacher Connection *(www.artteacherconnection.com)*: integrating computer technology and visual arts.

ELEMENTARY ART TEACHER

Job Location: Glendora, California

Job Summary: The Foothills Elementary School anticipates the need for an Art Teacher. Responsibilities include teaching art classes to preschool through sixth-graders, as well as facilitating open studio hours. In addition, participation in art shows, performances, and other events is required. Must be excited about working as part of an integrated Arts Team that also includes a librarian, music teacher, French teacher, and physical education teacher.

■ **Qualifications**

California licensure as an art teacher

Entry-level accepted

Bachelor's degree from an accredited institution preferred

Application Essay Questions (limit answers to 4,000 characters each):

1. What is your favorite Art material? Why are you passionate about this particular material, and how will you share that passion with children?
2. Why is Art an integral part of the school curriculum? How will you advocate for Arts education in our school and community?

LANGUAGE

Opportunities for language teachers are expected to grow faster than those for many other types of teachers as an emphasis on global competition increases. According to recent research, only 44 percent of high school students are enrolled in foreign language courses, compared with compulsory enrollment in schools throughout Asia and Europe. The U.S. Department of Education reports, for example, that 200 million Chinese students are learning English while approximately 24,000 (out of 54 million) American elementary and secondary school students are studying Chinese. The recognition of a need for the U.S. workforce to communicate and compete in a global economy has increased federal funding and expanded language programs throughout the country.

The number of languages offered in American schools varies greatly. Every high school provides access to instruction in at least a few languages, with French and Spanish being the most popular. However, a greater emphasis is being placed both on the teaching of "critical need languages" (such as Arabic, Chinese, Japanese, and Korean) and earlier exposure to language learning (in elementary and middle schools).

Resources

1. The American Council on the Teaching of Foreign Languages *(www.actfl. org/i4a/pages/index.cfm?pageid=1)*: publishes The Language Educator, holds conventions, and provides professional development opportunities.
2. The National Network for Early Language Learning *(http://nnell.org)*: for educators, parents, and policymakers, supporting the successful teaching of a second language to young students.
3. Foreign Language Teaching Forum *(www.cortland.edu/flteach)*: State University of New York Cortland's site; includes a foreign language listserv for communicating with other teachers.

ELEMENTARY SPANISH TEACHER

Job Location: Allentown, Pennsylvania

Job Summary: Johnson School is looking for an Elementary Spanish Language Teacher for a K–5 position. Ideal candidates should have experience designing and implementing curriculum, working with students with varied learning styles and levels of mastery; maintain a nurturing, student-centered classroom environment; demonstrate superior written and oral communication skills; and be able to develop cooperative relationships with parents, faculty, staff, and students.

■ **Qualifications**

Must possess a Pennsylvania Instructional One Teaching Certificate

Have successful classroom experience in an elementary or Spanish language classroom

Possess or at least be working toward a master's degree

PHYSICAL EDUCATION/HEALTH

The job of physical education (PE) and health instructors has undergone great changes in the last decade. What many call "the New PE" emphasizes fitness rather than sports. Physical education and health teachers are responding to the needs of a student population that has become increasingly overweight and sedentary by teaching the benefits of being physically active and healthy. The goal is to get students "hooked" on fitness for life.

In elementary schools, physical education teachers lead classes in indoor and outdoor activities that vary depending on the facility. Running, rock climbing, biking, jump roping, cross-country skiing, and swimming are age-appropriate activities, as are old stand-bys such as basketball and softball. Middle school students can begin weight training, sprinting, long distance running, and other more advanced physical activities. By high school, physical education classes can look like a trip to the health club; many schools have cardio and weight resistance machines, and students are taught to monitor body fat and calorie intake. Classes in racquet sports, yoga, gymnastics, and tai chi are not uncommon.

Physical education teachers often also teach health classes; indeed, most undergraduate PE curricula include classes in health education. Health teachers are typically certified to teach K–12, and work with district-, state-, or national-mandated class content. For example, Kansas uses the National Committee for Health Education Standards content areas: mental and emotional health; family living; growth and development; nutrition; personal health and physical activity; alcohol, tobacco, and other drugs; communicable and chronic diseases; injury prevention and safety; consumer health; and environmental health.

Resources

1. American Alliance for Health, Physical Education, Recreation, and Dance *(www.aahperd.org):* alliance of five groups, including the National Association for Sport and Physical Education and the American Association of Health Education.
2. PE Central *(www.pecentral.org):* information for PE and health teachers on best practices, assessment, and programs for every grade and ability level.
3. PBS Teacher Source Health and Fitness *(www.pbs.org/teachersource/health .htm):* lesson plans and activities searchable by age group and topic.

MIDDLE SCHOOL PHYSICAL EDUCATION AND HEALTH TEACHER

Job Location: Streamside Middle School, Duxbury, Vermont

Job Summary: The ideal candidate will have experience working with early adolescents and will have experience with PE and Health education. The position includes both PE instruction (75 percent) for grades 5–8 and health instruction (25 percent) with grades 7–8. The teacher will be part of a two-teacher PE/Health team; in addition, this position is part of a larger Unified Arts Team.

■ **Qualifications**

State certification and bachelor's degree

Must be considered to be a Highly Qualified Teacher

Must have taken PRAXIS

Must have been fingerprinted in Vermont

ENGLISH AS A SECOND LANGUAGE

Teachers of English as a second language (ESL) provide instruction in many different settings. Some may have their own classroom in which they teach various groups during the day. Others provide support to students within another teacher's classroom. ESL teachers may also work with individual students, helping them improve their language skills.

Other possible duties include completing screenings of English language learners and tracking students' progress and reporting to administrators, other teachers, and parents. ESL teachers are sometimes required to provide in-service training to other teachers, presenting techniques, strategies, and materials that help improve English language learning.

Most states require certification for ESL teachers; there are accredited schools in every state that offer undergraduate ESL courses. For those who enjoy travel, there are many opportunities worldwide for ESL teachers.

Resources

1. Teachers of English to Speakers of Other Languages, Inc. (TESOL) (*www.tesol.org/s_tesol/index.asp*): resource page for emerging teachers, publications, conferences, and professional development opportunities.
2. Ohio University's ESL Teacher Resources page (*www.ohiou.edu/Esl/teacher/*): links to skill- and content-based instruction sites, testing and assessment information, employment opportunities, and more.
3. *Teaching English as a Foreign or Second Language: A Teacher Self-development and Methodology Guide,* by Jerry G. Gebhard (University of Michigan Press, 1996). Aimed at the new teacher, with an emphasis on self-development.

ESL TEACHER

Job Location: Roosevelt High School, East Lansing, Michigan

Job Summary: Provide classroom instruction in English to international students in grades 9–10 and 11–12; teach according to the English as a Second Language Curriculum Guide. Coaching openings available.

■ **Qualifications**

Current Michigan Teaching Certificate with ESL Endorsement

Experience in teaching English as a Second Language

Background in working with international students

CHAPTER 6

Teaching Specializations Outside the Classroom

Teachers have many career options in addition to the traditional classroom role. Some of the jobs described in this chapter require further education, and others may be held in conjunction with a traditional teaching position. Not all jobs are offered at all schools or in all school districts; program supervisors, for example, are typically hired only by large school districts. But the following vocational options show the wide range of opportunities available to teachers looking to enhance or expand their careers.

TEACHER MENTOR

Twenty years ago, new teachers who asked about induction support would have probably been viewed as having weak qualifications. On the other hand, if school officials had volunteered their assistance to new teachers, they might have been misinterpreted as assuming candidates were unprepared. Today, we recognize how challenging teaching is and how mentors can help incoming teachers be successful in effective teaching practices.

Teacher mentoring programs are a relatively new professional development tool. They are designed to help new teachers develop their skills in a supportive environment, effectively doing away with the old "sink or swim" mentality. Studies show that retention of quality teachers is greatly improved when those teachers are provided with a mentor. These programs recognize and rely on the knowledge and skills of an experienced teacher who has much to share with a recently hired colleague. Mentors perform structured tasks, such as developing teaching assignments, acting as safety nets, answering questions, and providing guidance when needed. Most mentoring programs include instruction and support for their mentors through initial and ongoing training sessions, print and Web-based materials, and mentor meetings.

Mentors are hired internally, within the school in which they already teach. Mentor positions are therefore not advertised as other jobs are. Mentors are selected in various ways; some schools form selection committees that review résumés and interview prospective mentors, while at other schools, the principal selects mentors.

Resources

1. The Mentor Center: (*http://teachermentors.com*): dozens of links, advice, and other information for mentors.
2. Teacher's Network (*www.teachnet.org/TNPI/research/prep/index.htm*): research on mentoring.
3. *The Good Teacher Mentor: Setting the Standard for Support and Success,* by Sidney Trubowitz, Maureen Picard Robins, and Seymour Bernard Sarason (Teachers College Press, 2003).

TUTOR

Tutors work with individual students or small groups of students and reinforce classroom instruction. Tutoring positions may be full- or part-time in schools or created by individual teachers who wish to supplement their income or work fewer hours. In-school tutors are also referred to as "support technicians" or "support teachers."

Successful tutors are motivating and inspiring; their role is not simply to impart information, but to work with students' self-confidence, time management, and study skills issues. Their primary focus is on helping students learn how to learn; this can mean teaching a student how to slow down and take in smaller bits of information at a time, or it can mean reformatting content to make it more comprehensible to the student. Every strategy has as its goal the improvement of a student's ability to process and retain information.

Attributes of a good tutor include the following:

- A genuine desire to help others
- Reliability and enthusiasm
- An open mind and a positive outlook
- The ability to take initiative
- Patience, understanding, and empathy

Resources

1. National Tutoring Association *(www.ntatutor.org)*: offers certification program, holds conferences, supports research.
2. Association for the Tutoring Profession *(www.jsu.edu/depart/edprof/atp)*: offers workshops and grants, links to job openings.
3. *www.crla.net/tutoringexchangenewsletter.pdf*: link to the College Reading and Language Association's Tutoring Exchange newsletter.

ACADEMIC SUPPORT TECHNICIAN

Job Location: Baltimore, Maryland

Job Summary: The Academic Support Technician is responsible for tutoring academic subjects to at-risk students, for the ongoing assessment of students, and for maintaining required program documents and data for evaluation purposes. He or she will work with identified students individually or in small groups in core content areas for one to two hours per week as assigned by administration and determined by student need. Additionally, the AST will collaborate with administrative and instructional staff members and other school officials for the purpose of assessment and will communicate with parents for the purpose of informing them of individual student academic progress.

■ **Qualifications**

Bachelor's degree

Oral and written English language proficiency

Ability to work with students and teachers

Ability to reinforce academic skills

READING OR LITERACY SPECIALIST

Reading specialists are responsible for the literacy performance of students, and may be hired to work in one school or in many. They provide expert instruction, assessment, and leadership not only for students, but also for teachers of reading. In some states, reading specialists, like teacher mentors, may continue teaching in the classroom while working as specialists. Ohio, for example, is one of a growing number of states that offers a teaching license with a literacy specialist endorsement. The Ohio Board of Education describes the license as a "career advancement alternative." Teachers who hold it can continue in the classroom while also working as reading coaches or mentors to the other teachers in their school.

The standards for a reading specialist, as with most education positions, vary from state to state. However, most states do not have strict requirements. *Education Statistics Quarterly* [part of the U.S. Department of Education (DOE); *http://nces. ed.gov/programs/quarterly*] reports that two-thirds of reading specialists do not have graduate degrees, but rather earned a bachelor's degree in elementary education without a concentration in reading theory, assessment, and instruction.

The International Reading Association formulated recommendations for the role of the reading specialist, which includes instruction, assessment, and leadership. These roles involve working closely with classroom teachers to supplement standard curriculum, accurately diagnosing reading problems and designing schoolwide and individual student solutions, and acting as a resource and support person for faculty. States such as Ohio look to these recommendations when developing standards for reading specialists.

Resources

1. International Reading Association *(www.reading.org)*: membership organization that holds conferences, publishes newsletters, offers information and instruction on Response to Intervention.
2. Reading is Fundamental *(www.rif.org)*: educator Web pages include lesson plans, research articles, and links to other useful sites
3. Center for the Improvement of Early Reading Achievement *(CIERA, www.ciera.org)*: solutions to persistent problems in reading geared toward teachers, teacher educators, parents, policymakers, and others.

TEACHER, READING SPECIALIST

Job Location: Virginia Beach, Virginia

Job Summary: Position is responsible for implementing a comprehensive literacy program at the assigned school through coaching, supporting, and guiding teachers in the best practices for literacy instruction. Position conducts staff development, models lessons, conducts classroom visitations, and provides feedback to teachers and administrators on the school's literacy program. Position is responsible for analyzing school literacy data and planning for future literacy needs. Position is responsible for instructing students individually or in groups to enable students to develop literacy skills.

■ Qualifications

Valid Virginia Teaching License with an endorsement in reading

Applicant with teaching experience must have an acceptable rating for such teaching; teaching experience preferred

Ability to work collaboratively with colleagues and supervisors

Ability to monitor academic and social behavior of students

Ability to move about in room to monitor students and check work in classrooms with varied seating and desk organization patterns

Ability to prepare required written reports

PROGRAM SUPERVISOR/DEPARTMENT HEAD

The position of program supervisor may be offered in one school or within a school district. It is an oversight job performed alone or in conjunction with a classroom position. Program supervisors work with teachers to design and implement programs such as special education and gifted and talented. In some larger schools, and most high schools, department heads are hired to oversee one subject. Many department heads, like program supervisors, continue to hold a classroom position.

There are no state regulations for program supervisors or department heads. Experience and education are the most important qualifications; teaching experience in the program or department is critical, and an advanced degree is often sought by employers.

Resources

See listings under Administration Leadership later in this chapter and under individual subjects in this chapter.

SUPERVISOR, SCIENCE

Job Location: Granville, Ohio, School District

Job Summary: Supervise K–12 science curriculum and instruction to ensure program continuity and quality. Evaluate the effectiveness of present programs in meeting the needs of students, and the system's goals. Provide science support for district teachers and administrators as required.

■ **Qualifications**

Five years' experience teaching science

Ohio teaching license in earth sciences, integrated science, life sciences, or physical sciences

Masters degree or higher in related field

Managerial skills to supervise work of 15-teacher department

Knowledge of curriculum and ability to implement changes as necessary

MATHEMATICS SPECIALIST

Mathematics specialists are teacher leaders with strong preparation and background in mathematics content and instructional strategies. They can be based in elementary, middle, and high schools and are current or former classroom teachers. Mathematics specialists support the professional growth of their colleagues by strengthening their understanding of content, providing opportunities for improved math instruction, sharing research concerning how math is learned, and helping them use more effective teaching practices. Their goal is to increase and improve all students' math achievement.

Other duties may include:

- Collaborating with individual teachers through co-planning, co-teaching, and coaching
- Assisting administrative and instructional staff in interpreting data and designing approaches to improve student achievement and instruction
- Ensuring the curriculum is aligned with state and national standards and with their school division's mathematics curriculum
- Promoting teachers' delivery and understanding of the school curriculum through collaborative long- and short-range planning
- Facilitating teachers' use of successful, research-based instructional strategies, including differentiated instruction for diverse learners such as those with limited English proficiency or disabilities
- Working with parent/guardians and community leaders to foster continuing home/school/community partnerships that are focused on students' learning of mathematics
- Collaborating with administrators to provide leadership and vision for a schoolwide mathematics program

Resources

1. National Council for Teachers of Mathematics *(www.nctm.org)*: contains professional development, publications, page on "Be a Math Teacher."
2. American Mathematical Society *(www.ams.org)*: career information and guidance; message boards.
3. Mathematical Association of America *(www.maa.org)*: research and other resources.

MATHEMATICS SPECIALIST

Job Location: Amarillo High School, Amarillo, Texas

Job Summary: Candidates must:

Demonstrate expertise in teaching and working with the Texas Essential Knowledge and Skills (TEKS) of Mathematics

Possess effective interpersonal skills and willingness to work collaboratively with teachers and administrators plus effective coaching, problem solving, and conferencing skills

Demonstrate commitment to professional growth and learning

Demonstrate use of best teaching practices

Possess an understanding of and ability to use teacher development research

Be able to obtain and use evaluative data to examine curriculum and instruction program effectiveness

Provide effective staff development activities that incorporate the mathematics mission of the district

Plan the necessary time, resources, and materials necessary to support the accomplishment of campus/district goals

Align instruction and assessments

■ **Qualifications**

Valid SBEC Mathematics Teaching Certification

ADMINISTRATION LEADERSHIP: SUPERINTENDENT, PRINCIPAL, VICE OR ASSISTANT SUPERINTENDENT AND PRINCIPAL

Education administrators oversee all aspects of a school district (superintendent) or a school (principal). They develop educational standards, establish policies, and supervise staff. Superintendents and principals relate not only internally, with students and staff, but also handle communication with parents, the school board, and the community. In larger districts, assistants to these positions are hired, and duties are divided between the superintendent or principal and his assistant.

More specifically, a superintendent is the chief administrative officer of a school district and is hired by that district's school board. Superintendents must oversee not only the employees of the school district, but also the students. They must have a relationship with the school board and the community of which the school district is a part. Here is a typical job description for a Superintendent of Schools:

1. For Students:
   a. Keeps the needs of children paramount in the performance of all other duties.
   b. Serves as the curricular leader of schools, maintaining at all times the highest possible standards for the instructional programs of the school district.

2. For Employees:
    a. Develops an organizational chart that clearly shows the lines of authority and responsibility of all employees within the school district.
    b. Develops job descriptions for all positions of employment.
    c. Establishes a procedure for the written annual evaluation of each full-time employee. The supervisor responsible for each evaluation shall be clearly identified by the organizational chart.
    d. Establishes, with the approval of the school board, a procedure for encouraging the professional growth of all employees.
    e. Develops a system of collaborative management that includes both board and administration in development of goals and procedures for improvement.
3. For the Community:
    a. Represents the school district to the community.
    b. Encourages community participation in their schools.
    c. Assists in development of action plans to assure the community of continued improvement of our schools.
    d. Maintains the highest standards for all school facilities.
4. For the Board:
    a. Implements school board policy by developing administrative regulations that reflect the will of the board.
    b. Monitors the effectiveness of board policy and assists the board in investigating changes that would benefit the operation of the school district.
    c. Recommends to the board all candidates for employment, and includes in the recommendation a report of their academic credentials. In the case of administrative employees, meets with the board prior to the posting of any opening to discuss the procedures to be used in the selection process.
    d. Accepts, on behalf of the board, all employee resignations except her own. Once the superintendent has accepted a resignation, it may not be rescinded without board approval.
    e. Submits to the board, in a timely manner, the annual budget of the school corporation.
    f. Accounts to the board for all funds of the school corporation.
    g. Meets with the board president in a timely fashion to set the formal agenda for all board meetings.
    h. Keeps the board informed of significant changes occurring within the school district.
    i. Performs such other duties as the board may from time to time delegate.

Principals manage elementary, middle, and secondary schools, setting school policies and goals. They hire staff, evaluate performance, and create professional development opportunities. They work with their staff to improve student performance and curriculum standards. Principals also make budgets, oversee record keeping, and, in many cases, work to obtain financial support for their schools.

As the emphasis on national standardized testing increases, and school funding becomes more dependent on test performance, principals' involvement in the test preparation process also increases. The DOE can order that schools with poor test scores be taken over by the federal government. Some states or districts directly tie principals' bonuses, salaries, and even employment to their schools' performance. The accountability of the school to achievement mandates therefore often rests with the administration. Principals must become very familiar with the tests and work with teachers to create plans to address students' readiness and the possibility of low scores.

Other tasks include:

- Community relations
- Dealing with parental questions, concerns, complaints, etc.
- Disciplining students
- Facility management/coordination
- School safety
- Student and teacher assessment

Every state has standards for superintendents and principals. Most require at least three years of teaching experience, state certification as a school administrator, and an advanced degree (typically in education administration or educational leadership). Some states administer a test as part of the certification or licensure process. In addition, skills such as leadership, decision making, organizational abilities, and confidence, are required.

Resources

1. *www.superintendentofschools.com:* New York–based site with good general information about the position and professional development.
2. American Association of School Administrators *(www.aasa.org):* membership organization offering conferences, research, and publications.
3. Public School Administrator magazine *(www.freetradepubs.com/details.php? itemID=60598):* information on improving school performance, reporting on the best practices in public school administration.

ELEMENTARY SCHOOL PRINCIPAL

Job Location: Houston, Texas

Job Summary: The job of Elementary School Principal is for the purpose(s) of maintaining overall instructional and support operations at assigned elementary school including receiving, distributing, and communicating information to enforce school, district, and state policies; maintaining safety of school environment; coordinating school activities; communicating information to staff; addressing situations, problems, and/or conflicts that could negatively affect the school; developing school policies, vision, and mission goals; and guiding the instruction of programs.

■ **Qualifications**

Master's degree; Texas certification as a school principal

Teaching experience (3–5 years); educational administration/supervision experience (3–5 years)

Evidence of understanding of elementary education, including early childhood and primary levels

Evidence of leadership ability necessary for the improvement of instruction; evidence of compensatory education program knowledge, including special education, Chapter I, and other title programs of a federal and state nature

Demonstrated mastery of communications, decision-making, and human relation skills

ADMINISTRATION: CURRICULUM DIRECTOR

Curriculum director is typically a school district, as opposed to an individual school, position. Curriculum administrators work to develop and improve the quality of what is taught in classrooms. They work with the faculty of each school in their district and, in larger districts, may manage curriculum committees and/or curriculum coordinators. Curriculum directors also work closely with the school board and with state and national testing administrators.

Most curriculum directors work as teachers for a number of years before moving into this administrative position. State requirements vary, but most include an advanced degree, experience in teaching and/or administration, and a valid teacher's license or certificate.

Typical duties include:

- Planning and coordinating the development and implementation of curriculum areas
- Assisting with development and updating of course content
- Assisting and developing new curriculum guidelines
- Serving as a liaison between various organizations (e.g., regional office of education) and faculty concerning new information on educational programs and procedures

- Aligning all curriculum to state standards
- Compliance with state and national testing and other policies
- Assisting faculty with textbook selection and purchases

Resources

1. Center for Curriculum Renewal *(www.curriculumrenewal.com):* supports curriculum directors on- and offsite.
2. "Curriculum Director's Legal Insider" *(www.brownstone.com/products/ product.cfm?product_id=193):* newsletter dealing with federal regulations, the U.S. Department of Education, and more general curriculum issues.
3. *www.uml.edu/College/Education/Faculty/lebaron/ppsites.html#School:* University of Massachusetts Lowell's links to curriculum improvement and development information.

CURRICULUM DIRECTOR

Job Location: Knollwood High School, Baton Rouge, Louisiana

Job Summary: The curriculum director shall:

1. Plan for improvement of curriculum and instruction
2. Coordinate assessment writing and assist the principal in the development of the annual school improvement plan
3. Coordinate professional development activities, the mentoring program, and the advanced placement program
4. Interpret the curriculum to the staff, administration, Board of Education, and general public
5. Assist in the preparation and coordination of institute and in-service programs
6. Establish procedures for placement, evaluation, assignment, and reappraisal of students with regard to the Title I program
7. Assist in the recruitment, selection, and recommendation for hiring in the instructional programs
8. Assume division chair responsibilities

- **Qualifications**

Master's degree or higher with a major in educational administration or supervision from an accredited college or university

Must meet Louisiana certification requirements

At least 5 years teaching experience

At least 5 years administrative or quasi-administrative (division head or department head) experience

Practical experience in development and implementation of program and services at the secondary level involving the following: curriculum development, assessment development, school improvement activities, professional development, and evaluation of staff

PART THREE

Going Back to School

CHAPTER 7

The Investment in Yourself

The prospect of going back to school can be daunting for many career changers. Whether you need a few credits or a degree, a return to the classroom can seem complicated or impractical. You may ask, "With a family, a job, and other responsibilities, how can I fit school into an already busy schedule? Besides, I wasn't a great student the last time. And isn't school expensive? How can I afford it?"

The chapters in Part 1 of this book were designed to help you make a decision about a career change, exploring the teaching profession, as well as the required adjustments you'd need to make in your schedule and your life in order to change careers. In this chapter, we'll look more closely at the issues surrounding a return to the classroom—with you as the student. But the verdict is already out; it may not be easy, but the investment you make in yourself by going back to school will have a tremendous payoff. When you work in a career that you chose carefully and enjoy, you'll succeed not only on the job, but in terms of personal satisfaction and happiness as well.

THE ADULT STUDENT

There are more than six million "re-entry" or adult students attending college in the United States. In fact, the U.S. Department of Education (DOE) estimates that more than 40 percent of college students are over the age of 25, and the percentage continues to rise. Some go back to school to further career goals, while others need training as new business practices and technologies are introduced to their workplace. Still others, like you, return because they want a change.

Chances are, then, you won't be the only adult on the other side of the lectern. And your teachers will welcome you. Many college professors report that they find it easier to teach adult students. They cite as reasons their seriousness, willingness to ask questions, and general desire to get the most from every course.

If you've been out of school for many years, and remember your classroom days with less than fondness, consider this: You're a different person than you were years ago. The experiences you've had and the challenges you've faced have brought wisdom and maturity. Both of these qualities will serve you well as you go back to school. In addition, your motivation is probably very different. You're planning to go back to school because you've chosen a new career and are willing to do what it takes to have it. Strong motivation, wisdom, and maturity will make you a better, more focused student this time.

ARE YOU READY TO MAKE THE COMMITMENT?

Going back to school will affect every area of your life. You'll need to spend time attending classes and studying—time that you already fill taking care of other responsibilities. And your finances will feel the effect; even if you go back to school on a full scholarship, you're probably giving up a job, or at least some working hours, to do so. A temporary loss of income means, for most returning students, a change in lifestyle. Chapter 8 deals with these changes, and how you can fit school into your life, both in terms of time and money.

OPTIONS FOR ACCELERATING AN EDUCATION PROGRAM

There are many ways to ease the burden of going back to school. One option that addresses concerns regarding time and money is acceleration. A number of programs can help you get credit for courses you haven't taken—in some cases, you can take an exam to show that you have already mastered the course content. CLEP (College Level Examination Program) exams, for example, are just $60 each and free to military personnel. Compare that with the hundreds or thousands of dollars a college course costs. In other cases, your "portfolio," or résumé, can provide proof that your life and career experiences fulfilled the requirements of one or more courses.

Some benefits of taking these tests are as follows:

- Earn credit for previously learned knowledge
- Reach your career goals without taking time off from work to be a full-time student

- Gain confidence performing at a college level
- Improve your chances for college or university admission
- Make up missed courses
- Graduate in a shorter period of time

The requirements for education programs, whether to earn a degree or certification, vary. But most colleges and universities require a minimum of credits earned in residency (e.g., from them). They may also limit the number of transferred credits and those received through the programs described in this section. Some schools may allow up to half of the credits you need to be earned elsewhere or by acceleration, and others allow only a few credits to be earned out of residency. These restrictions mean it's important to check the requirements of the programs you are interested in to make an informed decision about where and how to get the education you need.

Credit by Exam Programs

These four types of tests are the most common and are recommended by the American Council on Education (ACE).

CLEP (College Level Examination Program)

CLEP is the most popular and widely accepted acceleration program in the country. More than 2,900 colleges and universities give credit for CLEP scores. The tests are 90 minutes long and are mostly multiple-choice with some fill-ins. (The exceptions are the composition tests, which include an essay, and a handful of other tests that contain fill-in-the-blank questions.) There are 36 different CLEP exams within five subjects:

Composition and Literature: American Literature, Analyzing and Interpreting Literature, English Composition, English Literature, Freshman College Composition, Humanities

Foreign Languages: French (levels 1 and 2), German (levels 1 and 2), Spanish (levels 1 and 2)

History and Social Sciences: American Government, Human Growth and Development, Introduction to Educational Psychology, Introductory Psychology, Introductory Sociology, Principles of Macroeconomics, Principles of Microeconomics, Social Sciences and History, U.S. History I (Early Colonizations to 1877), U.S. History II (1865 to present), Western Civilization I (Ancient Near East to 1648), Western Civilization II (1648 to present)

Science and Mathematics: Biology, Calculus, Chemistry, College Algebra, College Mathematics, Natural Sciences, Precalculus

Business: Financial Accounting, Introductory Business Law, Information Systems and Computer Applications, Principles of Marketing, Principles of Management

For more information, and to download study guides, check: *www.collegboard. com/student/testing/clep/about.html.*

DSST (DANTES Subject Standardized Tests)

DSST tests are accepted for credit at more than 1,900 colleges and universities across the country. There are currently 37 DSSTs within six subjects:

Applied Technology: Technical Writing

Mathematics: Fundamentals of College Algebra, Principles of Statistics

Social Science: Art of the Western World, Western Europe since 1945, An Introduction to the Modern Middle East, Human/Cultural Geography, Rise and Fall of the Soviet Union, A History of the Vietnam War, The Civil War and Reconstruction, Foundations of Education, Lifespan Developmental Psychology, General Anthropology, Drug and Alcohol Abuse, Introduction to Law Enforcement, Criminal Justice, Fundamentals of Counseling

Business: Principles of Finance, Principles of Financial Accounting, Human Resource Management, Organizational Behavior, Principles of Supervision, Business Law II, Introduction to Computing, Introduction to Business, Money and Banking, Personal Finance, Management Information Systems, Business Mathematics

Physical Science: Astronomy; Here's to Your Health, Environment and Humanity: The Race to Save the Planet; Principles of Physical Science I, Physical Geology

Humanities: Ethics in America, Introduction to World Religions, Principles of Public Speaking

Each test earns a recommended three credit hours (the equivalent of a one-semester course) and costs $60. For study guides, tests centers, and other information, log onto *www.getcollegecredit.com.*

Excelsior College Exams (ECE)

There are 44 ECEs that are accepted for credit at almost 900 colleges and universities, including 23 in Nursing and the rest in:

Arts and Sciences: Abnormal Psychology, American Dream, Anatomy and Physiology, Anatomy and Physiology Practice Exam, College Writing, Cultural Diversity, English Composition, Ethics Practice Exam, Ethics: Theory and Practice, Foundations of Gerontology, Juvenile Delinquency, Life Span Developmental Psychology, Life Span Practice Exam, Microbiology, Microbiology Practice Exam, Pathophysiology, Psychology of Adulthood and Aging, Religions of the World, Research Methods in Psychology, Social Psychology, Statistics, World Conflicts, World Population

Business: Organizational Behavior, Labor Relations, Human Resource Management

Education: Literacy Instruction in the Elementary School

Free study guides, a list of schools that accept ECEs, and other information may be found at *www.excelsior.edu.*

Individual College and University Programs

Many colleges and universities administer their own credit-by-exam programs. An Internet search with the terms "credit by exam" or "course challenging" will yield hundreds of hits for participating schools. Examples include Kansas State University, Ohio State University, Western Illinois University, University of Maryland, and University of North Carolina. The University of Maryland's program, called College Park Departmental Proficiency Examinations, offers tests similar to final exams in many areas. They cost $30 each, and most award three credit hours, as opposed to more than $1,200 in tuition (for a resident of Maryland) to take the course. Check the programs you are interested in for details.

ACE Programs for Corporate, Military, or Professional Training

The American Council on Education has two programs for granting college credit for corporate, military, and other professional training programs. The College Credit Recommendation Service (CREDIT) helps re-entry students get academic credit for formal courses and exams completed in the workplace, including certifications, apprenticeship programs, and training courses. The 25 approved certification programs include American Council on the Teaching of Foreign Languages Inc.,

Institute for Certification of Computer Professionals, and United States Marine Corps, Military Academic Credit Examination (MACE), and Law Enforcement. Hundreds of training programs offered by employers and organizations, including A.G. Edwards and Sons Inc., Educational Resources Inc., and IBM Corporation, are also approved for college credit. Complete listings of approved programs, as well as more detailed information about CREDIT, may be found at *www.acenet.edu.*

The ACE Military Program has been evaluating courses and occupational training programs offered by all branches of the armed forces since 1945. They then recommend appropriate college credit for successful completion of those courses and programs. ACE publishes the *Guide to the Evaluation of Educational Experiences in the Armed Services* biennially; it may be searched at *http://militaryguides.acenet.edu.*

The National Program on Noncollegiate Sponsored Instruction (PONSI)

The New York State Education Department established PONSI in 1973 to translate various nonclassroom learning experiences to college credit. PONSI evaluates instruction that takes place in cultural institutions, large corporations, government agencies, health care organizations, labor unions, and professional and volunteer organizations. It then makes the results available to colleges to use as a guide in awarding credit for noncollegiate course work in the online publication College Credit Recommendations (CCR). More than 1,500 colleges and universities consider awarding credit based on PONSI's recommendations. For more information, and to read the CCR, go to *www.nationalponsi.org.*

Credit for Life Experience (Portfolio Credit)

Experiential learning is honored by many colleges and universities through programs called "credit for life experience," "life experience portfolio," and "life/work experience portfolio," among other titles. These programs are typically more time-consuming and expensive than other acceleration methods, but they vary from institution to institution. At Cleveland State University, portfolios documenting life experience equivalent to a course are reviewed for a fee of $35 per credit requested. Prescott College in Prescott, Arizona, charges $50 to $300 for each portfolio review. Students can write a paper or submit evidence of "structured education" received during employment, military service, seminars, or workshops. A student teacher challenge is also available; students who have a year or more of approved classroom experience may receive credit and have their student teaching requirement waived.

THE MONEY ISSUE

The cost of education programs varies widely, and it's an important consideration when making the decision to go back to school. If you think you can't afford it, or are worried that your education will strain your financial resources, keep reading. There are a number of ways to alleviate the burden, from reducing the cost of going back to school (including the acceleration methods described earlier), to finding grant money, low-interest loans, scholarships, and work/study programs.

Types of Financial Aid

Many re-entry students mistakenly believe that financial aid, whether in the form of state loans, scholarships, or work/study programs, is only available to full-time traditional students. In fact, most types of financial aid do not have age limits and are open to students taking as few as one course a semester.

Another belief mistakenly held by many re-entry (and traditional) students is that the process of figuring out and applying for financial aid is so complicated that it's not worth the effort. In fact, it is much simpler than it appears. For instance, you apply for all types of federal student aid with just one form, the Free Application for Federal Student Aid (FAFSA). By approaching the search for financial aid logically using the three steps outlined here, you can easily determine the aid you are eligible for.

Federal Aid

Your first step is exploring federal aid. The DOE's Federal Student Aid (FSA) programs provide most of the financial aid in the country (more than $60 billion a year). FSA programs include a number of different grants, loans, and work/study programs. In addition to the DOE, other federal agencies provide aid in the form of internships, scholarships, and grants. Learn how to apply, who is eligible, and terms of loans from their website at *www.studentaid.ed.gov.* You will also find links to other federal agencies that award financial aid.

To apply for any of these aid programs, fill out the Free Application for Federal Student Aid (FAFSA), which may be found at *www.fafsa.ed.gov.*

1. *Pell Grant:* the "foundation" of federal aid. Other types of aid from federal and nonfederal sources are added to this grant, and their size may be determined by the amount of the Pell grant. Pell grants are given typically to undergraduate students but are also available for those enrolling in post-baccalaureate teacher certificate programs. Grants, unlike loans, do not have

to be repaid. Currently, the maximum award is $4,050, but this amount can change annually. The amount you are eligible to receive depends on four factors:

- Financial need
- Cost of your education
- Full- or part-time student status
- Plans to attend school for a full or partial academic year

If you are eligible, your school will let you know how much money you have been awarded, and how they plan to pay you. Some schools credit your account, some pay you directly (and you pay the school), and others use a combination of these methods. The amount of other student aid you might qualify for does not affect the amount of your Pell grant. You can receive only one Pell grant in an award year, and you cannot receive Pell grant funds from more than one school at a time.

2. *Federal Supplemental Educational Opportunity Grants (FSEOG):* for undergraduates with "exceptional financial need." FSEOGs range from $100 to $4,000 a year and do not have to be paid back. The size of your award is based on your financial need, when you apply, funding at your school, policies of your school's financial aid office, and other aid you might receive. Keep in mind that other aid you receive can reduce the amount of your FSEOG award, and because each school that participates in this receives a certain amount of funds from the DOE, if those funds run out before the year is up, then no more awards can be made for that year.

   As with Pell grants, your school will tell you the size of your award and how they will disburse it (methods are also the same as Pell grants).

3. *Federal Work/Study (FWS):* program for undergraduate and graduate students that provides part-time jobs (20 hours per week or less) based on financial need. Most jobs are based at the school the student attends, but there are also FWS jobs at private nonprofit organizations and public agencies. Pay must be at the current federal minimum wage or higher. Your total FWS award depends on when you apply, your level of financial need, and your school's funding level. An advantage of working under the FWS program is that your earnings are exempt from FICA taxes if you are enrolled full-time and are working less than half-time. For more information about Federal Work/Study programs, visit the website of the Corporation for National Service (*cns.gov*), which oversees programs such as AmeriCorps and VISTA. These programs offer money for tuition in exchange for service (typically for 11 months).

4. *Federal Perkins Loans:* up to $4,000 a year for undergraduate part-time or full-time study ($20,000 total for four years) is available to students with "exceptional" financial need. Graduate and professional students may also apply. The loan money is provided by the federal government to your school's financial aid office, which then acts as your lender. Nine months after you graduate, you must begin paying the full amount of the loan back your school, plus 5 percent interest.

5. *Stafford Loans:* available to undergraduate, graduate, and professional students, who must be enrolled at least as a half-time student. Stafford loans may be need based or non-need based. Current lifetime limits for independent students are $46,000 for undergraduates and $138,500 for graduate students. The loan must be paid back after graduation at a rate of 6.8 percent. For more information on these financial aid programs, visit *http://studentaid.ed.gov/ students/attachments/siteresources/StudentGuide.pdf.*

6. *Graduate PLUS Loans:* graduate students may borrow up to the full amount of their education costs with this program. The yearly limit on a Graduate PLUS Loan is equal to the cost of attendance minus any other financial aid you receive. There are five repayment options, all of which offer some kind of interest rate reduction. The highest rate of interest charged is 8.5 percent. Like its undergraduate counterpart, the Grad PLUS Loan can be used to pay for the total cost of education less any aid you've already been awarded. Also like the undergraduate version, eligibility for this loan is largely dependent on the borrower's credit rating and history (the rating average that is considered "good" is usually 625 or better), as opposed to the purely financial-need-based Graduate Stafford Loan. Interest may be tax deductible, and Grad PLUS loans can be deferred while you are in school.

7. *Signature Student Loans:* another program that allows students (undergraduate and graduate) to borrow up to the full amount of their education costs when combined with a Stafford loan. Interest rates are variable and are based on the prime rate. To be eligible, a student must be enrolled at least part-time in a four- or five-year college, be working toward a degree, pass a credit check, and be in good standing academically.

8. *Teacher Loan Forgiveness Program:* this program helps pay back Stafford loans five or more years after you begin teaching. It forgives up to $17,500 for teachers who have been employed for five consecutive full years in a public elementary or secondary school that has been designated by the DOE as low income. For more information about this program, including a current list of designated low-income schools, visit *http://studentaid.ed.gov/ PORTALSWebApp/students/english/cancelstaff.jsp?tab=repaying.*

State Aid

Once you have determined the type(s) of federal aid you can receive, the second step is to look to your state. The Appendix lists contact information for every state's financial aid agency. Even if you're not applying for state aid, agency employees are trained to help you through the process of securing funding and are a great free resource, especially if you're not certain of your options.

Every state budget includes money for student assistance, and that assistance takes many forms. The Alabama Mentor *(www.alabamamentor.org)* for example, is an online resource that helps students choose a college, apply for admission, and secure financing for their education. Many states also offer grants, scholarships, loans, and reduced tuition for residents. The Midwest Student Exchange Program *(www.mhec. org/index.asp?pageid=1)* allows students living in Kansas, Michigan, Minnesota, Missouri, and Nebraska to enroll in colleges and universities in any of those member states and pay a reduced tuition rate.

Some states offer financial aid specifically for those entering teacher-training programs. South Carolina's Teacher Loan Program *(http://ed.sc.gov/agency/superintendent/sch_ scteacher.html)* provides career changers up to $15,000 a year. Portions of the loan may be canceled if, after completing certification requirements, a teacher is employed by a school in a "critical" geographic area or teaches in a "critical" subject area.

Private and School-based Aid

Finally, your third step is to search for private and school-based financial aid opportunities. Private aid, in the form of scholarships, is almost always awarded for academic merit or for special characteristics (e.g., ethnic heritage, interests, sports, college major, geographic location) rather than financial need. As with grants, you do not pay your award money back.

To find scholarship money, use one of the free search tools available on the Internet. After entering the appropriate information about yourself, a search takes place that ends with a list of those prizes for which you are eligible. Try *www.fastasp.org,* which bills itself as the world's largest and oldest private sector scholarship database. In addition, *www.college-scholarships.com* and *www.gripvision.com* are good sites for conducting searches. If you don't have easy access to the Internet, or want to expand your search, your state's financial aid agency, and even federal aid websites, also have plenty of information about available scholarship money.

To find private sources of aid, spend a few hours in the library looking at scholarships and fellowships. Many of these sources are also online. See Chapter 13 for search service contact information and scholarship book titles. Also contact some or all of the professional associations for teachers (listed in Chapters 13 and 14); some offer scholarships, while others offer information about where to find scholarships.

If you know which educational program you will attend, check with a financial aid administrator (FAA) in the financial aid department to find out if you qualify for any school-based scholarships or other aid. Many schools offer merit-based aid for students with a superior high school or college GPA or with high standardized entrance exam scores. Check the education program's academic department to see if they maintain a bulletin board or other method of posting available scholarships.

In addition, many colleges and universities have work/study programs independent of those run by the federal government. Your school's employment or financial aid office will have information about how to earn money while getting your education. Options for work/study programs typically include:

- Location (on- or off-campus)
- Duration (part-time to almost full-time)
- Future career base (e.g., in an on-campus preschool)
- General work (e.g., in the library or cafeteria)
- Direct pay (you apply toward educational expenses)
- Indirect pay (applied by the school toward loans)

Applying for Aid

Eligibility for every form of federal aid—from loans to grants, work/study to scholarships, and much of the state, school-based, and private sources of funding—is determined by the Free Application for Federal Student Aid (FAFSA). The FAFSA website *(www.fafsa.ed.gov)* allows you to work on your application online, save it until completed, and then submit it electronically. You can also get a copy by calling the Federal Student Aid Information Center (1-800-4-FED-AID) or from many public libraries, state financial aid agencies, and school financial aid offices.

To stay organized and meet all application deadlines, create a calendar as you begin the application process. Note the deadlines for each step of the financial aid process, beginning with the date(s) you completed and submitted the FAFSA. (To download your own FAFSA worksheet, log onto *www.fafsa.ed.gov/fafsaws67bw.pdf)*. The current deadline for the FAFSA is June 30. As you complete and submit other applications, and request letters of recommendation or financial records, add those dates and deadlines to your calendar. State application deadlines vary, but most are either April 15 or June 30. Check your state's financial aid agency for this important date, and note it on your calendar. Using and maintaining your calendar will ensure that the financial aid application process runs smoothly and that all deadlines are met.

Apply for financial aid in January of the year in which you want to enroll in school. Because the FAFSA requires financial information that is easily obtained from your most recent tax return, consider filing your taxes as early as possible (you should have all the necessary paperwork by the first week of February). If you decide to mail your application (rather than submit it electronically), use an original form (no photocopies) and original envelope.

About four weeks after you submit the FAFSA, you will be mailed a Student Aid Report (SAR). The SAR reveals the number used to determine your eligibility for federal student aid, the Expected Family Contribution (EFC). SARs are sent directly from the DOE to the schools to which you are applying.

You must reapply for financial aid every year. However, after your first year, you will receive a Student Aid Report (SAR) in the mail before the application deadline. If no corrections need to be made, you can just sign it and send it in.

Determining Financial Need

Many of the financial aid programs discussed in this chapter are awarded on the basis of need (some loans, such as the unsubsidized Stafford, scholarships, and grants are exceptions). When you submit the FAFSA, your financial information is put in a formula established by Congress. The formula determines your Expected Family Contribution (EFC), the financial contribution you are expected to make toward your education. If your EFC is low enough, and you meet the other eligibility requirements, you will be eligible for a Pell grant.

There is no maximum EFC that defines eligibility for other financial aid options. Instead, your EFC is used in an equation to determine your financial needs:

Cost of attendance – EFC = Financial need

Financial aid administrators at the schools you're applying to calculate your cost of attendance and subtract the amount you are expected to contribute toward that cost. If the calculation equals more than 0, you are considered to have financial need.

Weighing the Cost of Loans

Just because you are eligible, should you take out loans? If the answer is yes, how much is too much debt? Many federal loan programs allow up to 10 years to pay off the debt. However, for example, if you complete school with a $30,000 Perkins loan and choose the 10-year repayment option, with current interest rates, your monthly payment would be more than $300. The total interest paid on this loan over 10 years would exceed $8,000.

Some things to consider before taking out a loan: What is the average teacher salary in the area in which you plan to teach? Do you have other outstanding debts? What are your other financial obligations (mortgage, rent, transportation, other living expenses)? Use the DOE's Budget Plan, which you can download from *http://studentaid.ed.gov,* to help you decide how much debt you can carry.

Loans must be paid back in monthly installments (although there are no penalties for paying a loan off in a few large payments), regardless of whether you lose your job or otherwise have trouble coming up with the payment. There are options for those having financial difficulties, such as deferment and forbearance, but they only postpone the inevitable payback and increase the amount of interest paid over the life of the loan.

Situations such as reenrollment in school, unemployment, and economic hardship can qualify you for a *deferment,* which is a temporary suspension of loan payments. However, if you have an unsubsidized Federal Family Education Loan (FFEL) or Direct Stafford Loan, you must pay interest during the deferment period. Unpaid interest can accumulate and be added to the principal of your loan, meaning the amount you must repay will increase. To apply for a deferment, contact the servicer of your loan.

More Questions to Ask before You Take Out a Student Loan

1. What is the interest rate, and how often is the interest capitalized?

2. Are there fees, such as origination and guarantee fees, that will be charged and deducted from my loan amount?

3. Will I have to make any payments while still in school?

4. When do I need to make my first payment, and approximately how much will it be?

5. Who will be my loan servicer? To whom will I be sending payments? Who should I contact with questions or inform of changes in my situation?

6. Will I have the right to pre-pay the loan, without penalty, at any time?

DEFERMENT REQUIREMENTS

If you are enrolled at least half-time in a postsecondary school, or are studying in an approved graduate fellowship program or are in an approved rehabilitation training program for the disabled, you can receive a deferment for direct, FFEL, and Perkins loans.

If you are unable to find full-time employment or otherwise suffer from economic hardship, you may be approved for a deferment of up to three years for all types of loans.

If you are serving on active duty during a war or other military operation or national emergency, or performing qualifying National Guard duty during a war or other military operation or national emergency, you may receive a deferment during your time of service (up to three years).

There are some other circumstances in which your loan(s) may be deferred or even canceled (meaning you owe nothing). If you teach in a low-income school for five years, up to $5,000 of any type of loan may be forgiven. If you become totally and permanently disabled or die, or if your school closes before you can finish your program, 100 percent of your loan(s) is forgiven. In some cases, bankruptcy can also result in a deferment or complete loan cancellation. The Perkins loan has the most loan cancellation options for teachers, including teaching in designated "teacher shortage areas" (currently math, science, foreign languages, and bilingual education); doing so can entitle you to have up to 100 percent of your loan canceled. Check *http://studentaid.ed.gov* for more information.

If you have financial difficulties but are not eligible for a deferment, you can receive *forbearance*, which is a temporary postponement or reduction of payments. Forbearance can be granted for periods of up to a year at a time for a total of three years. During forbearance, interest accumulates on every type of loan and must be paid back.

Two other options are available to temporarily reduce the amount of loan payments. A *graduated payment plan* allows you to pay only the interest you owe for two years, at which time payments increase, and continue to do so every two years after the initial increase. An *income-sensitive repayment plan* calculates payments based on the annual salary of the borrower. The payments increase or decrease as his or her income goes up or down.

All of these options are preferable to defaulting, which is failing to make full payments on your loan as scheduled. Specifically, for Perkins loans, that means missing one payment, or paying it after the due date. For FFEL and Direct loans, default occurs when you are 270 days delinquent (for those paying monthly) or 330 days (for those paying less often than monthly). A loan agreement is a legally binding contract. When you sign it, you agree to pay back the money you borrow according to the terms of the loan and maintain that you understand the consequences for failing to do so. Default can have serious long-term financial consequences, which is why it is critical that you determine how much debt you can handle before you sign the loan agreement.

If you default, your servicer or loan guarantor, as well as state and federal governments, can attempt to recover the money you owe. That can mean one or more of the following:

- Your default will be reported to national credit bureaus, which will harm your credit rating and make it more difficult, and more expensive, to borrow money in the future. Landlords and employers can check your credit rating, so it can also be more difficult to rent an apartment or get a job.
- You will be ineligible for additional federal student aid.
- The entire loan amount, plus interest, can be due immediately.
- All deferment options will be closed to you.
- Your account may be turned over to a collection agency, which can increase the amount you owe with additional interest charges, late fees, collection costs, court costs, and/or attorney fees.
- Your employer may be required to deduct loan payments from your paycheck.
- State and federal income tax refunds can be withheld and applied toward the amount you owe.
- Some states can deny you certain professional licenses.

CHAPTER 8

Choosing and Applying to a Program

Most career changers do not relocate for their new teaching job; therefore, they look for programs that both fulfill their needs and are within reasonable commuting distance from their homes. If there is no such program, online study is often a reasonable alternative

But just because a program is conveniently located doesn't mean it's right for you. Chapter 4 explained the different types of programs available. This chapter explains what to look for and how to evaluate them, and gives an overview of the admission process. You'll also get ideas for making the most of your program, from joining an organization for nontraditional students to managing your time.

WHAT TO LOOK FOR

Every good teaching program is made up of three critical components: subject knowledge, the study of how to teach, and practice teaching. Most programs also include a fourth: fulfilling certification requirements. As you do some preliminary research into the program(s) you're interested in, look for these components first:

- Check the program's course list
- Talk with teachers who went through the program and/or current students in the program
- Call or email with any questions (current and former students can also give you an accurate picture of the reputation of the program, which is an important criteria for your future employer)

If you're planning to teach social studies in a California high school, for example, check the history and political science departments. How many courses are available, and how many does your program require? Will fulfilling these requirements adequately prepare you to teach your subject? How long is the student teaching segment of the program? Does it involve observation, or do you begin teaching immediately? What kind of supervision and/or feedback will you receive?

If any of the critical components are missing or weak, move on. If the program does not include certification requirements, find out what you would need to do after you complete the program in order to be licensed by your state. You may decide to look for a program that includes licensure requirements.

Once you've determined that the program can meet your needs, continue your investigation by looking further. Here are some important questions to ask:

1. *Is the program accredited by your state?* Check with the U.S. Department of Education (DOE) (see the Appendix for contact information) for a list of accredited programs. These are the programs your state accepts because they have met a set of standards. In addition, the program should be accredited by the National Council for Accreditation of Teacher Education (NCATE, *www.ncate.org*). This organization has been evaluating teacher-training programs for more than 50 years. Currently, more than 600 colleges of education are accredited by NCATE.

   Another site to check is *www.teac.org,* the website of the Teacher Education Accreditation Council (TEAC). TEAC evaluates programs based on the success of their graduates. In other words, instead of looking at faculty, course offerings, facilities, etc., TEAC measures the program's ability to prepare "competent, caring, and qualified professional educators." Its website contains a list of current accredited programs.

2. *Is the faculty knowledgeable, spending enough time in classrooms other than their own to keep up with trends and the realities of K–12 environments?* Ph.D.'s who've written education textbooks have much to teach you, but you'll get the most out of a program that is taught by committed professionals who make a point of staying current and connected.

3. *Are the course offerings varied enough?* Do they include those important components listed earlier, including your state's requirements and testing for licensure? Will they prepare you to fulfill the job requirements of a teacher in the 21st century? For example, will you be taught how to spot learning disabilities or how to integrate computers and other technology in your curriculum?

4. *Does the program have a job placement office?* How successful are they in helping graduates find suitable positions? Do they have positive relationships

with schools in your area (this relates to the school's reputation, something you should have looked into in your preliminary investigation)? Look for résumé services, guidance counselors, career days, and/or job fairs, which are offered by many strong job placement offices.

EVALUATING ONLINE PROGRAMS

Many of the guidelines for regular programs also apply to those offered online. Look for a program that is accredited (most accreditations are for online master's degrees), that offers the four important education program components described earlier in this chapter, and that employs a knowledgeable, strong faculty.

In addition, there are other considerations to address if you will be preparing for your career over the Internet.

1. *What kind of interaction will you have with the faculty?* Will you receive feedback on assignments, quizzes and tests, and online postings? Those teaching online courses should provide access through email as well as a discussion board. They should be clear about how prompt their responses will be, and what, if any, limits they place on emailing. Similarly, if there are guidelines regarding appropriate content for discussion boards, those should be spelled out.

2. *What kind of interaction will you have with fellow students?* Is there an online forum or discussion scheduled? Is it weekly, biweekly? What is expected of students in discussions (is it required)? How many students will participate (as with any class, the lower the student/teacher ration, the better)?

3. *What kind of technical support is available?* If you have trouble logging onto the program's website, for example, can you call for help, or is support offered only via email? Are there limited hours for technical support? Many students who choose an online option do so because they can work at night and on weekends.

4. *What is the timeline for the course?* Can you learn at your own pace throughout the course, or are there assignments and discussions scheduled for specific dates or at specific intervals? Deadlines are preferable, as they help students focus and stay organized. They also provide a connection with the teacher throughout the course.

THE APPLICATION PROCESS

Many career changers spent years on the job, and haven't been in a classroom for a decade or more. The intricacies of the application process may have been forgotten. If you are applying to a program that awards a bachelor's or master's degree, you'll need to get your application together in the fall. Although some schools use a rolling admissions system (in which students are accepted and begin study at intervals throughout the year), most have deadlines in the late fall or early winter and notify applicants of their decision in the spring. Study begins in the fall.

The application consists of four parts, one of which is completed by the applicant (often including an essay on a given topic). As you work on your application, you'll also need to make arrangements for the following to be sent to the admissions office:

1. Transcript (record of your grades; high school if applying for a bachelor's degree, college in applying for a master's degree)
2. Test scores (SAT or ACT for bachelor's degree, GRE for master's degree)
3. Letters of recommendation (from former teachers; letters from supervisors are often acceptable for applicants who have not attended school in many years)

If the program to which you're applying does not use a rolling admissions system, you will follow a timetable similar to the following:

Fall of Year before Beginning School:

1. Get application(s).
2. Study for and take standardized test(s); have scores sent to programs to which you're applying.
3. Ask for recommendations (include necessary forms from the application if applicable).
4. Write application essay(s) if required.
5. Contact high school or college and request transcript copies be sent to programs to which you're applying.

Winter:

1. Complete application(s) and make copies of everything before mailing (or emailing).
2. Submit application(s) before due date (generally between January 1 and February 15).

Spring:

Decisions should be received in April. Programs allow a few weeks in which to respond.

What Tests Do I Need to Take?

Entrance exam scores are an important part of the application. Therefore, you'll need to study for and take the required test(s) months before you apply. Websites are listed for all of the tests described here; they give testing schedules and locations, online registration, and practice tests.

ACT: multiple-choice test required by most colleges and universities (some accept the SAT as an alternative); covers four skill areas: English, mathematics, reading, and science. There is an optional writing test *(www.act.org)*.

GRE General Test: required by most graduate schools of students applying for advanced degrees (master's and/or doctorate); measures critical thinking, analytical writing, verbal reasoning, and quantitative reasoning skills that have been acquired over a long period of time and that are not related to any specific field of study *(www.ets.org)*.

GRE subject tests: measures undergraduate achievement in eight areas: biochemistry and cell and molecular biology; biology; chemistry; computer science; literature in English; mathematics; physics; and psychology. Typically taken by those who wish to teach secondary school *(www.ets.org)*.

SAT Reasoning Test: required by most four-year programs; tests mathematics, critical reading, and writing *(www.collegeboard.com)*.

SAT subject tests: required or recommended by many colleges and universities; offered in English (literature), history and social studies (U.S. History and World History), mathematics (levels 1 and 2), science (biology, chemistry, physics), and languages (Chinese, French, German, Spanish, modern Hebrew, Italian, Latin, Japanese, and Korean) *(www.collegeboard.com)*.

ENTERING A PROGRAM

What are the realities of going back to school? Since the last time you were in a classroom, your life has probably changed significantly. Specifically, you have more responsibilities and less time. Juggling family, career, and school isn't easy, but there are solutions to help make it more manageable. And there are advantages to being an older student. To make your way successfully through your education program, you'll need to understand what is expected of you and how to maximize your advantages.

Program Flexibility

To meet the demands of the increasing number of re-entry students, colleges and universities are making it easier to take courses while also attending to family and career responsibilities. Many schools offer classes at night, on weekends, and online. Broadcast television and video conferencing are also used to make attending class easier.

Colleges have also responded by restructuring education program schedules; some allow students to take one or two courses a semester, while others provide accelerated formats in which students complete all requirements in a full-time condensed schedule. Additionally, leave of absence options are sometimes available to adult students who are unable to attend school for a semester or more due to work or family obligations. As the re-entry student population grows, so does schools' flexibility. Finding a program that fits into your life is not only possible—it's probable.

Support Systems

Some schools call it "Adult College Experience (ACE)," others call it "Nontraditional Student Organization (NTSO)," while still others use the more popular title "Returning Adult Student Organization (RASO)." In any case, there are clubs exclusively for re-entry students at hundreds of schools. These organizations support adult students academically, socially, and emotionally. Academic support is provided through advisors who are familiar with the challenges faced by this unique population. They may sponsor workshops and individual lessons or tutoring sessions on topics such as study skills, test-taking, and single subject review and support. Help in locating and securing sources of financial aid is also part of the mission of most RASOs.

Socially, RASOs may hold parties, concerts, and lectures where students can meet one another and network. Many schools, including the University of Wisconsin, also designate lounge space where adult students can relax between classes and get to know each other. Emotionally, the adult student may be supported through counseling services, weekly or monthly meetings of the RASO, and on-campus child care centers.

In addition to student organizations, many colleges and universities, in response to the growing number of adult learners, have offices or departments that specifically support these students. For example, Pennsylvania State University has a Center for Adult Students that offers a variety of academic and other support services, including help with registering, finding financial aid, and providing child care financial assistance. Eastern Wyoming College provides adult peer counselors who work with individual students and sponsor events such as study nights with free child care, support groups, and academic and career counseling. Search the Internet with terms such as "nontraditional student" and "returning adult student" for more information about the kinds of services colleges and universities offer their re-entry populations.

A KEY RELATIONSHIP

Many returning students first feel out of place on a campus populated by classmates in their older teens and young twenties. But your age can work in your favor. As we noted earlier, professors like older students because they tend to be more serious about their studies and produce better work than their younger counterparts. So you'll be met with positive expectations. In addition, older students are closer in age to (and sometimes older than) their professors. That means outside the classroom, your teachers are your peers. They may have the same kinds of family and career responsibilities that you do. Other life experiences may also be similar. Your professors' high expectations coupled with the natural understanding of peers can give you a significant advantage.

What can you gain from developing positive relationships with your professors? Think of it this way: Professors not only help prepare you for your future profession, they can help you establish relationships in it, too. They are already part of a large network of education professionals. They know many local administrators and teachers, make student teacher placements, and recommend students to area schools for employment.

Professors know the trends and important issues in education. Many of them conduct research and write papers and journal articles for publication or presentations at conferences. Students are often sought to help with research and other related tasks. Some schools also provide opportunities for student research projects that are mentored by professors. Your involvement in these kinds of projects can give you insights into education that you can't get from class assignments. It can also set you apart from classmates when job hunting begins.

To develop valuable relationships with professors, you need to take advantage of their office hours. Many younger students feel intimidated or otherwise worry that they will "bother" a teacher by asking a question or use up valuable time that other students might need. Don't make this mistake. Office hours are part of the job, and many professors report that their only complaint about scheduling that office time is that they get too few visits from students. If it's not possible for you to make posted office hours, ask for an appointment at a more convenient time.

You don't want to make an appointment for small talk, though. Be prepared with specific questions about coursework or career-related issues. If you're having trouble writing a paper, bring a rough draft or outline. If you don't understand a lesson or concept, bring concrete examples for clarification. Write down your questions, and be prepared to take notes. Be direct, and listen carefully.

As a result of these visits, you'll make the kinds of connections with your professors that are hard to make during class. You can get to know each other and begin building relationships. As the semester advances, continue to use office hours to let your professors know your career plans, and ask for advice. Professors who know you, and who value your efforts, are the ones who will think of you when they hear about suitable opportunities. They may ask for help with research, or help you find the right job at the right school. Don't ignore or undervalue this critical relationship.

TIME MANAGEMENT

Another difference between re-entry students and their younger classmates is their access to a very important resource: time. Younger students may be enrolled full-time, live on campus, and have no responsibilities aside from getting good grades. They've got plenty of time to get their reading done, solve every equation, perform hours of research, and write draft after draft of each paper (whether they do or not is another issue).

Before you begin school, examine how you already spend your time. How much is spent at work? Planning, shopping for, and preparing meals? Taking care of children or elderly parents? Cleaning and doing laundry? Make a list of your routine activities, with estimates as to how much time they take. Then, determine approximately how much time your classes, studying, and homework will take. (One estimate is that you should plan to spend two hours on homework, studying, and paper writing for every hour you spending class.) If you're like most returning students, the number of hours you have free is less than the number of hours required by your education. Because adding hours to your days or week is out of the question, the only way to balance the equation is to reduce the amount of time you spend doing routine activities, and making every study minute count.

Improving Time Management

The British Broadcasting Company's *Return to Learning* has an excellent time management tool on its website. To use it, log onto *www.bbc.co.uk/learning/returning/learninglives/time/index.shtml* and click on "time planner." You'll find a blank grid with each hour of every day mapped out. Block out the time you sleep, work, participate in leisure activities, and take care of home-related responsibilities. The spaces left blank represent the time you have currently available to attend class and study, and their total can be automatically calculated. You can also print your completed schedule.

Deciding on what is variable in your daily schedule is highly individual. Can you get help with child care or housework from a family member? Can you afford to hire help? Is there flexibility in a work schedule? Some students choose to let housework slide so they can continue to spend the same amount of time with family, while others can't imagine living in anything but a pristine environment. Prioritize your routine activities, and brainstorm ways to shrink or eliminate those that aren't at the top of your list.

As you prioritize and brainstorm, notice the close link between money and time. For example, having room in the budget for help with daily chores can add significant amounts of free time to your schedule. But when extra dollars are in as short supply as time, you may need to get creative. In fact, creativity can be an important factor in making the time/money equation balance. These are some of the solutions used by teachers we interviewed:

- Getting up an hour earlier, or staying up an hour later, to study
- Turning off the phone and email programs while studying
- Selling a newer car and purchasing an older, more energy-efficient model to make and save money
- Spending quality time with family members when not studying
- Carpooling to share travel expenses
- Moving to a less expensive apartment and/or getting a roommate
- Buying a new or used laptop computer to squeeze in work/study time anywhere
- Creating a budget and keeping track of spending

Streamlining Study Time

When time is tight, you need to make every minute count. Remember that your goal is to spend two hours studying and completing assignments for every one hour spent in class—and those hours add up quickly. So it makes sense to learn how to save time, and get better grades, by taking good notes, reading assignments more thoroughly, and studying and taking tests more effectively (especially if the last time you were in school your study skills were weak).

1. *Organization.* Set up a system for success. Have a notebook or file folder for each course, and keep notes and assignments together, in order. Use a PDA or calendar to write the dates of all tests, assignments, etc., for the entire semester. You'll be able to see when you've got extra time to work on a long-term project and when you'll be working overtime completing a number of demanding assignments simultaneously. Once your system is in place, use it! Organization is a day-by-day process, not a twice-a-semester blitz to regain order. To stay with it, write daily to-do lists, and complete them. Update your calendar frequently to keep it accurate and relevant.

2. *Note-taking.* During class, you'll need to create a written record of the lesson being presented. This will be easier if you read the related assignment on time, before you go to class. If you took notes on your reading (see item 3), you can add the lecture notes to your reading notes. Note-taking doesn't mean writing down every word—you'll only be able to record about 25 words a minute, as opposed to the hundreds that will be spoken in that time. Write down the key concepts.

   Make your notes legible enough so you can read them later that day, copying them neatly in outline form and noting any questions you may have. You can also fill in important information learned through a reading assignment completed after the lecture. The idea is to review for 10 or 15 minutes daily through the rewrite, rather than waiting weeks until a quiz or exam when you might find that you didn't understand all that was presented.

3. *Reading assignments.* When reading a textbook or other assigned material, you'll also want to take notes. The format of the book will help you easily transfer what you're reading to outline form. Chapters and headings within chapters divide information into neat sections, so pay careful attention to them. Use these headings and subheadings to organize, and fill in with key concepts, details, and definitions. If you have questions, write them into your outline and either star, highlight, or otherwise mark them so you can get clarification in class or during office hours.

The SQ3R method (developed by Francis Robinson in *Effective Study*, 1970), of assigned reading is highly effective because it uses five different techniques to help understand and retain information:

- *Survey.* Pay attention to headings and subheadings, as just described. Check out illustrations, charts, captions, graphs, and maps. If your professor handed out questions or a study guide, review the relevant section before reading. Finally, read the introduction and conclusion to the chapter or other assigned reading.
- Question. Turn your survey into a series of questions. What is this chapter/section/subsection about? What question is it trying to answer? Do I have questions that this chapter/section/subsection can answer? What do I already know about this subject? Every title, heading, and subheading can be turned into a question.
- Read (first of three Rs). Concentrate as you read the assignment. Look for the answers to the questions you formulated.
- Recite-Write. As you complete each section, answer your questions aloud (remember, the more senses you use, the better you'll remember information). Then write the main points in your notes. Don't copy—your notes should be in your own words. If possible, underline or highlight those main points in the text.
- Review. Go over your questions again (without looking at your answers) and quiz yourself. If any answers are unclear, reread the corresponding section of the chapter.

4. *Writing papers or research reports.* Almost every college-level course requires writing. In fact, schools are so concerned about their students' ability to write well that they requested that writing evaluations be included in standardized admissions tests such as the SAT and ACT. Most require at least one essay on their application. Academic writing differs from other types of writing in many important ways. It often involves research that must be carefully analyzed and documented. The tone and style of an academic paper must reflect they correct audience, which is typically a peer group assumed to have prior knowledge of the subject. Time, knowledge, and skill are needed to succeed with these types of papers and reports.

If it's been a while since you did any academic writing, it's worth refreshing your memory before classes begin. One great resource is *Kaplan's Writing Source: The Smarter Way to Improve Your Writing* (Simon & Schuster, 2005). Its chapter on academic writing addresses issues such as style guides, audience, exam essays, and research. The rest of the book interactively reviews grammar and mechanics, brainstorming, editing and proofreading, and many other writing issues. There are also many valuable academic writing websites, most of which are university based. Search the Internet with the terms "academic writing" or "writing course" to find examples.

5. *Studying for quizzes and exams.* If you follow the advice for note taking and reading assignments, you'll already be reviewing on a regular basis, taking a lot of pressure off when a test approaches. A few weeks before the test, check with your professor to see if he or she makes past exams available—they can be an invaluable resource.

Many adult students use a study technique called "mind mapping" that was developed by Tony Buzan. Mind mapping involves the relationships among a group of key points or ideas. Rather than creating a standard outline, mind mappers use looser formats such as circles or webs to represent those relationships. Because mind maps engage another sense (vision), they help you to understand and remember information more easily. For more information, check *www.mind-map.org* or the Study Guides and Strategies website at *www.studyg.net.*

Study groups are another great way to reinforce information, and you can take advantage of the notes of your more diligent classmates, too. Some study groups divide the class material in sections, and then assign sections to individuals or small groups. The individuals or groups then prepare study guides, and every one reviews together. If you decide to join a study group, remember that its success depends on the quality of its members. Everyone in the group should be motivated and hard working; otherwise, you may end up shouldering too much responsibility and wasting your time.

6. *Test-taking.* If you're prepared, the only things standing in your way of a great grade are your nerves and common mistakes that can be simply corrected. Confident test-taking is the result of both knowing your material and having experience. If it's been a while since you've taken an exam, you'll have to create your own experience. Ask to see exams your professor gave in the past, and find out how much time was allotted to complete them. The only way to know what the time pressure feels like is to time yourself as you take the practice exam.

Simple mistakes include:
- Cramming the night before or otherwise disrupting your sleep
- Going to an exam on an empty stomach
- Casually glancing at the directions
- Writing illegibly
- Losing track of time
- Forgetting required items (writing instruments, calculator, identification, etc.)

The Memory Game

Have you noticed that you can remember the lyrics to a song that was popular when you were in high school, but you can't seem to recall your cell phone number or what you ate for dinner last night? You're not alone. Memory skills decline over time, and for adult students, that can make studying and test-taking even more anxiety producing. For exams that are designed to determine how much information you've retained (as opposed to those that require you to assess and analyze information and then draw conclusions about it), memory skills are critical. But there are many techniques to help improve your memory.

First, use the study techniques we've listed. By taking good notes, and rewriting and/or reviewing them frequently, you'll learn small amounts of information over time. This is more effective than trying to cram a large amount of information into your memory quickly. The mind-mapping technique is especially useful, because it brings another sense (vision) to learning. But don't stop there. You can employ other senses as memory devices with great effect. Read your notes, delivering them as you would a speech. Stand up and move as you study. The more senses you use, the easier it will be to retain information.

That goes for study techniques, too. There are many of them, and the more you use, the better your information retention will become. Review the SQ3R process, and use it for every reading assignment. The "S," "Q," and third "R" (review) in particular are also great techniques for studying. You can review silently, or recite as you review. Rewrite the answers to your reading questions, and rewrite main points, definitions, and important terms. If there are questions at the end of a chapter, use them to test yourself. Again, the more methods you use, the better you'll understanding and retain the material.

These are all easily remedied. Get a good night's sleep, eat a balanced meal, print neatly, and check and double check test-taking requirements before an exam. It's also a good idea to wear a watch to your exams. Take time to carefully read the directions. Should you guess if you're not sure of an answer, or are there penalties for wrong answers? Sometimes missing one word, such as "not," can mean the difference between a passing and failing grade.

Advice for Taking Timed Essay Exams

Do:

Research your exam. Your professor will give you an idea of the subject and type of essay she expects you to write. If you don't understand something, ask for clarification.

Begin by brainstorming and creating an outline. Jumping into writing usually means your introduction will be a weak guesstimate of where you're headed, and you could easily veer off topic.

Use examples and details to illustrate and substantiate your point. Unless the essay is meant to be opinion only, you need to ground your argument in facts.

Don't:

Use your conclusion to refute anything you've already said, or to introduce new ideas.

Veer off the topic. Your grade will suffer if you don't fully address the subject of the essay.

Lose track of time. Be aware of your watch and gauge your progress so you'll have time to write a strong conclusion.

A REAL LOOK AT COURSES

Depending on the type of program you enroll in, the number and types of courses you'll need to take will vary. But these descriptions of common education courses will give you an idea of what to expect. Listed are typical course loads, followed by descriptions, for three options: an undergraduate degree, a licensing or certificate program, and a graduate degree.

Undergraduate Degree in Elementary Education

Required Courses

University Core requirements

ENG 101	English Composition
ENG 140 or 150	English or American literature
MTH	2 math courses
EDU 200	Introduction to Education and Society
EDU 201	Historical and Philosophical Foundations of Education
EDU 250	Educational Psychology
EDU 274	Methods of Mathematics Instruction
EDU 275	Teaching Language Arts and Reading
EDU 277	Children's Literature
EDU 280	Standards-Based Curriculum and Assessment
EDU 330	Instructional Technology in Education
MUSC 099	Theoretical and Applied Concepts of the Arts
BIOL 010	Issues in Human Biology
EENV 101, 102, 103, or 104	Environmental Sciences

or

ECOL:100	Science of Ecology
HIST 111 or 112	U.S. History
COMM 192	Public Speaking
POLI 111	American Government
PSYC 101	Principles of Psychology
EDUC 100	Intro to Human Geography

or

ANTH 162	Cultural Anthropology
EDUC 276	Principles of Learning and Teaching in Elementary Education

EDUC 281	Methods of Curriculum, Instruction, and Assessment in Elementary Education
EDUC 282	Classroom Management and Inclusionary Practice
EDUC 501	Preparation and Planning
EDUC 502	Student Teaching Practicum
EDUC 503	Classroom Management
EDUC 600	Seminar

Sample Course Descriptions

| EDU 275 | Teaching Language Arts and Reading |

Introduces knowledge and strategies for teaching language arts and reading at the elementary level. Students will learn about instructional strategies, developing a classroom context for literacy, and the relationship between reading and assessment. Topics include guided reading, literature circles, emergent literacy, comprehension, phonics, language conventions, and children's literature. School visits are a required component of EDU 275.

| EDU 330 | Instructional Technology in Education |

An introduction to applications of technology that will assist in efficient management and effective learning within the school environment. Experience will be gained in the development and use of instructional applications including computers and educational software.

| EDU 502 | Student Teaching Practicum |

The elementary credential candidate performs student teaching in participating schools for 7 to 8 weeks full-time for each course (15 weeks total) under the supervision of a cooperating teacher and university supervisor. The student teaching experience offers professional preparation and diversified teaching responsibilities for postbaccalaureate students pursuing the California Multiple Subject Teaching Credential.

Licensing or Certificate Program in Secondary Education (for students with a bachelor's degree in subject to be taught)

Required Courses

EDU 231	Schools and Society
EDU 271	Adolescent Development and Learning
EDU 343	Teaching Literacy in Secondary Schools
EDU 360	Cognition and Individual Differences
EDU 361	Current Trends in Secondary Education
EDU 417	Reflective Practices
EDU 424	Secondary Student Teaching
EDU 430	Senior Seminar: Secondary

Sample Course Descriptions

EDU 343   Teaching Literacy in Secondary Schools

Strategies for developing content-based reading/writing abilities, comprehension skills, and vocabulary of secondary students. Methods of teaching reading, writing, and language skills for English learners and speakers. Diagnostic assessment strategies.

EDU 361   Current Trends in Secondary Education

Surveys current curricular and instructional practices. Topics include components of professional practice, planning and preparation, classroom environment, classroom assessment, and professional development.

Graduate Degree in Teaching (Elementary Education Specialization)

Required Courses

EDU 510	Human Growth and Development
EDU 520	Foundations of Education
EDU 530	Education of Exceptional Children and Youth
EDU 540	Teaching and Learning
EDU 550	Technology in Education

EDU 600	Research in Curriculum and Instruction
EDU 621	Teaching for Mathematical Understanding
EDU 622	Teaching for Scientific Inquiry
EDU 623	Language, Literature, and Culture
EDU 624	Children's Literature
EDU 625	Constructing Meaning Through Literacy I
EDU 626	Constructing Meaning Through Literacy II
EDU 673	Student Teaching in Elementary Education (6 credits)
EDU 689	Advanced Seminar in Teaching

Sample Course Descriptions

EDU 600   Research in Curriculum and Instruction

Examines the relationship of curricula and instruction to current research in learning and knowledge construction, developing higher-order thinking in specific disciplines, and content areas and examines the role of understanding and metacognition in learning. Complex problems of pedagogy are identified and analyzed (e.g., interdisciplinary curricula, team teaching, collaborative learning), with attention to designing learning goals and outcomes with effective instructional strategies.

EDU 623   Language, Literature, and Culture

Applies contemporary research to processes and problems in teaching oral and written communication, with the basic assumption that listening, speaking, writing, and reading are integrated processes and should be taught as such. Covers analysis and use of instructional strategies for teaching developmental reading and writing, reading and writing in content areas, written correspondence, research reports, journal writing, poetry, and appreciation of children's literature.

EDUC 673   Student Teaching

Provides supervised field experience at a cooperating school designed to develop skills in instructional planning, pedagogy, motivation, classroom management and discipline, interrelationships among diverse populations within school settings, identification of instructional resources, and applications of current research on effective teaching.

CHAPTER 9

Licensing Exams

If your education program prepares you for state certification, you will probably need to study for and take at least one of the following exams (there are just six states that do not require a standardized test as part of their certification requirements). Timetables for taking theses tests vary by state—some may allow you to take them before you start coursework, or you can schedule them in the summer or during student teaching when you have less class, and studying, time to worry about.

PRAXIS

The most widely used licensing exam, required by 44 states, is the PRAXIS series. Many colleges and universities also use the PRAXIS series as an admission requirement for their education programs. There are three separate tests within the series, each designed to measure a different set of skills.

PRAXIS I at a Glance

Test	Items	Time
PPST Reading	40 multiple-choice questions	60 minutes
PPST Mathematics	40 multiple-choice questions	60 minutes
PPST Writing	38 multiple-choice questions	30 minutes
	Essay question	30 minutes

PRAXIS I, also known as pre-professional skills tests (PPSTs) is comprised of three tests that assess basic reading, writing, and math skills. The reading and math tests are multiple-choice; the writing test is multiple-choice and essay writing. They are each one hour long.

PRAXIS II is also made up of three separate tests. They are each two hours long and contain multiple-choice and short-answer items.

1. *Principles of Learning and Teaching (PLT):* a test of general pedagogical knowledge in four grade levels: early childhood, K–6, 5–9, and 7–12.
2. *Teaching Foundations Tests:* measure more specific pedagogical knowledge in five areas— elementary, English language arts, math, science, and social science.
3. *Subject Assessments:* given in more than 120 areas and gauge both core content knowledge and pedagogy. States whose licensing requirements include subject assessments determine the appropriate test(s) for each type of license. For example, to be certified to teach biology to grades 6–12 in Alabama, you must pass the Biology: Content Knowledge test. No test is required for a Biology 4–8 license.

PRAXIS Subject Assessment Tests (note that some of these tests are state-specific)

Agriculture	Biology and General Science
Agriculture (CA)	Biology: Content Essays
Agriculture (PA)	Biology: Content Knowledge, Part 1
Art: Content Knowledge	Biology: Content Knowledge, Part 2
Art: Content, Traditions, Criticism, and Aesthetics	Biology: Content Knowledge
	Business Education
Art Making	Chemistry: Content Essays
Audiology	

(continued)

PRAXIS Subject Assessment Tests *(continued)*

Chemistry: Content Knowledge

Chemistry, Physics, and General Science

Citizenship Education: Content Knowledge

Communication (PA)

Cooperative Education

Driver Education

Early Childhood: Content Knowledge

Early Childhood Education

Earth and Space Sciences: Content nowledge

Economics *(www.ets.org/Media/Tests/ PRAXIS/pdf/0910.pdf)*

Education of Deaf and Hard of Hearing Students

Education of Exceptional Students: Core Content Knowledge

Education of Exceptional Students: Learning Disabilities

Education of Exceptional Students: Mild to Moderate Disabilities

Education of Exceptional Students: Severe to Profound Disabilities

Education of Young Children

Educational Leadership: Administration and Supervision

Elementary Education: Content Area Exercises

Elementary Education: Content Knowledge

Elementary Education: Curriculum, Instruction, and Assessment *(www.ets.org/ Media/Tests/PRAXIS/pdf/0011.pdf)*

Elementary Education: Curriculum, Instruction, and Assessment K-5 *(www.ets. org/Media/Tests/PRAXIS/pdf/0016.pdf)*

English Language, Literature, and Composition: Content Knowledge

English Language, Literature, and Composition: Essays

English Language, Literature, and Composition: Pedagogy

English to Speakers of Other Languages

Environmental Education

Family and Consumer Sciences

Foreign Language Pedagogy

French: Content Knowledge (contains listening section)

PRAXIS Subject Assessment Tests *(continued)*

French: Productive Language Skills *(www. ets.org/Media/Tests/PRAXIS/pdf/0171.pdf)*

Fundamental Subjects: Content Knowledge

General Mathematics (WV)

General Science: Content Essays

General Science: Content Knowledge, Part 1

General Science: Content Knowledge, Part 2

General Science: Content Knowledge

Geography

German: Content Knowledge *(www.ets. org/Media/Tests/PRAXIS/pdf/0181.pdf)*

German: Productive Language Skills

Gifted Education

Government/Political Science

Health and Physical Education: Content Knowledge *(www.ets.org/Media/Tests/ PRAXIS/pdf/0856.pdf)*

Health Education

Introduction to the Teaching of Reading

Latin

Library Media Specialist

Life Science: Pedagogy

Marketing Education

Mathematics: Content Knowledge *(www. ets.org/Media/Tests/PRAXIS/pdf/0061.pdf)*

Mathematics: Pedagogy

Mathematics: Proofs, Models, and Problems, Part 1

Middle School: Content Knowledge

Middle School English Language Arts

Middle School Mathematics

Middle School Science

Middle School Social Studies *(www.ets. org/Media/Tests/PRAXIS/pdf/0089.pdf)*

Music: Analysis (contains listening section)

Music: Concepts and Processes

Music: Content Knowledge

Physical Education: Content Knowledge

Physical Education: Movement Forms— Analysis and Design *(www.ets.org/Media/ Tests/PRAXIS/pdf/0092.pdf)*

(continued)

PRAXIS Subject Assessment Tests *(continued)*

Physical Education: Movement Forms—Video Evaluation (contains video section)

Physical Science: Content Knowledge

Physical Science: Pedagogy

Physics: Content Essays

Physics: Content Knowledge (1 hour)

Physics: Content Knowledge (2 hour)Pre-Kindergarten Education

Psychology

Reading Across the Curriculum: Elementary

Reading Across the Curriculum: Secondary *(www.ets.org/Media/Tests/PRAXIS/pdf/0202.pdf)*

Reading Specialist

Safety/Driver Education *(www.ets.org/Media/Tests/PRAXIS/pdf/0860.pdf)*

School Guidance and Counseling

School Psychologist

School Social Worker: Content Knowledge *(www.ets.org/Media/Tests/PRAXIS/pdf/0211.pdf)*

Social Sciences: Content Knowledge

Social Studies: Analytical Essays

Social Studies: Content Knowledge *(www.ets.org/Media/Tests/PRAXIS/pdf/0081.pdf)*

Social Studies: Interpretation and Analysis

Social Studies: Interpretation of Materials

Social Studies: Pedagogy

Sociology *(www.ets.org/Media/Tests/PRAXIS/pdf/0950.pdf)*

Spanish: Content Knowledge *(www.ets.org/Media/Tests/PRAXIS/pdf/0191.pdf)*

Spanish: Pedagogy

Spanish: Productive Language Skills *(www.ets.org/Media/Tests/PRAXIS/pdf/0192.pdf)*

Special Education: Application of Core Principles Across Categories of Disability

Special Education: Knowledge-Based Core Principles

Special Education: Preschool/Early Childhood

Special Education: Teaching Students with Behavioral Disorders/Emotional Disturbances

Special Education: Teaching Students with Learning Disabilities

Special Education: Teaching Students with Mental Retardation *(www.ets.org/Media/*

PRAXIS Subject Assessment Tests *(continued)*

Tests/PRAXIS/pdf/0321.pdf)

Speech Communication

Speech-Language Pathology

Teaching Foundations: History—Social Science

Teaching Foundations: Mathematics

Teaching Foundations: English

Teaching Foundations: Science

Teaching Foundations: Multiple Subjects *(www.ets.org/Media/Tests/PRAXIS/pdf/0528.pdf)*

Teaching Speech to Students with

Language Impairments *(www.ets.org/Media/Tests/PRAXIS/pdf/0880.pdf)*

Teaching Students with Orthopedic Impairments

Teaching Students with Visual Impairments

Technology Education *(www.ets.org/Media/Tests/PRAXIS/pdf/0050.pdf)*

Theatre

Vocational General Knowledge

World and U.S. History

World and U.S. History: Content Knowledge

Both PRAXIS I and PRAXIS II tests may be taken on paper or computer. Computer-based tests are given by appointment at Prometric Testing Centers around the country. Many of these sites are located in Sylvan Learning Centers (*www.ets.org* has a complete list of all sites). If you opt for the computer-based test, your test time is doubled to include tutorials, in which you are taught how the computerized test works, and a collection of test-takers' background information.

PRAXIS III, or Classroom Performance Assessments, measure the skills of new teachers by observing them in their classrooms, reviewing a class profile and instruction profile completed by the teacher, and interviews. PRAXIS III is performed by an assessor who is trained to observe and rate a new teacher in four areas: lesson planning, classroom environment, instruction, and professionalism.

To determine whether your state has PRAXIS requirements, and what specific tests are required, check the PRAXIS website: *www.ets.org*.

CBEST

The California Basic Educational Skills Test™ (CBEST®) was designed to fulfill state laws regarding the credentialing of teachers. In 1984, Oregon added the CBEST to its licensing requirements. The CBEST differs from other standardized teacher exams in that it does not test pedagogy or the ability to teach. Rather, it focuses on the basic reading, mathematics, and writing skills needed by teachers.

The CBEST consists of three sections: reading, mathematics, and writing.

1. *Reading section.* Questions in this section test your ability to comprehend and analyze what you read. You are given a number of written passages, tables, and graphs and asked a total of 50 questions. All of the questions are based on information provided; there is no outside knowledge required. Questions that assess your critical analysis and evaluation skills are based on an excerpt from a book, article, or report and will ask you, for example, to compare and contrast information in one passage or from different sources, find support for the author's main idea, make predictions, identify the author's opinion or bias, or identify the target audience of the passage. Questions that assess your comprehension and research skills may require you to locate information using an index or table of contents, determine the meaning of a word through its context, or draw conclusions. Approximately 20 questions are drawn from the critical analysis and evaluation area, and approximately 30 questions are drawn from the comprehension and research skills area.

2. *Mathematics section.* These questions assess your skills in three areas: estimation, measurement, and statistical principles; computation and problem solving; and numerical and graphic relationships. Most of the 50 multiple-choice questions are word problems. Questions about estimation, measurement, and statistical principles (approximately 30 percent of the test) will, for example, ask you to estimate the result of a math problem; test your understanding of standard measures of length, temperature, weight, and capacity; and interpret the meaning of test scores. The approximately 17 questions in the computation and problem-solving area will ask you to solve various problems, including those with positive and negative numbers, fractions and decimals, and an unknown (simple algebra). Numerical and graphic relationships questions also total about 17 and involve using numbers found in graphs to solve problems, recognizing relationships among numbers, and identifying mathematical equivalents.

3. *Writing section.* This section gauges your ability to write with clarity and focus; observe the conventions of standard written English; develop ideas using supportive details; demonstrate knowledge of the difference between

fact and opinion; and avoid the use of non sequiturs, contradictions, and baseless conclusions. You must respond to two topics: one requires your use of analytical skills, and the other calls for expressive writing about a personal experience.

CSET

California's prospective teachers have the option of taking exams to meet their subject matter competence requirement for certification. The California Commission on Teacher Credentialing (CCTC) developed the California Subject Examinations for Teachers (CSET) to meet this requirement. CSET is offered in most credential areas, replacing the NES and PRAXIS single-subject tests, and reflect the K–12 California Student Academic Content Standards.

All multiple- and single-subject teaching credentials require knowledge and skills in the uses of educational technology. Therefore, all candidates must pass the CSET: Preliminary Educational Technology (test codes 133 and 134) before the Professional Clear Credential can be issued, no matter what subject they apply for single-subject credentialing for. Passing scores on the appropriate CSET must be achieved before student teaching commences.

Most subject tests are self-explanatory. Special credential authorizations include:

1. *Foundational-Level Mathematics.* This credential authorization allows the teaching of selected content areas to K–12 mathematics students (non–advanced placement). Eligible content areas are general mathematics, algebra, geometry, probability and statistics, and consumer mathematics. To achieve the credential authorization, candidates must pass CSET: Mathematics Subtests I and II.

2. *Science (specialized).* This credential authorization allows the teaching of biological sciences (specialized), chemistry (specialized), physics (specialized), and geosciences (specialized). It does not allow the teaching of general or integrated science. Candidates must pass CSET: Science Subtests III and IV in their specific science area.

CSET Subject Areas

Multiple Subjects (Subtest I: Reading, Language, and Literature; History and Social Science. Subtest II: Science; Mathematics. Subtest III: Physical Education; Human Development; Visual and Performing Arts)

Agriculture	Mandarin
American Sign Language	Mathematics
Art Business	Music
English	Physical Education
French	Preliminary Educational Technology
German	Punjabi
Health Science	Russian
Home Economics	Science
Industrial and Technology Education	Social Science
Japanese	Spanish
Korean	Vietnamese

NYSTCE

The New York State Teacher Certification Examinations (NYSTCE) were developed to meet the state law requiring teachers to demonstrate knowledge and skills before receiving a license. The NYSTCE program includes seven tests. Candidates seeking an initial teaching certificate must pass the Liberal Arts and Sciences Test (LAST), the elementary or the secondary version of the Assessment of Teaching Skills—Written (ATS–W), and a Content Specialty Test (CST) in their area of certification. Those seeking a bilingual education extension to a teaching certificate must pass the Bilingual Education Assessment (BEA) in the appropriate language.

1. *Liberal Arts and Sciences Test (LAST)*. This test measures conceptual and analytical skills, critical-thinking and communication skills, and multicultural

awareness. It examines scientific, mathematical, and technological processes; historical and social scientific awareness; artistic expression and the humanities; communication and research skills; and written analysis and expression. The LAST uses multiple-choice questions and a written assignment.

2. *Elementary Assessment of Teaching Skills—Written (ATS–W).* The ATS-W assesses pedagogical and professional knowledge at the birth–grade 2 and grades 1–6 levels. ATS-Ws use multiple-choice questions and a written assignment.

3. *Secondary Assessment of Teaching Skills—Written (ATS–W).* This test assesses pedagogical and professional knowledge at the grades 5–9 and 7–12 levels. ATS-Ws consist of multiple-choice questions and a written assignment.

4. *Content Specialty Tests (CSTs).* CSTs assess knowledge and skills in the field of certification. Except for those for languages other than English, they consist of multiple-choice questions and a written assignment. Tests for languages other than English measure listening comprehension, reading comprehension, language structures, cultural understanding, written expression, and oral expression through written, listening, and speaking assignments.

Content Specialty Tests

Agriculture	English to Speakers of Other Languages
American Sign Language	Family and Consumer Sciences
Biology	Gifted Education
Blind and Visually Repaired	Health Education
Business and Marketing	Latin
Chemistry	Library Media Specialist
Dance	Literacy
Deaf and Hard of Hearing	Mathematics
Earth Science	Modern Languages Other Than English (Cantonese, French, German, Greek, Hebrew, Italian, Japanese, Mandarin, Russian, Spanish)
Educational Technology Specialist	
English	

(continued)

Content Specialty Tests *(continued)*

Multisubject	Students with Disabilities
Music	Technology Education
Physical Education	Theater
Physics	Visual Arts
Social Studies	

5. *Bilingual Education Assessments (BEAs).* These tests are a requirement for candidates who are adding a bilingual education extension to an existing certificate. BEAs include listening, speaking, reading, and writing assignments in English and the appropriate foreign language. Multiple-choice and short-answer items are used.

6. *Communication and Quantitative Skills Test (CQST).* This is a multiple-choice test that is a requirement for the Transitional A certificate (nondegree route) in career and technical education subjects.

7. *Assessment of Teaching Skills—Performance (ATS–P) (Video).* Candidates must produce a 20- to 30-minute video of their classroom teaching. The students in the class must be those the teacher regularly teaches. This test is not required of candidates who received an initial certification after February 2, 2004.

TEXES

Teacher certification requirements in Texas include TExES (Texas Examinations of Educator Standards) tests. This requirement applies not only to those new to the field of education, but to also to certified teachers who wish to add an additional standard certificate in another area of certification. TExES tests are primarily made up of multiple-choice questions, although some tests also use short-answer items.

Current TExES Tests

Superintendent Part I

Superintendent Part II

Principal

Pedagogy and Professional Responsibilities EC–4

Generalist EC–4

Bilingual Education Supplemental EC–4

Bilingual Generalist EC–4

English as a Second Language EC–4

Pedagogy and Professional Responsibilities 4–8

Generalist 4–8

Bilingual Education Supplemental 4–8

Social Studies 4–6

Mathematics/Science 4–8

Science 4–8

English Language Arts and Reading 4–8

Social Studies 4–8

Bilingual Generalist 4–8

English as a Second Language/ Generalist 4–8

Pedagogy and Professional Responsibilities 8–12

English Language Arts and Reading 8–12

Social Studies 8–12

History 8–12

Mathematics 8–12

Science 8–12

Physical Science 8–12

Life Science 8–12

Technology Applications 8–12

Chemistry 8–12

Computer Science 8–12

Technology Applications EC–12

Mathematics/Physics 8–12

School Librarian

Reading Specialist

School Counselor

Educational Diagnostician

English as a Second Language Supplemental

Speech 8–12

Journalism 8–12

Health EC–12

Current TExES Tests *(continued)*

Physical Education EC–12

Pedagogy and Professional Responsibilities EC–12

Special Education EC–12

Gifted and Talented Supplemental

Special Education Supplemental

Pedagogy and Professional Responsibilities for Trade and Industrial Education 8–12

Technology Education 6–12

Agricultural Science and Technology 6–12

Health Science Technology Education 8–12

Mathematics/Physical Science/ Engineering 8–12

Marketing Education 8–12

Music EC–12

Dance 8–12

Theater EC–12

Deaf and Hard of Hearing

Visually Impaired/Braille

American Sign Language

The TExES Program includes three other tests

1. *Texas Oral Proficiency Test (TOPT)*. This test assesses a candidate's ability to speak Spanish or French and is required for those who plan to teach Spanish or French or plan to teach in a bilingual setting. The TOPT consists of speaking tasks that require recorded responses.
2. *Texas Assessment of Sign Communication (TASC)*. TASC is required for those who plan to teach deaf students. It measures sign communication proficiency within one or more of the many sign communication systems used in Texas classrooms and uses an interview format.
3. *Texas Assessment of Sign Communication—American Sign Language (TASC-ASL)*. This test must be taken by those who plan to teach students who are hard of hearing. It also uses an interview format, but it measures proficiency in American Sign Language only.

Those who are seeking their first teaching certificate must pass a TExES content test and a pedagogy test that corresponds with the grade level the candidate plans to teach. Certified teachers who seek to add an additional certification must pass a corresponding content test. For more specific information about requirements, including those for Temporary Teacher Certificates, check the TExES website, *www.texes.nesinc.com.*

INTASC

The Interstate New Teacher Assessment and Support Consortium (INTASC) is a group of 34 state education agencies and national educational organizations. Its mission is to improve teacher preparation, licensing, and professional development.

INTASC is currently developing tools, including a "Test for Teaching Knowledge" (TTK) that member states can use to reform their own licensing standards. The TTK assesses a prospective educator's ability to meet INTASC's model "core standards," the essential skills needed to be an effective teacher. It is comprised of three tests; INTASC recommends that all tests be required in order for a state to issue a permanent teaching license.

The first is a test of content knowledge (knowledge of the subject one is preparing to teach). The second is pedagogy, which includes topics such as theories of teaching and learning; cognitive, social, and physical development; diagnostic and evaluative assessments; language acquisition; and the role of student background in the learning process. The third test is an assessment of the prospective teacher's portfolio and includes documents and other evidence that represent the quality of the candidate's teaching.

The first two TTKs are to be given at the end of a teacher education program by a testing service and, if passed, allow the issuing of a provisional license that covers the first few years of teaching. The third test is to be given after the first or second year of teaching. Portfolios are scored by experienced teachers who look at instruction materials, videotapes of instruction in the classroom, examples of students' work, and commentary by the candidate. Teachers who pass this test receive a permanent license.

INTASC is also creating an Elementary Portfolio with the Wisconsin Department of Public Instruction, the University of Michigan, and the University of California—Berkeley. Currently, the TTK, Portfolio, and Elementary Portfolio are still in development, but member states may incorporate them as licensing requirements within the next few years.

Members of INTASC

Alabama	Iowa
Nevada	Arkansas
Kansas	New Jersey
Connecticut	Kentucky
New York	Delaware
Louisiana	North Carolina
Maine	South Dakota
Tennessee	Texas
District of Columbia	

PRAXIS I SAMPLE QUESTIONS AND ANSWERS

Reading

1. Halley's Comet has been around since at least 240 B.C. and possibly since 1059 B.C. Its most famous appearance was in A.D. 1066 when it appeared right before the Battle of Hastings. It was named after the astronomer Edmund Halley, who calculated its orbit. He determined that the comets seen in 1530 and 1606 were the same object following a 76-year orbit. Unfortunately, Halley died in 1742, never living to see his prediction come true when the comet returned on Christmas Eve 1758.

It can be inferred from the passage that the last sighting of the Halley's Comet recorded before the death of Edmund Halley took place in

(A) 1066.
(B) 1530.
(C) 1606.
(D) 1682
(E) 1758.

1. **D**

This is a slightly tricky inference question because a lot of dates are mentioned in the passage. Nonetheless, the passage states that Halley determined that the comet followed a 76-year orbit. He never lived to see the comet that appeared in 1758, so it follows that the last time the comet appeared before his death took place 76 years earlier, or 1758 − 76 = 1682, choice (D).

Mathematics

2. One-fourth of the 1,600 sales representatives employed by a company work in its corporate headquarters. Of these, 62.5 percent met or exceeded their sales goals last year. Which computation shows the number of sales representatives working at the corporate office who failed to meet their goals last year?

(A) 375 × 400
(B) 37.5 × 400
(C) 3.75 × 400
(D) 0.375 × 400
(E) 0.0375 × 400

2. **D**

1,600 ÷ 4 = 400 sales representatives who work at the company's corporate headquarters. Because 62.5 percent of these met or exceeded their sales goals last year, 100 percent − 62.5 percent = 37.5 percent who failed to meet their goals. Convert 37.5 percent into a decimal by dividing by 100: 37.5 ÷ 100 = 0.375. The number of sales representatives who work at the corporate headquarters who failed to meet their sales goals last year can thus be found by multiplying 0.375 by 400, choice (D).

Writing

Directions: For the following question, choose the best answer from the given choices and darken the corresponding oval.
The following sentence contains problems in grammar, usage, diction (choice of words), and idiom. The error, if there is one in the sentence,

is underlined and lettered. Parts of the sentence that are not underlined are correct and cannot be changed. In selecting an answer, follow the requirements of standard written English. If there is an error, choose the <u>one underlined part</u> that must be changed to make the sentence correct and fill in the corresponding oval on your answer grid.

If there is no error, fill in oval E.

3. Before <u>the advent of</u> modern surgical
        A
   techniques, <u>bleeding patients</u> with
                    B
   leeches <u>were considered</u> therapeutically
                    C
   <u>effective.</u> <u>No error</u>
        D   E

3. **C**

Bleeding, the gerund, is the subject of the verb *to be considered,* so you need to change the sentence to read *bleeding...was considered.*

Directions: The following sentence tests accuracy and effectiveness of expression. In selecting an answer, follow the rules of standard written English; in other words, consider grammar, choice of words, sentence construction, and punctuation. In the following sentence, a portion or all of the sentence is underlined. Under the sentence you will find five ways of phrasing the underlined portion. Choice A repeats the original underlined portion; the other four choices provide alternative phrasings. Select the choice that best expresses the meaning of the original sentence. If the original sentence is better than any of the alternative phrasings, choose A; otherwise,

select one of the alternatives. Your selection should construct the most effective sentence—clear and precise with no awkwardness or ambiguity.

4. In *War and Peace,* Tolstoy presented his theories on history and <u>illustrated them</u> with a slanted account of actual historical events.

   (A) illustrated them
   (B) also illustrating them
   (C) he also was illustrating these ideas
   (D) then illustrated the theories also
   (E) then he went about illustrating them

4. **A**

The original sentence is best.

Written Assignment

5. With more violent acts occurring in our schools, there is a call for more obvious security measures, such as metal detectors, security guards in the hallway, banning backpacks, and requiring students to wear uniforms.

   Do you believe these or other security measures are a good idea or bad idea?

   Write an essay to support your position.

5. The following is an example of a strong response to the written assignment.

I believe that some security measures in a school are important. If the idea of the security is actually to keep children safe while at school, it is a very good idea. If the idea has no safety value but infringes on the rights of students, I would not be in favor of them. Let me explain my position with examples.

Security guards in the school, and even a local police precinct located in a school, can be a very positive thing for all involved. In this way, students and police generally get to know each other on a more personal basis and can begin to trust and respect each other. If a police-person knew the students on a personal, informal basis, it might help him or her not to jump to conclusions based on a student's appearance or perceived behavior. It also might afford the students the opportunity to talk to the police when they thought trouble might be coming.

Since it is easy to hide a weapon in a backpack, another safeguard that might be helpful is not allowing students to carry backpacks to class. The backpacks can be kept in the lockers and only books carried to class. Schools might need to adjust the time allowed for changing between classes so students have the time to go their lockers to exchange their books. This would be a minor modification and could mean a big difference in the safety of all the students.

An example that I believe is not a good safety measure would be requiring students to wear uniforms. Granted, in some schools, certain dress may have the appearance of gang clothing, but I think this is a limited argument. Dress, as long as it does not contain obscene material and sufficiently covers the student, is a matter of personal style. I do not believe it is the school's job to try to make everyone alike. Schools attempt to create individuals who can think critically and take a stand on an issue. By making everyone look alike, they tend to send the message that everyone should think alike. I do not believe that this is the job of school.

In summary, I believe that there are measures that can be taken to improve safety in schools. They should be well thought-out and not unduly infringe on the rights of students in the school. In other words, the measure taken should have the sole purpose of improving safety of everyone in the school.

CBEST SAMPLE QUESTIONS AND ANSWERS

Reading

Our galaxy, home to our solar system, is called the "Milky Way" in the West. The Japanese call it the "Silver River of Heaven." It contains 100 billion suns and many more planets, moons, and asteroids than that. The "Milky Way" moves through space like a wheel and carries our sun a full revolution once in every 230 million years.

1. The author's intent in this passage is probably

   (A) to present many facts.
   (B) to capture the reader's attention.
   (C) to attract students to the study of astronomy.
   (D) to inform and educate.
   (E) to impress the reader with numbers.

1. **D**

(D) is the best answer because of all the information presented. The other answer choices, (A) and (E), are not appropriate purposes. (B) is incorrect because it doesn't capture the reader's attention, and (C) is incorrect because the selection is too brief to attract students to the study of astronomy.

Mathematics

2. Which of the following numbers is between 0.003 and 0.08?

   (A) 0.0035
   (B) 0.35
   (C) 0.0835
   (D) 0.8
   (E) 0.00035

2. **A**

The only one between 0.003 and 0.08 is 0.0035. (B), (C), and (D), 0.35, 0.0835, and 0.8 are all greater than 0.08. (E) 0.00035 is less than 0.003.

CSET SAMPLE QUESTIONS AND ANSWERS

Reading, Language, and Literature

1. Which of the following statements is *not* a good pedagogical reason for a teacher to dictate *grill* and *girl* to her third-grade students?

   (A) Students will need to listen for subtle differences in sound.
   (B) The dictation will encourage phonological awareness.
   (C) Students will begin to understand the influence of vowel-like consonants—in this case *r*—on a vowel—in this case *i*.
   (D) Students will better understand prescriptive grammar.

1. **D**

Choices (A), (B), and (C) are all appropriate pedagogical reasons to dictate close-sounding words. Choice (D) is incorrect because this particular dictation would reflect issues of structural linguistics, not prescriptive (or traditional) grammar.

History and Social Science

2. Which of the following modern disciplines was NOT influenced by the civilization of ancient Greece?

   (A) Philosophy
   (B) Anthropology
   (C) Theater
   (D) Mathematics

2. **B**

Anthropology—the study of peoples—was not founded as a discipline until the 20th century. Today's philosophy (Aristotle, Socrates, Plato), theater (Sophocles, Aristophanes, tragedy as a form), and mathematics (particularly geometry) were all greatly influenced by the ancient Greeks, as were art, architecture, medicine, and many other disciplines. The Greeks were also our predecessors in practicing an early form of democracy.

Science

3. Which of the following is a correct association?

   (A) Mitochondria: transport of materials from the nucleus to the cytoplasm
   (B) Golgi apparatus: modification and glycosylation of proteins
   (C) Endoplasmic reticulum: selective barrier for the cell
   (D) Ribosomes: digestive enzymes most active at acidic pH

3. **B**

The Golgi apparatus consists of a stack of membrane-enclosed sacs. The Golgi receives vesicles and their contents from the smooth ER, modifies them (as in glycosylation), repackages them into vesicles, and distributes them. In (A), mitochondria are involved in cellular respiration, and in (C), the ER transports polypeptides around the cell and to the Golgi apparatus for packaging. The ribosome (D) is the site of protein synthesis.

Mathematics

4. Four basketball players took part in a free-throw shooting contest. They each shot 8 free throws. Jasmine made 5 of her shots, Juniper made just over 87 percent of her shots, Marcia made 50 percent less shots than Juniper, and Reece made a quarter of her shots. What is the correct order of participants from the player that made the least number of shots to the player that made the most?

   (A) Jasmine, Marcia, Juniper, Reece
   (B) Reece, Marcia, Juniper, Jasmine
   (C) Reece, Jasmine, Marcia, Juniper
   (D) Reece, Marcia, Jasmine, Juniper

4. **D**

This problem requires converting numbers to percents. Jasmine's 5 out of 8 is equivalent to 62.5 percent, Juniper made over 87 percent, Marcia made about 43.5 percent (roughly half of Juniper's shots), and Reece made 25 percent of her shots. From here, the order from least to greatest becomes clear.

Constructed-Response Question

Complete the exercise that follows.

5. Using your knowledge of the components of physical fitness and age-appropriate activities, discuss how to design activities that enhance development of the following in your class of third graders:

   Flexibility
   Muscle strength
   Muscle endurance
   Cardio-respiratory endurance

5. Constructed-response sample essay:

The four components of physical fitness often form various combinations during games and sports. For example, I might enhance flexibility (range of motion at the joints) by having my third graders devise floor routines with stretching, swaying, and tumbling on mats in time to rhythms. My students could combine nonlocomotor and locomotor movements to build flexibility and grace by trying various travel patterns in relation to music. This assignment might include basic flips, cartwheels, and handstands—building muscular strength, which is developed through stress and tension applied during repetition.

A par-course or obstacle course that includes chin-ups, leg lifts, jumping, and skipping will improve muscle strength as well as muscle endurance—the ability of muscles to continue performing without fatigue. My students might dribble a ball continuously, using the hands and feet to control it, building both endurance and flexibility. Maintaining aerobic activity for a specified time is important for developing cardio-respiratory endurance, which refers to the circulatory and respiratory systems' ability to deliver oxygen to the body during exercise. My third graders might increase their endurance by running longer and longer relays, which might also involve passing a baton to a teammate for coordination and teamwork skills.

Human Development from Birth through Adolescence

6. What would be the best way for a teacher to influence a typical 13-year-old to stop smoking?

(A) Tell her she will eventually be caught and have to serve detention
(B) Remind her it is against the law
(C) Ask her concerned friends to tell her they honestly think smoking is a disgusting and uncool habit
(D) Tell her that she will cause future heart and lung damage to herself

6. **C**

An average 13-year-old, according to Kohlberg's Theory of Moral Development, will not care as much about punishment (A), society's laws (B), or abstract ideas about the future (D), as she will care about peer pressure and the opinions of friends (C).

Visual and Performing Arts

7. In dance, the qualities of movement are called sustained, percussive, suspended, swinging, and collapsing. What is the term for the release of potential energy into movement (also called the dynamics of dance)?

(A) Force
(B) Gesture
(C) Space
(D) Phrasing

7. **A**

Force is the term for releasing potential energy into movement; gesture (B) is all expressive movements of the body not supporting weight; space (C) refers to the location of a performed dance or the immediate spherical space surrounding the body; phrasing (D) is the way in which the parts of a dance are organized.

NYSTCE SAMPLE QUESTIONS AND ANSWERS

LAST

1. Identify the underlined section containing the error in the following sentence. If there is no error in the sentence, select choice (D).

   "Actually, <u>we never</u> married," <u>said Gwen</u>,
                     A   B
   the <u>5-foot-11</u> songstress. <u>No error</u>
                  C   D

1. **D**

This sentence is correct as written.

2. PLAYWRIGHT : PAPER :: PAINTER :

   _____

   (A) BRUSHES
   (B) PAINT
   (C) CANVAS
   (D) EASEL

2. **C**

We can make this bridge: A PLAYWRIGHT creates his work on PAPER. Likewise, a PAINTER creates his work on a CANVAS. Response (A) would be correct if the question was stated as PLAYWRIGHT : PENCIL. But as it stands, *brushes* are tools for a painter, and that does not complete our bridge. The same goes for (B) *paint*—it's a tool for a painter. In (D), an *easel* is just a prop for the painter.

ATS-W

Use the information below to answer the question below.

Mike O'Grady is a first-year second grade teacher. He has a positive outlook and holds high expectations for his students.

3. Mr. O'Grady wants his students to engage in activities that will promote their development of higher-order thinking skills. Which of the following tasks is most likely to achieve his purpose?

   (A) Filling in missing components of a pattern
   (B) Naming the characters of a favorite story
   (C) Writing a thank-you letter
   (D) Writing a recipe for "silly putty"

3. **A**

The primary focus of this question is Objective 005:
Understand learning processes and apply strategies that foster student learning and promote student's active engagement in learning.

This is a priority-setting question. You must select the answer choice that is *most* likely to promote higher-order thinking skills. Eliminate (B) because naming the characters simply involves knowledge-level learning. Eliminate (C) because writing a thank-you letter can be done entirely by rote. Eliminate (D) because writing a recipe involves sequencing skills (putting things down one after another), but not higher-order thinking skills. Filling in missing components of a pattern requires the higher-order thinking skills of analysis (involving the ability to examine relationships of the parts of the pattern to one another) and synthesis (involving the ability to predict what part is missing). Choice (A) is the correct response.

4. Federal laws and regulations must be complied with in a New York State school district:

   (A) because the U.S. Congress has a constitutional mandate to regulate education in the United States.
   (B) at no time and in no situation because the power to regulate education in a state is constitutionally the province of that individual state.
   (C) only in cases that involve the civil rights of students.
   (D) whenever the school district accepts and receives federal monies.

4. **D**

The primary focus of this question is Objective 0017:

Understand the structure and organization of the New York State educational system and the role of education in the broader society. Eliminate (A) because the Constitution grants the regulation of education to the states. Eliminate (C) because it's too narrow an answer. While the laws about civil rights must be obeyed in schools, other federal laws must be obeyed also. This answer choice doesn't mention them. In theory, federal regulations should not affect the schools because the power to regulate education is a power granted to the states, not to the federal government. Federal regulations enter the picture because federal funds are available to public educations. The catch is that the schools accepting federal monies must comply with federal laws and regulations as a condition for receiving them. Eliminate (B) since it contradicts this reality. Choice (D) is the correct response.

CST

5. The purpose of *invented spelling* is

   (A) to help children become better spellers in the future.
   (B) to encourage students to use proper grammar and spelling when they write.
   (C) to allow students to express themselves in writing before they have mastered the conventions of grammar and spelling.
   (D) to require students to make attempts to spell words that the teacher then corrects.

5. C

Choice (C) is the correct choice because *invented spelling* (also called approximated spelling) allows young children to get their words down on paper and experience the joy of writing even before they have fully learned correct grammar and spelling. It does not help them become better spellers in the future, (A). To do that, students need word study and repeated exposure to words. The purpose of *invented spelling* is not about testing proper grammar and spelling, (C). Choice (D) is not correct because the teacher does not correct the spelling on invented spelling assignments.

6. The final line of a book a teacher is reading to her students is, "And the dog rolled over and wagged his tail." She reads the first part of each page aloud, but has the children join in to read the final line of each page. This is called

(A) guided reading.
(B) shared reading.
(C) interactive reading.
(D) independent reading.

6. B

Shared reading, (B), is the process of the teacher and the students reading aloud together. Typically, the teacher reads a few lines and then the students join in. This process is employed in the primary grades, especially in kindergarten. Choice (A) is not correct because guided reading is the process of a teacher introducing a leveled book to a small group to read quietly to themselves while she provides scaffolding. Choice (C) is not correct because interactive reading is the process of two or more students taking turns reading while helping one another as needed. Choice (D) is not correct because independent reading is the process of having students read individually and silently to themselves.

TEXES SAMPLE QUESTIONS AND ANSWERS

Pedagogy and Professional Responsibilities Test

1. Students in a seventh-grade history class have been discussing Stephen F. Austin's contributions to the state of Texas. Mr. Radcliffe has several English Language Learner (ELL) students in his class. Which of the following shows that Mr. Radcliffe understands student diversity issues?

   (A) Having the ELL students work with English-proficient partners to create dialogue or scenes about Stephen F. Austin and then dramatize the events

   (B) Having the ELL students complete a timeline of Austin's contributions to the state of Texas

   (C) Having the ELL students meet together and conduct research to learn more about Stephen F. Austin and then give a report

   (D) Having the ELL students create a map about the settling of Texas and the contributions made by Stephen F. Austin

1. **A**

This question addresses information from PPR Competency 002:
The teacher understands student diversity and knows how to plan learning experiences and design assessments that are responsive to differences among students and that promote all students' learning.

Eliminate (B) because a timeline is the lowest level of cognitive development and does not address the students' needs. Eliminate (C) because, although the students might enjoy working in a group, unless there is someone who is able to speak English, the action on the part of the teacher suggests Mr. Radcliffe is not aware of the needs of ELL students. Choice (D) will not further the development of English and the activity becomes a form of busywork. First of all, Mr. Radcliffe must realize the importance of becoming acquainted with each student's culture and then building on that culture. Because most English Language Learner (ELL) students require more time for learning activities than other students, Mr. Radcliffe has arranged activities for his ELL students to create dialogue and then dramatize their work. In doing so, the students and their English-proficient partner will have time to discuss unfamiliar material and work on translating or clarifying meaning. Choice (A) is the correct response.

2. Ms. Jackson has her first-grade class use centers while she is involved in teaching the guided reading program. The technology center is set up as an extension of her rock unit. The textbook publishing company has a website that is directly related to the teaching of rocks. Children have choices of finding out how to safely gather rocks, putting a rock puzzle together, or learning new vocabulary associated with rocks. Which of the following is a *primary* reason Ms. Jackson has the students use a computer rather than just looking at books on rocks?

(A) It satisfies the technology component of the Texas Essential Knowledge and Skills (TEKS).

(B) It provided for a variety of resources when studying the concept of rocks.

(C) It keeps the children well occupied while Ms. Jackson is working with guided reading.

(D) It ensures that the students will develop a more active role in science.

2. **B**

This question addresses information from PPR Competency 009:

The teacher incorporates the effective use of technology to plan, organize, deliver, and evaluate instruction for all students.

This is a priority-setting question asking you to determine the teacher's *primary* reason for having the students use the computer. Eliminate (A) because although it does satisfy the TEKS, it wouldn't be the primary reason for having students use technology.

Eliminate (C) because, even though having students work on the computer keeps them occupied while Ms. Jackson is teaching other students during guided reading, it would not be a primary reason. Choice (D) should be eliminated because the word *ensure* sets the tone that to incorporate technology, students will be more active in science and no teacher can predict those results. Ms. Jackson is providing for a variety of resources during the rock unit. By extending the program with the use of the computer, Ms. Jackson is allowing students to interact with technology. She has shown she understands how to acquire and evaluate electronic information. Choice (B) is the correct response.

Ms. Brown's second-grade class is beginning an integrated unit that will focus on important information about the state of Texas, particularly on its historical figures. Ms. Brown introduces information about heroes, biographers, songs, and legends that she finds available from a variety of sources. During the language arts period, Ms. Brown reads poetry and stories that relate to famous Texans. During geography, they look at maps of Texas and discover famous trails, and during math they compare such data as the number of Mexican soldiers and Texas soldiers who fought at the Alamo.

3. As the class continues to study about Texas and famous Texans, Ms. Brown asks students if they can identify various community or state landmarks. The students are quick to point out that there are several schools as well as streets named after significant individuals. Ms. Brown's *main* purpose in using familiarity of landmarks is to

(A) integrate historical facts so children will do well on the TAKS.
(B) impact students' learning by planning activities that include the community and the student.
(C) increase time spent on history because it is Ms. Brown's favorite subject, and she wants to help students develop this desire for the past.
(D) provide a means whereby students will experience success using higher-order thinking skills.

3. **B**

This question addresses information from PPR Competency 004:
The teacher understands learning processes and factors that impact student learning and demonstrates this knowledge by planning effective, engaging instruction and appropriate assessments.
This is a priority-setting question as you are asked to determine the *main* purpose in using familiarity of landmarks. Eliminate (A) because although these facts are important, it should not be the main reason. Eliminate (C) because, although history is Ms. Brown's favorite subject, that would not be a main purpose in discussing famous landmarks.

Eliminate choice (D) because you don't have enough information on the type of questioning Ms. Brown is using. Ms. Brown wants to make sure the students have an opportunity to learn about resources in the community and how these contacts impact their learning. Choice (B) is the correct response.

4. The fourth-grade teacher is a first-year teacher and is having difficulty with behavior management. She talks with her mentor and is give advice. Which of the following is the *least* likely to help with the problem?

(A) Have three to five rules for behavior management created by students and teacher
(B) Wait several weeks before she begins to enforce the rules and consequences
(C) Present and explain the rules and consequences on the first day of school
(D) By day three, have the students practice appropriate behavior through role playing

4. **B**

This question addresses information from PPR Competency 006:
The teacher understands strategies for creating an organized and productive learning environment and for managing student behavior.

This is a priority-setting question. Which choice is *least* likely to help with behavior management? This question is about strategies for making students want to learn. Eliminate choices (A), (C), and (D) because these are all good ways to improve behavior problems. The least likely to help is the correct answer. Choose (B). Teachers must begin day one of school being fair, yet consistent with following the rules. If choices (A), (C), and (D) are done each year, teachers will have fewer behavior problems.

5. Mr. Line recently noticed that one student in his classroom is very talented in geometry. The student is normally considered lazy because he often falls asleep in class. Mr. Line knows that the student is bright and could someday have a promising career in math. He confers with the student after class one day and finds that the student has a job at a fast-food restaurant from 8 P.M. until 12 A.M. each night. The boy explains that his father and mother are both out of work and he must work to support the family. What is the *best* thing for Mr. Line to do?

(A) Meet with the family and the school social worker to try and find a solution to the student working such late hours
(B) Meet with the parents and arrange for the family to get a short-term loan from the bank until summer vacation
(C) Call the Salvation Army and see if the family can get financial assistance
(D) Call the state employment agency and arrange for the parents to go in for a job interview

5. **A**

This question addresses information from PPR Competency 011:
The teacher understands the importance of family involvement in children's education and knows how to interact and communicate effectively with families.
This is a priority-setting question. This question is about using family support resources. Remember, the teacher's job is to teach. Eliminate choices (B), (C), and (D) because the teacher is acting as a social worker, not a teacher. Choice (A) is the correct answer. The teacher should put the family in touch with the school social worker and the social worker will provide the family with support resources.

PART FOUR

Landing a Job

CHAPTER 10

Searching for a Teaching Job

Despite a national shortage of teachers, conducting a job search can be a time-consuming process. In most districts, there is a shortage in only certain subject areas, such as science, math, and special education. Those districts, for example, may turn down dozens of applicants for positions in English or elementary classrooms. That means a search for a teaching job needs to be as thorough and well planned as a search for any other professional position.

You're probably already familiar with job searches, and much of the process is similar for most professional careers. But there are some key differences that set a teacher job search apart, beginning with steps you can take before you officially enter the job market.

BECOMING A DESIRABLE JOB CANDIDATE

While you're pursuing your license, you can take steps to ensure that you'll be hired once you've got it. Because you're probably reading this book in anticipation of a career change, you've got plenty of time to become the job candidate schools are looking for. But who is that candidate? Administrators around the country generally agree that the newly certified teachers who get hired first have the following qualifications:

- Are passionate about teaching and optimistic about every child's capacity to learn
- Can teach more than one academic area
- Are bilingual

- Have coaching experience
- Have work experience that relates to teaching (mentoring, tutoring, camp counseling, etc.)
- Know about their school and demonstrate that knowledge during the interview

What can you do with this information? First, don't panic. If languages have never come easily to you, and you consider sports a nightmare, that still leaves four areas in which to excel. The first is obvious and is rarely an issue with career changers—passion for teaching is a widely held quality among those in this group. But you can enhance your image as a professional who is passionate about her new career in a number of ways. Consider joining a professional organization; many have student memberships that allow you to attend workshops and conferences and network with other members. You could become a member of a general teaching organization, such as the National Education Association (NEA) and the Association of Teacher Educators (ATE). Or, join a subject specific organization; the National Council of Teachers of English, for example, accepts student memberships. A comprehensive list of educator organizations may be found in Chapter 13.

Another option is to attend seminars or workshops. The range of opportunities is wide—organizations run hundreds of different workshops on subjects such as literacy teaching techniques, technology in the classroom, and introductions to new curriculum. Individual sites, such as museums, educational companies, and libraries hold seminars on topics pertaining to their offerings. Experts travel around the country holding workshops for teachers and future teachers. Your attendance at these kinds of events should be listed on your résumé, offering further proof of your passionate interest in your chosen field.

The second quality, the ability to teach in more than one area, requires some research. If you want to teach science, for example, explore your options by studying state certification requirements. What would you need to do to become certified in biology and life sciences? Is it possible to take a few courses to add a middle school license to the high school one you're pursuing? Many certifications have similar requirements, making it easy to get two, or more, instead of one in the same amount of time. Does your bachelor's degree offer certification or endorsement potential? You may already have the schooling you need and may simply have to pass a test in another area of study. The more areas you can teach, the more job opportunities you'll be eligible for.

Work experience, the third quality, is critical for new teachers who haven't had their own classroom. The right jobs, whether paid positions or volunteer, can make you

Teacher Workshops

Here is a sampling of workshops offered across the country; all are open to students:

- Constitutional Seminar—Being an American: Exploring the Ideals That Unite Us: one-day seminar given by the Bill of Rights Institute *(www.billofrightsinstitute. org)*.
- Teaching the Holocaust: online workshop presented by the Education Division of the Holocaust Museum in Washington, D.C. *(www.ushmm.org/education/ foreducators/guidelines)*.
- Inclusion in the Standards-Based Classroom: four-day conference presented by the Teacher's Workshop and Corwin Press Conference Series *(www. teachersworkshop.com)*.
- Passport to the Future Teacher Workshop: a one- or three-day option offered by the American Institute of Aeronautics and Astronautics for those who "want to explain the aerospace industry and demystify math and science for [their] students" *(www.aiaa.org)*.
- National Teacher's Workshop on Africa: three-day program in which participants attend sessions at the State Department, the World Bank, and National Geographic; presented by the World Affairs Councils of America *(www. worldaffairscouncils.org/news/pressreleases/teacherworkshop)*.

more marketable than other candidates. In addition, if they're in a school, you are making yourself known to the administrators and other teachers. See the section on networking later in this chapter for ideas about how to pursue these contacts when you're looking for a job.

What kinds of experience enhance your job candidacy, provide solid experience, and are looked upon favorably by hiring administrators? Here are some ideas:

- Find a job at a learning center. National companies such as Kaplan, Huntington, and Kumon, as well as smaller local companies, hire teachers to work with individual students and small groups. Instruction is needed in subjects such as math (elementary, algebra, geometry, etc.), reading, study skills, and test preparation. For more information, try searching the Internet with the terms "learning center."

Should You Substitute Teach?

There are at least seven great advantages to working as a substitute:

1. You'll be in the school, getting the best, closest perspective on what it's like to work there.

2. You'll get classroom experience that looks good on your résumé.

3. You'll get on the inside track to find out about job openings.

4. You can network with teachers. They may be able to help you find a job opening, even if it's not at their school.

5. Substituting is a flexible position; if you need to take a day or two off, you can do it with ease.

6. You'll find out if teaching really is what you want to do, and you can narrow down the age group that appeals to you most.

7. You'll get paid while reaping the benefits of the other six advantages!

- Work during the summer as a camp counselor. The skills you develop in managing and motivating campers translate into success in the classroom. At the end of the summer, ask your supervisor for a recommendation that specifically details the positive effects you've had on your campers. Libraries often have directories of local camps, or try searching the Internet with the terms "camp counselor jobs." Directories such as Camp Channel *(www. campchannel.com)* are also good resources.

- Volunteer or find a paying position as a tutor. Many students simply post signs at local business or place classified ads noting their qualifications and availability. Tutoring companies (such as *www.tutorsteach.com*) hire tutors to travel to students' homes, and Internet sites hire "virtual" tutors who work with students live online or via email. Volunteer programs such as Boys and Girls Clubs of America and Big Brother/Big Sister use tutors, and many colleges and universities provide tutoring services to young area students.

- Volunteer at a school that interests you. Any way you make positive contact with a school you are considering for employment can help your chances of landing a job. Your hobbies and interests can be used to create a volunteer role as, for example, a drama coach, a story reader in the library, or a gymnastics club assistant. You might also consider joining a volunteer program already in place, such as a Parent Teacher Organization (PTO).

■ Make the most of your student teaching experience. Invite the principal, vice principal, or department chair to observe you. After the observation, thank him or her and ask for a letter of recommendation. Become an integral part of the school by volunteering to assist with activities including extracurricular activities. Show your professionalism and dedication by arriving early and staying late.

■ Consider taking a long-term substitute position. These jobs typically arise when a teacher takes a scheduled (e.g., maternity leave) or unscheduled (e.g., illness in the family) leave of absence. The school with this kind of opening looks for a substitute who can carry out the teacher's plans for a month or more, providing continuity for the students. If the teacher on leave decides not to return, you could be on the short list of candidates interviewed to replace her.

DOING YOUR HOMEWORK

The next step in your job search should also begin before you finish your education program and certification requirements. In the first part of this proactive step, you will make a list of appropriate schools (in other words, don't list elementary schools if you're working toward a secondary certification). Each school should be within what you consider a reasonable commuting distance: No matter how perfect the position, you'll probably grow to dislike it if you spend more time commuting than you're comfortable with. However, be aware that the narrower your geographic confines, the fewer job opportunities you'll probably find. There should be a balance between the commute you're willing to make and your willingness to make some sacrifices for the right position.

Once you've compiled your list, begin researching the schools. Research will help you narrow down your list, so you'll eventually apply for positions only at the schools you've determined will offer the best "fit." What does that mean? A good fit refers to both tangible and intangible qualities of a school:

■ A school culture that's a good match with your values and goals
■ Location (urban, rural, suburban)
■ School size
■ Support from mentoring programs
■ Administrators who treat their teachers with respect and offer creative leeway
■ Up-to-date technology resources

- Communities that support their schools financially and ideologically
- Parents who are interested and involved in the school's programs
- Professional growth and development opportunities
- Diversity in the community and classroom

You'll need to consider what is important to you when evaluating potential employers, and those considerations may grow and change as you do your research.

Public school district websites, as well as sites for individual public and private schools, are your first stop. A school's mission, philosophy, and programs should be easy to find. Salary ranges are typically included on district sites, and you may choose to remove schools from your list based on those numbers. Read each site completely, and make sure to complete this step during the school year, because many schools' sites are less vital or even dormant during summer months.

Once you've scoured the school and district sites, call the district office and find out how to get a copy of their "school report card." Most schools or districts publish an annual report that includes statistics regarding standardized testing, budget details, recent or upcoming changes in staffing, and many other topics. Reading these reports in conjunction with the websites (which can be of a more promotional nature) can help you get a more accurate picture. Figure 10.1 shows two actual report cards, one from a high school in New Jersey, and the other from an elementary school in Bellingham, Washington. Notice the concerns of each school and how they differ.

FIGURE 10.1—Parsippany Hills 2004–2005 School Report Card

School Environment

Length of School Day	
Amount of time school is in session on a normal school day.	
School	6 hours: 36 minutes
State Average	6 hours: 49 minutes

Average Class Size	2004-2005	
	School	State
Grade 9	17.4	21.4
Grade 10	21.9	21.1
Grade 11	21.9	20.4
Grade 12	23.0	20.0
Special Ed. (ungraded)	9.5	8.8
Total School	20.6	19.2

Instructional Time	
Amount of time per day students are engaged in instructional activities.	
School	5 hours: 24 minutes
State Average	5 hours: 52 minutes

Student/Computer Ratio		
Numbers of students per computer available for the purposes of supervised instruction.		
	School	State Average
2004-05	4.3	3.7
2003-04	4.2	3.7
2002-03	4.5	3.9

Student Information

Enrollment by Grade				
Counts of students "on-roll" by grade in October of each school year				
Grade	2004-2005	2003-2004	2002-2003	2001-2002
Grade 9	295.0	291.0	312.0	271.0
Grade 10	307.0	314.0	280.0	283.0
Grade 11	307.0	275.0	274.0	262.5
Grade 12	276.5	260.0	248.0	309.0
Special Ed. (ungraded)	9.5	10.0	9.5	10.0
Total School	1195	1150	124	1136

Students with Disabilities	
Percentage of students with IEPs (Individualized Eduation Program) regardless of placement/programs:	15.1%

Language Diversity	
First language spoken at home in order of frequency	
Language	Percent
English	70.0%
Gujarati	10.8%
Spanish	5.0%
Mandarin	2.5%
Korean	1.2%
Hindi	1.0%
Taiwanese	1.0%

<u>**Student Performance Indicators**</u>

ASSESSMENTS

High School Proficiency Assessment (HSPA) LANGUAGE ARTS LITERACY		Year	Number Tested	Proficiency Percentages		
				Partial	Proficient	Advanced
All Students »details for subgroups for Language Arts Literacy	School	2004-05	316	13.9%	57.6%	28.5%
		2003-04	280	10.0%	64.3%	25.7%
	District	2004-05	559	15.7%	57.2%	27.0%
		2003-04	532	9.8%	67.5%	22.7%
	DFG	2004-05	17808	9.4%	65.2%	25.4%
		2003-04	×	×	×	×
	State	2004-05	94858	16.8%	63.6%	19.6%
		2003-04	90946	17.8%	65.0%	17.2%

*To protect the privacy of students, the Department of Education suppresses sufficient information to eliminate the possibility that personally identifiable information will be disclosed.

× The DFG data for 2003-04 were omitted because they were based on the 1990 Census. For 2004-05, the source for DFG data is the 2000 Census.

High School Proficiency Assessment (HSPA) MATHEMATICS		Year	Number Tested	Proficiency Percentages		
				Partial	Proficient	Advanced
All Students »details for subgroups for	School	2004-05	314	12.7%	46.5%	40.8%
		2003-04	280	14.3%	49.3%	36.4%
	District	2004-05	558	15.8%	45.7%	38.5%
		2003-04	532	17.5%	50.4%	32.1%
	DFG	2004-05	17659	14.7%	48.6%	36.7%
		2003-04	×	×	×	×
	State	2004-05	93939	24.5%	47.1%	28.4%
		2003-04	90712	30.0%	45.6%	24.5%

*To protect the privacy of students, the Department of Education suppresses sufficient information to eliminate the possibility that personally identifiable information will be disclosed.

× The DFG data for 2003-04 were omitted because they were based on the 1990 Census. For 2004-05, the source for DFG data is the 2000 Census.

Scholastic Assessment Test (SAT) Results										
	Students Taking Test		Mathematics				Verbal			
	#	%	Average Score	Percentile Scores			Average Score	Percentile Scores		
				25th	50th	75th		25th	50th	75th
2004-05										
School	228	83%	558	470	560	650	515	440	520	590
DFG	13712	85%	543	460	540	620	521	450	520	590
State	64612	75%	519	430	520	600	501	420	500	580
2003-04										
School	226	87%	552	470	550	640	512	440	510	590
DFG	×	×	×	×	×	×	×	×	×	×
State	60936	73%	516	446	515	586	499	432	498	566
2002-03										
School	205	83%	557	470	560	630	514	440	520	600
DFG	×	×	×	×	×	×	×	×	×	×
State	60196	75%	518	448	518	589	499	433	499	566

× The DFG data for 2003-04 were omitted because they were based on the 1990 Census. For 2004-05, the source for DFG data is the 2000 Census.

Advanced Placement Results

Test Name	# of Students in Class	# of Students Taking Test
CHEMISTRY	22	11
COMPUTER SCIENCE AB	10	5
ENGLISH LITERATURE & COMP	19	15
EUROPEAN HISTORY	15	13
GERMAN LANGUAGE	0	2
MATH - CALCULUS AB	16	9
MATH - CALCULUS BC	0	7
MUSIC - THEORY	15	6
PHYSICS C - ELEC & MAGNET	0	9
PHYSICS C - MECHANICS	18	12
SPANISH LANGUAGE	9	4
STATISTICS	25	15
UNITED STATES HISTORY	99	40
TOTAL*	248	148

*This number is a duplicated number, because students may take more than one course.

Advanced Placement Results Summary

▶Number of test scores 3 or higher: **127**

Advanced Placement Participation for Grades 11 and 12

	School	State Average
2004-05	13.7%	14.8%
2003-04	15.0%	15.5%
2002-03	13.0%	15.8%

Graduation Rate

	School	State Average
Class of 2005 (2004-05)	95.7%	91.3%
Class of 2004 (2003-04)	96.5%	90.5%
Class of 2003 (2002-03)	95.0%	89.5%

Staff Information

Student/Administrator Ratio		
Numbers of students per administrator.		
	School	State Average
2004-05	398.3	182.3
2003-04	383.3	186.7
2002-03	280.9	189.6

Student/Faculty Ratio		
Numbers of students per faculty member.		
	School	State Average
2004-05	10.6	11.4
2003-04	11.9	11.6
2002-03	11.1	11.6

Faculty Attendance Rate		
Percentage of faculty present on average each day.		
	School	State Average
2004-05	98.5	96.3
2003-04	98.4	96.2
2002-03	98.4	96.1

There are three essential components of a highly qualified teacher in accordance with the *No Child Left Behind (NCLB) Act*:

- Hold at least a bachelor's degree;
- Be fully certified/licensed by New Jersey; and
- Demonstrate competence in each of the core academic subjects in which the teacher teaches.

Teachers can demonstrate competence in the subject(s) they teach by either:

- Passing a rigorous state test or completing an academic major, graduate degree, coursework equivalent to an undergraduate academic major, or national certification or credentialing; OR
- Meeting the requirements of the NJ High, Objective Uniform State Evaluation (HOUSE) Standard.

Teacher Information			
Percentage of teachers teaching with emergency or conditional certificates.			
	School	District	State
2004-05	0.0%	0.6%	1.6%

Faculty and Administrator Credentials			
Percentage of faculty and administrators possessing a bachelor's, master's, or doctoral degree.			
	BA/BS	MA/MS	PhD/EdD
2004-05	50.9%	46.3%	2.8%
2003-04	55.0%	42.0%	3.0%
2002-03	55.7%	41.5%	2.8%

National Board Certification			
Number of teachers who have been certified by the National Board for Professional Teaching Standards.			
	School	District	State
2004-05	0	0	98
2003-04	0	0	63
2002-03	0	0	16

District Financial Data

Administrative and Faculty Personnel								
In FTE (Full-time Equivalents).								
	# of Administrators		# of Schools		# of Students per Administrator		# of Faculty per Administrator	
	District	State Average	District	State Average	District	State Average	District	State Average
2004-05	31	28	14	7.5	227.8	165.4	22.1	15.1
2003-04	32	27	14	7.5	216.1	168.5	21.4	15.2
2002-03	33	27	14	7.4	204.1	165.5	20.4	14.8

Median Salary and Years of Experience of Administrative and Faculty Personnel	2004-05	2003-04	2002-03
Administrators			
Salary - District	$104,990	$102,143	$98,970
Salary - State	$102,755	$99,483	$96,282
Years of Experience - District	25	25	30
Years of Experience - State	26	26	26
Faculty			
Salary - District	$55,865	$61,835	$66,040
Salary - State	$52,563	$51,809	$51,137
Years of Experience - District	10	10	12
Years of Experience - State	10	10	11

Teacher Salaries and Benefits				
Percents of teacher salaries and benefits of the total comparative expenditures. The percent increase or decrease represents the expenditure change in teacher salaries/benefits from one year to the next.				
	% for Teachers Salaries/Benefits		% Change - Increase/Decrease (+/-)	
	District	State Average	District	State Average
2004-05	58%	55%	6%	8%
2003-04	58%	55%	7%	4%
2002-03	59%	56%	4%	8%

Source: Report card reprinted with permission from the New Jersey Department of Education; *http://education. state.nj.us*.

FIGURE 10.2—Birchwood Elementary School Report Card

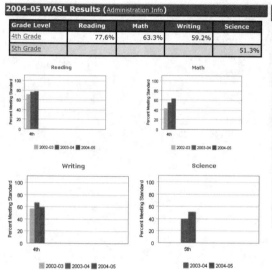

2004-05 WASL Results (Administration Info)

Grade Level	Reading	Math	Writing	Science
4th Grade	77.6%	63.3%	59.2%	
5th Grade				51.3%

Reading — 2002-03 ■ 2003-04 ■ 2004-05

Math — 2002-03 ■ 2003-04 ■ 2004-05

Writing — 2002-03 ■ 2003-04 ■ 2004-05

Science — 2003-04 ■ 2004-05

Student Demographics

Enrollment	
October 2004 Student Count	342
Gender (October 2004)	
Male	52.3%
Female	47.7%
Ethnicity (October 2004)	
American Indian/Alaskan Native	2.9%
Asian	6.4%
Black	3.8%
Hispanic	17.8%
White	68.4%
Special Programs	
Free or Reduced-Price Meals (May 2005)	61.6%
Special Education (May 2005)	12.7%
Transitional Bilingual (May 2005)	10.8%
Migrant (May 2005)	0.0%
Other Information (more info)	
Unexcused Absence Rate (2004-05)	0.2%

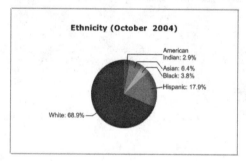

Ethnicity (October 2004)

American Indian: 2.9%
Asian: 6.4%
Black: 3.8%
Hispanic: 17.9%
White: 68.9%

ITBS/ITED Trend

This displays student performance information for the Iowa Tests of Basic Skills (ITBS) at grades 3 and 6 and the Iowa Tests of Educational Development (ITED) at grade 9. This trend shows the National Percentile Rank (NPR).

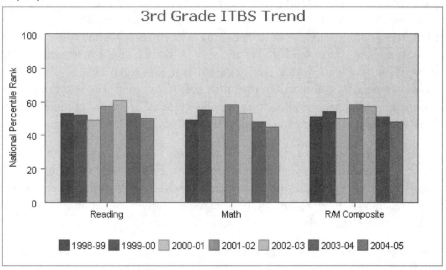

Grade 3	1998-99	1999-00	2000-01	2001-02	2002-03	2003-04	2004-05
Reading	53	52	49	57	61	53	50
Math	49	55	51	58	53	48	45
R/M Composite	51	54	50	58	57	51	48

Adequate Yearly Progress Summary

Yes Group met AYP.		**N<Required** Group has fewer than required.	
No Group did not meet AYP.		**N/A** There are no students in this group.	

4th Grade	Met Proficiency Goal		Met Participation Goal		Other Indicator
Student Group	**Reading**	**Math**	**Reading**	**Math**	Yes
All	Yes	Yes	Yes	Yes	
American Indian	N<Required	N<Required	N<Required	N<Required	
Asian	N<Required	N<Required	N/A	N/A	
Black	N<Required	N<Required	N<Required	N<Required	
Hispanic	N<Required	N<Required	N<Required	N<Required	
White	Yes	Yes	Yes	Yes	
Limited English	N<Required	N<Required	N/A	N/A	
Special Education	N<Required	N<Required	N<Required	N<Required	
Low Income	N<Required	N<Required	N<Required	N<Required	
Number of Yes: 9	**Number of No:** 0	**% of Yes/Total:** 100.0%	**Number of N<Required:** 24	**Number of NA:** 4	

Another valuable source of information is your local paper and local papers outside your area; most are now online. If the sites include archives and are searchable, look for articles on the schools you're interested in. You may find that a local school board and the teachers in that district don't get along. They may have had difficulty negotiating salaries and may have held strikes recently. A school might have strong community support, or have won awards. Active Parent Teacher Organizations (PTOs) are usually a sign of a healthy school. All of this information can help you better understand each school. If local paper websites don't include archives, or are not completely searchable, head to your local library to complete this research.

Next, use the resources at the school where your education program is located. The career services office, as well as your professors, probably know about the schools on your list. Ask around. Do they know new teachers who work in those schools? Are those teachers happy? You might be able to get contact information for a new teacher who is willing to answer your questions.

The final research step is contacting the schools directly. If you have teacher contacts, use them. Call or email and ask about their willingness to answer your questions. You may also be able to arrange to be a "shadow," following a teacher through his day to get a sense of what it's like to work in his school.

If you don't have teacher contacts, you'll need to call an administrator. Ask the principal or vice principal for an informational interview. This will give you an opportunity to introduce yourself, ask questions, present your résumé, and arrange a shadow day. Remember, you're not trying to get hired, but rather trying to determine where you want to get hired. That doesn't mean you should treat an informational interview casually—keep in mind that you might eventually apply for a job at the school. Prepare as you would for any interview (see Chapter 11). But keep your goal in mind: Learn as much about the school as you can to determine whether it's a good fit.

JOB SEEKING TIMELINE

If you are seeking certification through an alternate route, some of these steps may vary. In general, though, this timeline works for most teaching candidates.

What	When	Where
Find opportunities to gain experience with children (see "Becoming a Desirable Job Candidate" in this chapter)	During your education program or before job seeking	See "Becoming a Desirable Job Candidate"
Join a teacher's organization; attend workshop(s) and/or seminar(s)	During your education program or before job seeking	See "Becoming a Desirable Job Candidate"
Begin your résumé and cover letter.	September of senior year or year before job seeking	On your own, but use career services or other resource for oversight
Research potential employers (see "Doing Your Homework" earlier in this chapter)	During your education program or before job seeking	See "Doing Your Homework"
Visit career services office to determine how they can help you find a job	September of senior year or year before job seeking	On campus
Prepare for interviews	Within six months of licensing	On your own, but use career services or other resource for oversight
Begin job search calendar	Within one or two months of licensing	Ideas found earlier in this chapter
Attend job fairs	Within one or two months of licensing	On campus, other locations
Apply for job openings	Within one or two months of licensing	At job fairs or hiring schools
Send thank-you notes after interviews; maintain calendar until you accept a position	Within one or two months of licensing or later	On your own

FINDING JOB OPENINGS

There are a number of ways to find out who's hiring. Many are traditional job search techniques, and others are specific to a career in teaching.

Schools' Career Services or Placement Centers

The education departments of colleges and universities publish their success rates for placing graduates in jobs, and their overall quality is measured in part on these rates, which makes them very motivated to help students find a job. They have numerous ways in which they accomplish that goal. Various placement services are provided through the Career Services Office (known at some schools as the Career Placement Center), which offers both direct and indirect assistance.

Most important are the contacts maintained by Career Services. Working closely with the school's Education Department, they form relationships with area administrators and human resources offices. When teaching positions open, Career Services is contacted and can either post the position or recommend students with appropriate qualifications. Some hiring districts send representatives to perform on-campus interviews, which prospective teachers can sign up for. Career Services has specific contact information and can give students accurate and extensive information to help them decide which positions to apply for and how to prepare for interviews.

Career Services offices also help students with the job application process. At many schools, the office opens a "teacher placement file" when you begin student teaching. This file is a package of documents, including your transcript and recommendations that can be forwarded to hiring schools. When you hear of an opening, you simply email the Career Placement office requesting that they send your file to the appropriate school. Other schools help you develop an "e-portfolio," which is more extensive than a placement file. It is an online portfolio that includes samples of lesson plans, student work, and even audio or video of teaching in the classroom.

Because the placement file is often maintained indefinitely, it is up to you to continue to take advantage of this service by keeping your file up to date. When you find a job, update your résumé and get it into your file. Letters of recommendation from every position you hold that remotely relates to your teaching career (substitute teaching, volunteer positions, tutoring, etc.) should also be added. As your teaching career continues, update the file at Career Services. If you decide to look for another position, work toward an advanced degree, or complete additional coursework, this file can be of great value in the application process. The service is free at most schools, so there is no excuse not to take advantage of it.

Indirect job placement assistance takes many forms. Career Services typically offers workshops on résumé and cover letter writing and may schedule job fairs at which area school districts can present information about their schools and even conduct interviews. Career Services provides individual assessments of résumés, interview practice, and help with other general job search skills both in person and through online resources.

Did You Know?

Any school of higher education must offer their career services to past graduates. Even if you attended 20 years ago or more, you can access the Career Placement office and take advantage of their teacher placement services.

Direct Contact

The research you conduct before job searching will help you compile a targeted list of schools in which you're interested. You should have already contacted those schools or school districts directly to gather information and inquire about informational interviews and shadow days. Now, you need to make contact again—this time, to inquire about job openings.

Call every school on your list, and ask to speak with the principal or personnel office. If you visited the school previously, remind them. Then, be direct. Let them know you are interested in their school and are planning to apply when openings arise. Follow up each call immediately by sending your résumé and a brief cover letter reiterating your desire to work at their school.

Don't worry about the timing of your calls. Openings can happen at any time, although most become known late in the school year. Some of the teachers we interviewed noted that they found out about a job in early spring, summer, or even September. Because openings aren't typically scheduled ahead of time, ask the principal, personnel official, or district human resources department about their application procedures. Do they maintain a file of applications to be assessed when and if an opening occurs, or do they prefer applications to be submitted for known openings only?

If the first round of calls ends with no suitable openings, don't hesitate to begin again. A second call a few months after the first won't be seen as badgering—schools know only too well the unscheduled nature of their job openings. You don't need to send a résumé each time you make contact, but a second or third call could, unintentionally, put you in the mind of an administrator who just found out he or she has a position to fill. In other words, you can create your own luck, or the conditions wherein a lucky break can happen, the more often you make direct contact.

Newspapers

Once the standard venue for job classifieds, newspapers are being supplanted by other forms of advertising, especially the Internet. The U.S. Department of Labor reports that only 5 percent of job seekers found a new position by responding to a classified ad. However, schools of every size, from urban to rural areas, still advertise openings in newspapers. Part of your job search routine, therefore, should include a daily check of your local paper's classified section (without relying on it as your primary source of information).

When you find a job opening that interests you, read the ad carefully. Most ads explain exactly how to respond and give you the information you need to position yourself as an ideal candidate.

Before you respond, evaluate the ad. Research the school using the methods described earlier in this chapter. Is it a good fit for you? Is the salary range acceptable? If you're interested in applying for the position, use the phone rather than email for a more personal contact. Ask for the address to which you should mail your résumé and cover letter, and determine whether other documents, such as recommendations, should also be sent. If possible, schedule an interview. Finally, find out when you'll get a response to your résumé. Some schools suggest you call back after two weeks if you haven't received a reply, while others use a "don't call us, we'll call you" policy.

Because the ad is very clear about their preference, make certain you emphasize how well your skills match their needs. If you can teach biology and English as a second language, let them know. Or, if you are certified to teach biology both to middle and high school students, mention that, too. There might be a middle school opening in the same district. In addition, stress your certification, and demonstrate your knowledge of the school in your response. For example:

123 Main Street
Tacoma, Washington 98406
Central High School
Murphy, Washington

Dear Mrs. Lee,

It was a pleasure speaking with you this morning regarding the biology teacher opening at your school. The information you shared regarding the school's philosophy and emphasis on professional development was particularly helpful. My background and skills are an excellent match for this position.

As I mentioned, I worked for 15 years in Research and Development at ABC Labs before deciding to become a biology teacher. During that time, I volunteered with the Summer Science for Girls Project and in the Technology Education classroom at Ridge High School. As my résumé notes, I am certified to teach grades 5–8 and 6–12.

Thank you again for speaking with me this morning about your biology teacher position. I look forward to hearing from you.

Sincerely,

Janice Rodriguez

Professional Organizations

At the beginning of this chapter, you were advised to join a professional organization or association to enhance your image as a professional. Membership in one or more organizations offers another benefit when you begin your job search—they provide job search tools on their websites and offer a variety of opportunities for job seekers through workshops, meetings, and seminars.

For example, the National Council of Teachers of Mathematics, which offers a student membership, provides a searchable section of job listings *(www.nctm.org/ jobs/available.asp)*. Student members are encouraged to attend its annual meeting and regional conferences, at which registration is free or reduced. The American Council of Teachers of Foreign Languages has a Web-based Career Center where members can set up candidate profiles, post their résumés, search job listings, and have new openings that match their profiles emailed directly to them. Check the comprehensive list of educators' associations in Chapter 13 for contact information for both general and subject-specific organizations. Once you join one or more as a student member, take advantage of your membership by checking available career services.

Job/Career Fairs

Career Fairs, also known as Job Fairs, Job Expos, Career Information Days, and Career Information Conferences, offer a forum where administrators or their representatives from many schools come together to meet with prospective teachers. They may be organized by an individual school, a school district, an educational office (city, county, or state), or a college or university Career Services Office. Administrators often present short talks about their schools, designed to entice you to want to work there. Then, they are available to answer questions and explain their current and future employment needs. They may conduct interviews or collect résumés from interested students. On-site hiring may also take place.

The Career Fair will be publicized weeks in advance, giving you a chance to research the schools that will be attending and sign up for interviews. Many Career Fairs charge for registration, which you may need to pay for in advance. In addition, there are other steps you can take to prepare for a Career Fair:

1. *Set priorities.* At large Career Fairs, there may be more schools in attendance than time allows you to meet. Research them, and come up with a list of the schools you are most interested in. Don't waste time moving from representative to representative gathering superficial information. The schools' websites and other resources can help you determine who you want to meet.

2. *Preregister.* Some career fairs allow jobseekers to preregister for the event, which usually includes submitting a résumé or summary résumé. With more fairs going to the Web, preregistration will most likely become even more common. The idea behind preregistering, of course, is that employers get a chance to prescreen applicants and possibly make note of applicants they want to meet at the fair. Does preregistration guarantee that you will get noticed or that employers will even look at the registrations? No, but why would you not take advantage of such an easy step?

3. *Contact schools prior to the Career Fair.* Find out who will represent the schools you're most interested in, and write a brief letter of introduction to that person. Tell them you are looking forward to meeting them, and enclose a copy of your résumé.

4. *Organize your research.* In step 1, you researched the schools that plan to attend the Career Fair. Now, create note cards or an outline for each school. What did you like about what you learned, and why do you think you would fit in well at each school? Be prepared to explain how your skills are a great match for them. In addition, formulate some questions to ask the representative.

5. *Prepare for interviews.* Career Fair interviews are typically shorter than those held at other locations, but expect to be asked some of the following questions:
   - What is your teaching style?
   - What is your preferred classroom management style?
   - What can you contribute to our school?
   - What have you learned from your teaching experiences?
   - What is your philosophy of education?
   - Why did you choose teaching as a career?
   - Why will you be a successful teacher?
   - What subjects are you qualified to teach?
   - What are your strengths and weaknesses?
   - What skills did you develop in your previous career that will help you in the classroom?

   Write your answers to each question, and practice giving those answers. Be certain to identify yourself as a career changer, explaining why your passion for teaching brought you to the change.

6. *Get your résumé, and portfolio, if applicable, ready.* Make certain that any updates are included, and errors caught during proofreading are corrected. You'll need copies for every school you make contact with, so get them made and bring them in a briefcase or sturdy folder.

7. *Gather other necessary items:*
   - Proof of registration if you registered in advance (typically a printout of an email, or letter you received)
   - Cash if you're registering at the door
   - A notebook and pens for taking notes during meetings with school representatives
   - Application forms if you filled them out in advance
   - A teaching portfolio (if yours is online, consider printing recommendations and other important pages, and add the Web address to your résumé)

During the Career Fair, make sure you do the following:

- Check the listings when you arrive to see which schools that were not originally slated to attend are there. At larger Career Fairs, the lineup of attendees may change, bringing additional administrators who are hiring.
- Make contact with the representative during a break or at the end of the Fair if a school you're interested in has no interview openings. Express your interest, make it personal by recalling specific details about the school, and give him or her a copy of your résumé.
- Leave a positive impression. During an interview or less formal meeting, show your enthusiasm and professionalism by making eye contact and giving a firm handshake. Use body language to express openness and honesty, and dress professionally (see the interviewing tips in Chapter 11).
- Follow the proper procedures if you need to cancel an interview. At some Career Fairs, that means simply crossing your name off a list. At others, messages for interviewers are collected at a central location. Don't leave an unprofessional image by simply not showing up.
- Get the contact information you need to send a prompt thank-you note to your interviewer at the conclusion of the interview. Notes should be mailed the day after the Fair. Check the section on follow-up thank-you notes in Chapter 11 for more ideas and guidelines.

Networking

Networking is part of the vocabulary of job searches in every profession. It refers to the active making of contacts with potential employers, colleagues, and others, thus creating a "network" of people who can be invaluable resources not just for finding a job, but for providing assistance and information throughout your career. Through networking, you can:

- Learn more about the school(s) you're interested in
- Find a mentor
- Keep up-to-date on trends in education
- Be notified of unadvertised job openings

But while networking seems to be effortless for some job seekers, for others it is intimidating. Do you have to shake hands and introduce yourself to everyone you meet to build a network? No. Networking can be as successfully accomplished by shy people as by assertive ones. The key is to identify and understand the process and to incorporate networking skills into your life. As you read the steps for building an education network, notice how many of these steps incorporate actions that have already been described in earlier chapters. Networking can and should be a part of your life as you go through the process of changing careers—it probably is already, even if you're not aware of it.

1. *Tap into the existing network.* We've already explained how education departments and Career Services offices maintain relationships with area schools. Those relationships are part of a vast and powerful network. Once you are associated with a school and its placement office, you become a part of the network too. The people you can easily come into contact with—your professors, the education department chairperson, your student teaching coordinator, and the director of the placement office—should all know you. They are already aware that you are or will soon be looking for a job. If you follow the advice in Chapter 9, you will develop a relationship with your professors. Continue by contacting the placement office. If it is large, try to speak and meet with the same person each time. The more personal the contact, and the more specific you are about what you're looking for, the more this powerful existing network can help you.

2. *Do your homework.* No, you don't need to repeat your research. Simply be aware that the work you do creating a list of potential employers, and researching those on your list, is a part of networking. When you schedule an informal interview or shadow day, you've added an administrator, a teacher, or both, to your network. Even calling to find out about job openings gives you the opportunity to make a favorable impression on the person you speak with. You are reaching out to those who know, or will know, about the exact kind of openings you are hoping to find. Every contact in the field expands your network.

3. *Connect with teachers.* You probably already know many teachers. If you have children, you know their teachers. You know students you attended class with who are now in the field. If you substituted or volunteered in a school, you

185

met teachers. Social contacts can also add teachers to your list. All of these teachers should know about your job search and the kind of position you are looking for. Be direct; don't assume that they have this information. Ask them about their jobs and how they found them. They are on the inside track and can not only provide you with leads, but can offer advice and information to help you with your search.

4. *Expand your network.* Every contact in your network has her own network and can share some of her contacts with you. In other words, everyone in your network can provide more contacts. You could mention a school you're interested in and ask whether your contact knows anyone who teaches there. Or, simply ask if your contact knows another teacher in your subject or grade level. If you join a professional organization, you can expand your network by attending meetings, conferences, workshops, and seminars. Ask attendees about their jobs, and, if possible, volunteer to serve on a committee. Let fellow members know about the kind of job you're looking for and the schools you're interested in. They're already part of the vast education network and may be able to help you.

5. *Get organized.* Steps 1–4 put you in touch with dozens of people, creating a network that can ultimately help you find a job. But no matter how good your memory, keeping track of dozens of people isn't easy. Instead of relying on your powers of recall, create a system to help you easily connect and remember your contacts. That system can be as simple as a box of index cards or as technologically savvy as software for your computer or PDA. No matter how you choose to get organized, you'll want to make note of the following information for each of your contacts:

   - Name
   - Street and email address
   - Phone and fax numbers
   - School where employed
   - Grade/subject taught
   - Connection to you (how you met)
   - Connection(s) to others in your network
   - Topics of interest

When your system is established, and even after you find a job, maintain it. Continue to contact those in your network to get advice, ask questions, and share information. If a contact helped you land a job or put you in touch with someone else who helped you, send a thank-you note. Your network is a vital professional tool that can continue to provide benefits throughout your career.

Job Placement Services

Traditional education job placement services have been around for decades, and they are similar to those developed for finding other types of professional employees. These services are typically paid for by the schools or districts that are seeking suitable teachers, although some charge teachers for their service if they find a job through them.

Most of these placement services operate through websites, and some maintain offices where they conduct interviews and meet with school administrators. Before you sign up with a service, find out what they offer and how they are paid. Some placement services simply ask you to register and submit your résumé. Others are more comprehensive; they conduct an interview, review your résumé, and offer advice on how to improve your job search skills. They may even conduct a background check. Keep in mind that the more a service knows about you, the better they will be able to match you with an ideal position. As suitable job openings become known, you will be notified by phone, mail, or email.

National and Regional Job Placement Services

Don't limit yourself to the following list. Check the yellow pages of your local phone book for services that may have strong connections to area schools.

www.teachers-teachers.com: Free to registered teachers, this site lists job openings from more than 2,000 schools across the country. You create an online job application and apply electronically for the positions that interest you.

Education Placement Service (www.educatorjobs.com): Free registration; teacher is charged a fee if he accepts a job found through EPS. EPS assigns a Placement Specialist to each candidate who conducts an interview and screens credentials before referring him to schools. Interviews with potential employers are held in EPS offices.

GA Teachers Agency (www.teachersagency.com): Works with teachers in New York and New Jersey. After an in-person interview at their offices and submission of your résumé, transcript, certification, and other documentation, you are notified of suitable job openings. There is a fee if you accept a job through the service.

The National Association of Independent Schools (www.nais.org): Lists a number of job placement services that work specifically with private schools.

(continued)

National and Regional Job Placement Services *(continued)*

In addition to national and regional services, a number of states have responded to their teacher shortages by setting up their own job placement services. Some provide services that are run by private companies. These companies then charge school districts that list job openings. In Massachusetts, the state operates the service with the Massachusetts Association of School Personnel Administrators. It is free to both districts and educators and may be accessed through its Department of Education website. Check your state's Department of Education website (addresses are listed in the Appendix) to find out if a similar service is offered.

ONLINE SITES

These resources differ from placement services in that they provide job listings with few or no additional services. It's up to you (sometimes after paying a registration fee) to find suitable openings and apply for them. Find additional sites by searching the Internet with the terms "teacher job." Currently, the trend in education is for schools and school districts to utilize these sites more every month. As listings grow, so do your chances for finding a great opening on an Internet site.

Academic Employment Network (www.academply.com): listings in California, New Mexico, Ohio, and Wisconsin.

Education America Network (www.educationamerica.net): offers more than just job listings. You can post up to three résumés, get advice on how to improve your résumé, apply for jobs online, and get email updates of suitable job openings.

Education Week and Teacher Magazine (www.agentk-12.org): another site offering a few additional services. You can post your résumé and cover letter, have suitable openings emailed to you, and apply for jobs "in one click."

www.educationjobs.com: view thousands of teaching, coaching, and administration jobs.

Nationjob Network (www.nationjob.com/education): nationwide listings, including many for speech pathologists and support staff.

www.nowhiring.com: more than 2,000 listings from schools across the country.

www.schoolstaff.com: national job openings, including summer camp employment, searchable by state, job type, employer type.

OUT-OF-STATE JOB SEARCHES

Many of the same techniques used for local job searches are effective for out-of-state searches. Begin by following the steps outlined in the "Doing Your Homework" section earlier in this chapter. As you research the area you're interested in, begin compiling a list of schools. Geography will probably be a factor in your search, but visiting the area and its schools is the only way to know if the fit is right. You don't want to accept a position and move 1,000 miles only to find out that you should have stayed where you were.

Schedule a number of shadow experiences and informational interviews over the course of a couple of days. Leave time to explore the surrounding towns. The local newspapers will give you an idea of the housing or rental market.

Once you've got your list and know where you want to be, placement services and the Internet can help you find out-of-state job openings. Check state Department of Education sites, as well as regional Offices of Education. Both are great sources of vacancy information, and many use a simple application procedure (such as one application for any opening).

We've already explained how and why your Career Placement Office is the best place to get help with your job search. But if you are looking for a position out of state, that office won't be able to help you. The good news is that many Career Placement Offices, especially those at large universities, make their services available for a fee if you didn't attend their school. When you are researching schools, find out about nearby colleges and universities with strong education departments. Call the schools' Career Placement Offices and inquire about their willingness to help an out-of-state job seeker.

Although long-distance job searches are more difficult than local ones, states are continuing to make the process easier. Not only are they sending vacancy listings to many types of Internet sites, they also are adapting licensing procedures to make it less cumbersome for teachers from other states to obtain certificates. In other word, there has never been a better time to find and land an out-of-state position.

INTERNATIONAL JOB SEARCHES

If you are thinking about teaching outside the United States, there are a number of ways to explore your options. Different types of schools around the world employ American educators, seeking them to teach English and other subjects. Some schools are American, in which every subject is taught in English, and the student population is made up of the children of Americans living abroad (in some cases other English-speaking children

---

English Teaching Certificates

There is no standard international qualification for Teaching English as a Foreign Language, and no traditional accreditation for TEFL programs currently exists. Schools in Central America and the Far East look for candidates with bachelor's degrees. Those in the European Union, Central Europe, and South America require a degree and a 70-hour TEFL course (including observed teaching practice). There are a number of TEFL certificates offered through various schools, online, and as correspondence courses. The website *www.tefl.net* offers a searchable database of international TEFL programs. In addition, search the Internet for the following:

- Certificate in Teaching English as a Foreign Language (CTEFL)
- Teaching English to Speakers of Other Languages (TESOL)
- Cambridge ELT Certificate in English Language Teaching to Adults (CELTA).
- Diploma in English Language Teaching for Adults (DELTA)

---

attend as well). In these American schools, the faculty teaches every course in English, so openings for science, math, social studies, etc., are available.

Other schools add American teachers to their faculty solely to teach English. Because English is the second language of many countries throughout the world, there are numerous opportunities for those seeking these positions, including those in elementary, middle, and high schools; colleges; independent language schools; and businesses. Many overseas schools require that English teachers have a bachelor's degree and an English teaching certificate.

Doing Your Homework

Researching overseas job is much like researching local ones. You'll need to figure out where you want to teach and then narrow your search to a list of potential schools or placement programs. There are a number of excellent websites with general information about what international positions are like, including benefits and potential problems. Many offer links to job listings, as well as help with legal issues such as work visas.

Here's where to start your search:

- Overseas Teaching Digest *(www.overseasdigest.com/teacher1.html)*: interviews with international teachers, articles on job scams, and links to the employment pages of international schools.
- U.S. Department of State's Office of Overseas Schools *(www.state.gov/m/a/ os)*: information on the hundreds of International schools affiliated with the Department of State, located in Central and South America, Europe, Africa, and the Near East. Included are links to each school.
- Teach Abroad *(www.teachabroad.com)*: information on certificate programs; job postings from around the world; free newsletter.
- The International Educator (TIE) *(www.tieonline.com)*: plenty of free information on international jobs; also offers subscription service with résumé bank, email notifications of vacancies, and message boards.

If you are interested in finding a position in Europe, the Teach Europe program is a great place to start. It was developed by the Cultural Services of the Consulate General of Germany, the French Embassy, the Portuguese Embassy, the Consulate General of Italy, the Consulate General of Denmark as well as the American Association of Teachers of French (AATF), the American Association of Teachers of German (AATG), the Goethe-Institute, the Czech Center, and the Italian American Committee on Education (IACE) to prepare American teachers for work in Europe. It offers seminars for high school teachers of European Union languages, social studies, history, and art in Connecticut, New Jersey, New York, Pennsylvania, and Rhode Island that teach participants about the European Union.

> ### Languages of the European Union
>
> Czech, Danish, Dutch, English, Estonian, Finnish, French, German, Greek, Hungarian, Italian, Latvian, Lithuanian, Maltese, Polish, Portuguese, Slovak, Slovenian, Spanish, Swedish

During four workshops and a panel discussion, teachers work with professors, learn innovative teaching strategies, and receive a pedagogical resources kit. For more information, including a schedule of upcoming seminars, visit *www.teacheurope.org*.

Finding International Job Openings

The best ways to locate vacancies are to check online job postings (some of the sites already listed have posting and/or links to postings; search with the terms "international teaching" for more), placement services, and job fairs.

International School Services is a recruiting company that finds teachers for more than 200 international American schools. It holds International Recruitment Centers around the world for teachers registered with their service (you must apply to establish a professional file). The ISS website also has good general information about international job searches: *www.iss.edu.*

Another placement service is Search Associates *(www.search-associates.com).* They place more than 1,000 teachers each year, most of whom have at least two years of experience and the flexibility to consider positions in more than one country. However, Search Associates also places interns who are recent graduates with no teaching experience. These placements offer a great way to get experience in the classroom and travel abroad.

The University of Northern Iowa Overseas Placement Service for Educators holds the original International Fair for Educators. It has been an annual event for more than 30 years, and attracts representatives from 120 schools in more than 70 countries. After registering for the fair, candidates receive a subscription to the newsletter *Overseas Placement Matters,* which includes information and tips related to international teacher job searches, job listings, and strategies for success at the fair. UNI also provides credential and referral services *(www.uni.edu/placemnt/overseas).*

Special Considerations

International teaching positions offer the possibility of an incredible, once-in-a-lifetime experience. But they can also be risky. Before you accept a job offer, you'll want to research the country where you'll be teaching, including the culture, living conditions, local customs, school, and housing conditions. Find general information about living conditions from the U.S. Department of State and the CIA's *World Fact Book, www. cia.gov/cia/publications/factbook/,* including country descriptions, climate and terrain information, environmental and natural disaster risks, population and demographics, health concerns and access to medical facilities, government and legal systems, economic and commercial statistics, transportation, telecommunications, and any ongoing civil or transnational disputes.

If the contract and other paperwork you receive isn't as informative as you'd like, you'll need to ask questions. The school or placement service needs to tell you your salary and how it will be paid (weekly? monthly?), how many hours you'll be expected to work each week, the length of the contract (typically one to two years), how much vacation time you'll have and whether it is paid or unpaid, the benefits you will receive (especially medical), and what kind of housing is available. Some schools provide housing, while others expect you to find your own or place you with a local family. If you must find your own housing, determine the average cost of a furnished apartment or house within commuting distance of the school. Ask also about size, furnishings, cleanliness, security, heating, air conditioning, electricity, phones, Internet access, kitchen facilities, and bathrooms.

Finally, research the school. What kind of support is offered? Are you expected to provide supplies, or does the school supply everything you'll need? Are extracurricular commitments expected, and are you compensated additionally for them? What are typical work clothes for teachers?

Choosing a Placement Service

Most services are reputable and provide exactly what they say they will. However, like all companies, there are some bad ones.

Portrait of a Disreputable Company

- Ask for cash or a money order (untraceable payments allow them to hide income)
- Ask for payment in advance
- Use names that are very similar to reputable companies
- Ask for credit card and bank account numbers over the telephone
- Use their contract to tie you to unreasonable demands
- Don't provide you with a written contract
- Don't answer your questions satisfactorily
- Put pressure on you to make a hasty decision

Protect yourself by
- Paying by check and making a copy of it along with all paperwork
- Never giving out sensitive financial information over the phone
- Having an attorney check any contract before you sign
- Demanding a written contract if one has not been provided
- Researching the company, using the Better Business Bureau, the Office of Consumer Affairs in the state in which the company is based, former teachers, etc.
- Taking your time; if the offer sounds too good to be true, it probably is

CHAPTER 11

Applying for the Job

Once you locate a vacancy, you'll need to do more than just complete an application form. Marketing yourself to future employers involves a number of key ingredients: a résumé that highlights your skills and previous experiences, a portfolio that enthusiastically demonstrates your ability to teach, a well-crafted cover letter, and a practiced plan to ace interviews. Once you get a job offer (or two), how do you decide whether to take it? You'll need to weigh your options and compare the offer to what you can reasonably expect from other schools in your area.

RÉSUMÉ WORKSHOP

Résumé basics haven't changed much since the last time you had to create one. It's still a good idea, for example, to keep its appearance on the conservative side and have it proofread by at least two grammatically minded friends. But beyond the basics, the career changer's résumé needs thoughtful craftsmanship. How do you make the most of your limited teaching experience, and demonstrate the transferable skills you developed working in another profession?

Being a career changer means you already have work experience—and specifically the skills you have developed—and are able to talk concretely about how that will help you be an outstanding classroom teacher. Have your previous jobs made you an expert at time management? Talk about how you can apply that to the classroom. Did your past career make you an expert at crisis management? Talk about how that skill is applicable to the classroom.

The Basics

You probably still have a copy of an old résumé in a file cabinet, on a disk, or on your hard drive. Although it was geared toward landing a different kind of job, it's a great place to start. If you don't have a hard copy, print one—because you are creating a document that will ultimately be read in that form, editing on paper is more effective.

There should be four primary sections: heading (contact information and objective), education, work experience, and skills. Update your contact information if necessary, including name, complete street address, phone number, and email address. Then, write a concise phrase describing the position you are seeking. Use one or two lines (at most) for your description, such as: "Objective: to obtain a position in a secondary school teaching science and math." If appropriate for the job vacancy, add additional objectives and credentials such as "Qualified and interested in coaching basketball and hockey."

The education section should list all degrees in chronological order, placing your latest degree (in education) first. Degrees earned many years ago should not be described in great detail. The name of the college or university, dates of attendance, and specific

Old Résumé Advice That Still Works

- Create a professional look; use white or off-white paper and neat, traditional font no smaller than 10-point
- Use consistent section headings and dating styles
- Be concise—use phrases rather than complete sentences
- Choose specific words rather than vague ones (e.g., "six" rather than "many," "created and maintained file system" rather than "clerical duties")
- Use action words such as "accomplished," "implemented," "developed," "created"
- Organize to make information easy to locate
- Leave some "white space"; a résumé crammed with too much information is hard to read; use two pages if necessary
- Leave out personal information; height, weight, and marital status do not belong on a résumé
- Be relevant—leave out the part-time job at the auto parts store five years ago and anything referring to high school
- Proofread, proofread, proofread! Don't rely solely on spell- and grammar-check programs. Ask at least two other people to check for errors. There is no excuse for a spelling or grammar mistake.

degree earned are probably enough. Your future employer doesn't need to know if you were in a fraternity or played on the Division III championship field hockey team. However there is an exception: If a college experience is relative to your new career, mention it briefly. If you plan to coach a team, list all playing experiences with that sport. If you tutored or performed another teacher-like job, note that as well.

Your recent education, whether an advanced degree or a few courses for an alternative route program, should be placed ahead of previous education. A typical format lists the school attended, its location, your course of study (or courses), dates of attendance, and grade point average. However, if your GPA is less than impressive, leave it out!

Work experience should be subdivided into teaching experience and prior or other experience, with teaching placed first. Student teaching experience should be described in detail, including the subject and/or grade. Rather than listing the duties of all student teachers, focus on what made your experience unique. What makes your teaching special? How did you develop curriculum by devising a unique project or lesson? Did student achievement improve in some way as a result of your instruction? Did you implement a new program or initiate a new way to teach a

The One-Page Controversy

Should you or shouldn't you (create a two-page résumé)? Old résumé advice dictated the one-page rule. The theory went that if you were concise and relevant, you wouldn't need more than a page. But what if you had two student teaching experiences, worked with a professor on a research paper, and were heavily involved as a student member of an educator's organization? If one page is simply not enough to contain the information you need to convey, use two.

Obviously, if you need a second page, you must repeat your contact information in case the pages become separated. If you don't want to staple them together, a few of the teachers we spoke with gave the following ideas for creating a unique two-page résumé (but check school requirements before doing anything too unique—some schools and districts have length and style preferences).

The first is to use two sides of the same piece of paper, brochure-style. If you've never created a brochure, you can use software that guides you through the process of placing text on each panel. Or, you can print your résumé pages side-by-side on an 11×17 paper, and fold it in half. Use the blank "cover" to repeat your contact information.

Résumé Action Words That Make the Most of Your Experience

achieved	assessed	communicated
demonstrated	encouraged	evaluated
facilitated	implemented	instructed
integrated	lead	motivated
organized	planned	prepared
researched	supervised	wrote

lesson? Perhaps you invited a local author to speak to your class about prewriting techniques and then led the class in an energetic practice session. Or you had students prepare typical Greek foods for a special lunch at the end of a unit on ancient Athens. Describe anything that sets you apart from other student teachers.

Other teaching experience could include substitute teaching, practicums, working as a teacher's aide, volunteer positions (camp counselor, tutor, etc.), and other types of instruction, such as religious and fitness. Any experience that put you in a position of teaching others or studying teachers in action should be described.

When you write about prior work experience, stress the skills you developed that translate to the classroom. Time management, familiarity with technology, organization, and the ability to lead others are all examples of transferable skills.

Add other sections if your experiences and abilities warrant them. For example, if you are a member of a professional organization, you could include an Activities section. Describe your participation, workshops and seminars attended, positions held, etc. Other activities that could be relevant to your work in a school include newsletter writing (think school newspaper or yearbook advising), sports (coaching), travel (advisor or organizer of study abroad program), and hobbies (advisor to clubs such as chess, knitting, or cooking).

If you have received more than one award, whether at school, work, or through an organization or activity, or have otherwise had accomplishments recognized, highlight them with their own section.

Barbara Kendall
20 Vista Hill Road
Brandon, VT 05733
(802) 123-4567
bkendall@internet.com

Education: Saint Michael's College, Colchester, VT
Bachelor of Science in Biology; Magna Cum Laude, August 2006
Secondary Education: Science Licensure, March 2007
Seeking second endorsement in math
Trinity College of Vermont, Burlington VT, 2003–2005
Canton Agricultural and Technical College, Canton, NY
AAS in Chemistry; Biology minor, 1990
Honors: Kappa Delta Pi Educational Honor Society
St. Michael's Academic Scholarship
Skills: Strong interpersonal skills
Microsoft Word, Microsoft Excel, Printshop, and C programming

Practica: <u>Student Teaching</u>, Mountainview Middle School, Burlington VT, *Fall 2005*
Seventh Grade Science: Human Biology. Worked closely with a four-teacher team to instruct 75
students. Focused on instilling good scientific skills, but also used the tools of cultural anthropology
to understand similarities and differences in people from around the world. Created original units on
genetics and digestion.
<u>Curriculum Project</u>, Burlington School District, Burlington VT, *Summer 2005*
Worked closely with a team of Science and Technology teachers and the district curriculum coordinator
to rewrite the Science curriculum for grades 6–8.
<u>Relevant Teacher</u>, Central Middle School, Fairfax VT, *Fall 2007–present*

Experience: Science teacher on a team of either three or four other teachers and 75 students. Focused
on instilling good scientific and reading skills in seventh- and eighth-graders.
<u>Teacher</u>, St. Albans City School, St. Albans VT, *Spring 2006*
Eighth Grade Physical Science including standards-based instruction and labs in Chemistry, Force and
Motion, and Gravity. Also interaction/teaming with three other eighth grade teachers.
<u>Long-term Special Educator</u>, Central Middle School, Fairfax VT, *2001–2002*
Sixth Grade Math, Reading and Seventh Grade Language Arts
Whole group, small group, and individual instruction as well as development of original unit and lesson
plans for Math and Reading. Interaction with parents, colleagues, and administrators; provided input
for the writing and revision of IEP 157 and 504 plans.
<u>Long-term substitute</u>, Central Middle School, Fairfax VT, *Spring 2001*
Sixth Grade Social Studies, Language Arts, and Math
Planned original units on *Tuck Everlasting*, Geometry, and early exploration in North America.
Assessed student work and participated in parent/teacher conferences.

Work History: Sole proprietor of About the House Interiors. *1999–2001*
Chemical engineering technician at IBM. *1990–1999*

In addition, principals and other hiring administrators will read your résumé with an eye toward your standing as a professional. In particular, they look for four important criteria. Be sure to include as many as are applicable to your experience within your work and/or education sections:

1. Structure of your class (was there multi-age grouping, team teaching, collaboration?)
2. Diverse student population (highlights your ability to connect with all types of students)
3. Successful relationships with parents and community (makes job of principal easier and promotes school with local population)
4. Types of reading or math instructional materials used (include the publisher's name, showing your familiarity)

Electronic Résumés

Many school districts and education job sites ask for electronic (or text) résumé submissions. They may request that you send your résumé online, or mail or fax a text version that they scan when they receive. It saves them time because they can search all submitted résumés for the keywords they determine are important, quickly eliminating candidates. Electronic résumés are also easier to share if there is a committee making the hiring decision.

Text résumés differ from regular résumés in two important ways: The first way is the use of keywords as previously mentioned. Because your résumé will be searched electronically, you need to include the terms and jargon used in education to describe your skills, education, and experience. The second difference is the format. Although you will use the same major sections (header, job objective, education, work experience, etc.), the look of a text résumé is typically much simpler.

The content of your résumé, including your education and work experiences, should remain the same. But you will need to make important changes in the words you use to convey that content. How can you determine which keywords you should include? Obviously, they will vary depending on the type of teaching job you are looking for.

Here are some ideas for formulating a keyword list:

1. *Look for the roles and skills described in job advertisements.* Copy terminology that is repeated, as well as words and phrases that are particularly relevant to your position.
2. *Think about your coursework and student teaching experiences.* What jargon or buzz words are used not only in education, but also in your specialty?

Keyword Ideas

brain-based learning

classroom management

classroom monitoring

cultural sensitivity

curriculum design

curriculum development

curriculum planning

detail-oriented

discipline strategies

diversity

ESL or ESOL

flexibility

gifted and talented

hands-on instruction

inclusion

instruction

interdisciplinary teaching approaches

K–12

leadership

learner assessment

lesson planning

mainstream mentoring

parent-teacher relations

parental involvement

peer mentoring

peer tutoring

phonemic awareness

self-motivated

special needs

student involvement

student success

teaching and learning

teaching across the curriculum

teamwork

technology

testing

whole language

3. *Do your homework.* Check the hiring school and district websites for words they use to describe their teaching staff and school philosophy.
4. *If you belong to an educator's organization, check its website and promotional literature.* Find the websites of similar organizations, paying particular attention to language.
5. *Visit online forums, discussion boards, and chat venues for teachers.* You can ask directly for help or search stored messages (once you have a list of words, search for them on these sites to confirm their relevance. You may find additional or better examples).
6. *Once you have created a list of keywords, rewrite your résumé.* Write keywords in phrases that describe your experiences and accomplishments. They'll get maximum exposure if you put them in your job objective, because it is at the top of your résumé. Use restraint, though. Repetition of keywords looks just as bad to a reader as repetition of any other words.

If after you finish your rewrite you find that you weren't able to use as many keywords as you wanted to, add a new heading such as "Skills" or "Accomplishments." By describing results you achieved and skills you developed, you'll create another opportunity to use more keywords.

Some schools ask for a PDF version of your résumé, which can be made by simply opening your résumé document and saving it in PDF form. Others scan résumés or open them with a variety of software. They often prefer plain text versions because they are adaptable to these differing programs (because they are simply formatted). Some programs, for example, don't recognize bullets. Others interpret tab spacings as lines of text. Another bonus is that when plain text résumés are sent in hard copy before being scanned, they eliminate the risk of transmitting a computer virus. To create an electronic résumé using an existing standard résumé, check for and correct (if necessary) the following formatting issues:

- Font: standard only, such as Arial, Courier, Futura, Helvetica, Optima, Palatino, Times New Roman, or Univers
- Type size: between 11 and 14 points
- Characters per line: no more than 65 (type size may allow for a few more or less)
- Graphics and/or shading: eliminate
- Bold, italics, underlining: eliminate; for headings, use all caps
- Bullets and/or lines: eliminate; use one or two dashes to create "bulleted" lists, although each item must be flushed left
- Justify text: left (including heading)
- Heading: at top of every page

BARBARA KENDALL
20 Vista Hill Road
Brandon, VT 05733
(802) 123-4567
bkendall@internet.com

EDUCATION
Saint Michael's College, Colchester, VT
—Bachelor of Science in Biology; Magna Cum Laude, August 2006
—Secondary Education Science Licensure, March 2007
—Seeking second endorsement in math
Trinity College of Vermont, Burlington VT, 2003 - 2005
Canton Agricultural and Technical College, Canton, NY
—AAS in Chemistry, Biology minor, 1990
HONORS
Kappa Delta Pi Educational Honor Society
St. Michael's Academic Scholarship
SKILLS
Strong interpersonal skills, encouraging student success and parental involvement
Excellent classroom management using a variety of discipline strategies
Microsoft Word, Microsoft Excel, Printshop, and C programming
PRACTICA
Student Teaching, Mountainview Middle School, Burlington VT, Fall 2005
—Seventh Grade Science: Human Biology. Worked closely with a four-teacher team to instruct 75 students. Focused on instilling good scientific skills, but also used the tools of cultural anthropology to understand similarities and differences in people from around the world. Created original units on genetics and digestion.
Curriculum Project, Burlington School District, Burlington VT, Summer 2005
—Worked with a team of Science and Technology teachers and the district curriculum coordinator to rewrite the Science curriculum for grades 6 - 8.
EXPERIENCE
Teacher, Central Middle School, Fairfax VT, Fall 2007 - present
—Science teacher on a team of either three or four other teachers and 75 students. Used an interdisciplinary approach to instill good scientific and reading skills in seventh- and eighth-graders.
Teacher, St. Albans City School, St. Albans VT, Spring 2006
—Grade 8 Physical Science including standards-based instruction and labs in Chemistry, Force and Motion, and Gravity. Also interaction/teaming with three other eighth grade teachers.
Long-term Special Educator, Central Middle School, Fairfax VT, 2001 - 2002
—Sixth Grade Math and Reading, Seventh Grade Language Arts. Whole group, small group, and individual instruction of special needs students as well as development of original unit and lesson plans for Math and Reading. Interaction with parents, colleagues, and administrators; provided input for the writing and revision of IEP 157 and 504 plans.
Long-term substitute, Central Middle School, Fairfax, VT Spring 2001
—Sixth Grade Social Studies, Language Arts, and Math. Planned original units on Tuck Everlasting, Geometry, and early exploration in North America. Assessed student work and participated in parent/teacher conferences.
WORK HISTORY
Sole proprietor of About the House Interiors, 1999 - 2001
Chemical engineering technician, IBM, 1990 - 1999

- Printer: high quality laser printer or inkjet only
- Paper: white or off-white, 8 1/2×11

Note: Many schools have guidelines for electronic submissions either on their applications or websites. After you develop your basic text résumé, adapt it as necessary to conform to those guidelines.

See a text version on page 202 of the résumé found earlier in this chapter.

THE PORTFOLIO

Portfolios have long been a staple of job seekers in fields such as art and journalism, in which standard résumés don't do justice to the talents of the candidates. Think of them as "expanded résumés;" they may include samples of work, video and audio components, and copies of recommendations. Many schools and districts expect teacher candidates to come to their interviews with a portfolio (although check with the hiring school—those that routinely hire hundreds of teachers don't have time to spend reviewing them).

Why You Need a Portfolio

Portfolios engage many senses, drawing a broad picture of the candidate. The interviewer doesn't simply read about accomplishments, he sees evidence of them. Your skills, your experiences, and your accomplishments illustrate your potential as an educator. Portfolios are especially useful when a pool of job candidates have very similar educations and experiences.

As you create your portfolio, make a smaller version that can be left with your interviewers. Once you land a job, veteran teachers, and most career service centers, recommend that you maintain it. Keep a box in your classroom to store anything new that highlights your successes and growth in the profession. Once a year, go through the box and add those items that will best enhance your portfolio.

The experience of creating (and maintaining) a portfolio demands that you think seriously about your goals, where you've been, and where you'd like to go. You must evaluate your experiences and skills, deciding which are worthy of inclusion (no interviewer has the time to sift through a portfolio that's hundreds of pages in length!). Before an interview, a review of your portfolio reminds you of how you stand out as a job candidate and which skills and experiences to highlight.

Creating a Portfolio

Before you begin your portfolio, check with your Career Services Office or Department of Education. They probably have sample portfolios and may even be able to help you create yours. Some schools not only help students put portfolios together, but they store and update them throughout a former student's career as she submits material.

There are a few different formats used for portfolios. Most are created in a three-ring binder and include a table of contents. Tabs or dividers are used to separate sections of the portfolio. Some teachers use multimedia formats, including PowerPoint, video, and Web-based portfolios. These may be used in addition to a standard binder portfolio or in place of one. Because technology has become such an important part of curriculum, and principals look for candidates with strong computer skills, it makes sense to highlight those skills through your portfolio.

After choosing a format, you will need to decide how to organize content. Most educator portfolios include sections such as résumé and certification information; professional preparation and development; classroom planning, instruction, and evaluation; personal goals; committee work; and other educational activities. These sections can be labeled in your binder and/or used to create separate Web pages or links if you are developing an online portfolio.

When development is complete, the next step is to assemble the material you will include in your portfolio. What should you include? Begin with your résumé. What do you mention in it that could use more explanation? What could you "show" rather than "tell"? Then, consider what you want a potential employer to know about you. What qualities do you possess that make you stand apart from the crowd? In general terms, think about how you can showcase your education and experience with examples, evidence, and details of your work, skills, and accomplishments.

Here are some common elements of portfolios:

- *Personal goals.* Include your career objective, which should be broader than the job objective on your résumé. Where do you see yourself in five years? How will you grow as a teacher? What is important to you? Also include your mission statement, describing the philosophies you live by, and the direction you want your life to take.
- *Résumés.* Include both standard and scannable copies.
- *Certification information.* Include standardized test scores and other criteria used to grant your certification or license.

- *Professional preparation and development.* Include transcripts; descriptions of relevant courses taken; list of conferences, seminars, and workshops attended; membership in professional organizations.
- *Classroom management.* Describe your theory of this critical skill, and include specific techniques you use to create an orderly, respectful environment.
- *Skills.* Here is where you "show" rather than "tell." How have you demonstrated that you possess certain marketable skills? Examine specific experiences in detail. You might choose to include photos, lesson plans, test results, and highlights of your student teaching experience.
- *Work samples.* As with skills, include photos, examples of student work, lesson plans, audio, and/or video examples of your classroom. If you created a website or online material with your students, include screen shots and Web addresses. These samples should show the type of learning environment you create for your students.
- *Accomplishments.* Focus on teaching, but you may include highlights of your past career experiences. These include, but are not limited to, awards and other honors.
- *Letters of recommendation.* Include letters from other teachers, professors, administrators, and previous employers.
- *Volunteer work.* If it connects with your teaching ability, treat volunteering as work experience. Describe your duties, results, time commitment, etc. If it doesn't connect with your teaching ability, then this section should simply list the organizations for which you've volunteered, with dates of activity.
- *Other educational activities.* Think of these in terms of demonstrating other skills that could apply to your teaching career, such as coaching if you are an athlete and have experience in one or more organized sport. Other examples include acting, writing, computer, and public speaking abilities.
- *References.* List five people with full contact information and a brief description of how each person is familiar with your skills and experience.

When your portfolio is complete, make a copy to bring to interviews. In addition, select those key documents and other elements to include in a shorter version. Make multiple copies to be given to your interviewers. Finally, maintain your portfolio. Create a space to save important new documentation, and take the time to update it semiannually.

Here are components from an actual teacher portfolio, including the Table of Contents and key pages:

Table of Contents

Letter of Introduction to My Portfolio

Biographical Sketch: About the Author

Philosophy of Education

Résumé

Letter of Recommendation

Transcript

Student Teaching Evaluations

Awards and Certificates

Certification Documents

Training in Violence Prevention and Intervention

Training in Child Abuse and Maltreatment

NYS Teacher Exams

Domain 1: Motivation, Learning, and Development

Overview INTASC Standard 2: Knowledge of Human Development; INTASC Standard 5: Classroom Motivation and Management

Artifact rationale 1 INTASC Standard 2

Artifact: PISCES Lesson from Caterpillars to Butterflies

Artifact rationale 2 INTASC Standard 2

Artifact: Floor Plan

Artifact rationale 1 INTASC Standard 5

Artifact: Bulletin Board

Artifact rationale 2 INTASC Standard 5

Artifact: Classroom Learning Centers

Domain 2: Curriculum

Overview INTASC Standard 1: Knowledge of Subject Matter; INTASC Standard 2: Planning Instructional Skills

Artifact rationale 1 INTASC Standard 1

Artifact: The Rainforest Lesson

Artifact rationale 2 INTASC Standard 1

Artifact: Candy Heart Bar Graph Lesson

Artifact rationale 1 INTASC Standard 7

Artifact: *The Grouchy Ladybug*

Artifact rationale I INTASC Standard 7

Artifact: Permission Slip to Visit Long Island Jewish Hospital

Domain 3: Instruction

Overview INTASC Standard 3: Adapting Instruction to Diverse Learners; INTASC Standard 4: Multiple Instructional Strategies; INTASC Standard 6: Communication Skills

Artifact rationale 1 INTASC Standard 3

Artifact: Lesson Plan on Clocks for Inclusion Class

Artifact rationale 2 INTASC Standard 3

Artifact: Planning Adaptations in the Instructional Environment

Artifact rationale 1 INTASC Standard 4

Artifact: Fun with Balloons Lesson

Artifact rationale 2 INTASC Standard 4

Artifact: Lesson Plan on Descriptive Words

Artifact rationale 1 INTASC Standard 6

Artifact: Software Reviews

Artifact rationale 2 INTASC Standard 6

Artifact: Certificate for Behavior or Academic Performance

Domain 4: Assessment

Overview INTASC Standard 8: Assessment of Student Learning

Artifact rationale 1 INTASC Standard 8

Artifact: Kindergarten Writing Rubric

Artifact rationale 2 INTASC Standard 8

Artifact: ARI Case Study

Domain 5: Professionalism

Overview INTASC Standard 9: Reflection and Professional Development; INTASC Standard 10: Collaboration, Ethics, and Relationships

Reflections on the Past, Goals for the Future

Key Pages from Table of Contents:

Philosophy of Education

I believe that in order for children to learn, they must be active participants in the learning process. From my education courses, I have learned that retention of information is based on the number of modalities present in the lesson taught. Therefore, I want the children to see, hear, and perform activities that will help them retain the information I present. I want every child to reach his/her full potential. When a child is not successful, I want to convey to that child my belief that he/she can do better, and that together we can accomplish anything.

I want my understanding of children to create in my classroom an atmosphere where they feel safe, valued, and successful. In order to achieve this, I will develop meaningful relationships with my students, parents of my students, and my colleagues. In order to achieve this, I believe it is necessary to put forth effort outside of the classroom which will demonstrate my desire to be involved in my students' lives and the life of the community in which I work.

Teaching is a complex endeavor that requires high-level thinking and decision-making among multiple alternatives. The knowledge that I have now is a starting point that will be strengthened by attending conferences, workshops, and classes. Life is a journey and throughout life's journey, knowledge is gained. I need to continue to grow, learn, and be educated in order to be the best teacher I can be.

Under Domain 1: Motivation, Learning, and Development:

Artifact Rationale 2 INTASC Standard 5

Name of Artifact: Classroom Learning Centers

Children, by their very nature of being children, need to have a variety of activities to participate in throughout the school day. Therefore, I would have seven different learning areas within my classroom where the children can explore, create, imagine, and participate. This active involvement in learning by the children demonstrates INTASC Standard 5: Classroom Motivation and Management. When children are actively involved, the number of discipline issues will be lower. It also provides an opportunity to separate children who are having difficulty on a particular day socializing with certain other children.

Under Domain 2: Curriculum

Artifact Rationale 1 INTASC Standard 7

Name of Artifact: *The Grouchy Ladybug*

The lesson on *The Grouchy Ladybug* is built upon three learning objectives for the students. The activities the students perform will reinforce the learning objectives. Before beginning the story, I informed the students that we would be making predictions about the story, reiterating the order of what happened, and comparing the two ladybugs from the story. By stating clearly what the children should pay attention to, I set the stage for them to listen for specific information. This focuses on INTASC Standard 7, stating goals for the students before the lesson.

Lesson: *The Grouchy Ladybug*

Class/Grade: Kindergarten

I. Aim/Goal: Students will be able to listen to a story and recall information based on their listening.

Objective: While listening to the story, the students will orally predict events based on the context clues. They will construct the order in which the events occurred. They will compare the differences between the two ladybugs using words and pictures.

II. Materials Needed: *The Grouchy Ladybug* by Eric Carle

Ladybug puppet
Pictures of the two ladybugs
Words to place under the pictures
Pictures demonstrating different parts of the story

Procedures:

1. Before beginning the story, I will discuss the concept of "sharing" with the students. I will question them about sharing toys, a room, or food.
2. I will then use the ladybug puppet to introduce the book.
3. Next, I will read the book, *The Grouchy Ladybug.*
4. As the story progresses, I will ask the students to predict or guess what is going to happen next and why they made their predictions.
5. After the story is finished, I will hand out to three different groups of students three sets of cards that contain pictures of various parts of the story.

6. Using the cards, the students must line up events in the book according to the order that the events happened.
7. When all three groups have finished, I will have them form a triangle and compare their order with the order of the other groups.
8. The children will then judge which group is correct, if they do not all agree.
9. I will then have them sit and will place the two ladybug pictures on the chalkboard.
10. Along the chalkboard edge, I will place various words with pictures that describe the two ladybugs.
11. The children will then take turns deciding what word goes with what picture.

III. Culminating Activity: We will make ladybug cookies using vanilla wafers, red frosting, chocolate chips, and thin black licorice.

IV. Follow-Ups: I will give the students a ditto with different pictures of daily activities in their lives and have them place the activities in the correct order.

V. Other Activities: Discussion of facial expressions and feelings.

Play a game by having the children act out different feelings using facial expressions and have the class guess the feeling.

Self-Discovery: In my science-learning center, I would have a variety of activities that the children could work on independently. They would perform the experiment and then demonstrate what they learned as a result of the experiment. This would provide an opportunity for self-discovery. The child could then report the results either by drawing what they observed, talking into a recorder to explain what they observed, or writing down on paper what they observed.

Activity 1: Have a bowl of water available in the science center. Into the bowl of water, the children would drop a variety of objects—a tiny pebble, a cork, a feather, a tiny plastic boat, a small ball, a jack, a piece of paper, and other assorted objects. The children may add to this collection. They would then drop the objects into the water to see where they would go. They would report their findings in any method mentioned above.

THE COVER LETTER

Cover letters are written for two purposes: in response to a known job vacancy (often called a letter of application) and to ascertain whether there are job vacancies (often called a letter of inquiry). Both types are seeking the same result: an interview. How do you achieve the cover letter's purpose? Through the careful use of a number of techniques:

- Convey genuine interest in the school by being accurate and specific. Never send a cover letter addressed to "Dear Principal," or "Dear Sir or Madam." It takes one phone call or one visit to a website to find out the name of the person who's doing the hiring. Even if you are sending out dozens of letters, take the time to personalize each one.

- Demonstrate your knowledge of the school (gained through research), its philosophy, size, location, faculty, awards, etc. This is another way to convey your interest.

- Express your passion for teaching. You're not applying for a job on an assembly line or accounting firm. You want to work with children, to help them and to be a positive influence on them. Let your emotion show.

- Don't just enclose a résumé—draw attention to one or two highlights. The letter should by no means reword the résumé, but refer to its most positive features.

- Mention a contact at the school or other person who suggested you write, if any. Do you already know a member of the faculty who suggested you send your résumé? Did a professor recommend the school as a great match for your skills? Don't leave out an important piece of information that can leave a positive impression.

- Indicate your expectation of an interview. Maintain a tone that's confident without being pompous as you let the administrator know you expect to hear from her soon.

- Refer to previous contact(s) with the administrator, if any. If you had an informative discussion at a job fair, or even just called a few months ago to ask about vacancies, refresh her memory. Multiple contacts say you're very interested in the school.

- Don't use a cover letter template. Writing this letter isn't difficult—make your letter stand out by typing it yourself.

- If you are responding to a specific vacancy, provide or refer to any requested information. Many vacancy postings ask applicants to provide references or availability dates.

- For letters of inquiry, don't assume the administrator will contact you. Instead, take action. Write, "I am very interested in working at your school and will contact you within the week to find out about upcoming employment opportunities." Five days later, make the call.

■ For letters of application, you can also write that you will make contact, unless the vacancy posting specified "no phone calls."

Jennifer Johnson
59 West Main Street, Apt. 2B
Chico, CA 95928
(530) 898-1834
jjohnson@webmastermail.com

April 1, 2007

Devon Kingston, Principal
Valleydale Junior High School
16580 Union Boulevard
La Costa, CA 95240

Dear Mr. Kingston,

I read with great interest your anticipated junior high positions that were posted on your district website. My practicum professor, Everett Murphy, recommended your school highly. I am seeking full time employment as an English teacher for the 2007–2008 school year. The high standards of Valleydale Junior High School are well known, and it would be a privilege to be a member of your staff.

In May 2007, I will receive my Master of Arts degree in Education and a Multiple Subject Credential with a supplemental authorization in English at the State University of California. I received a Bachelor's Degree in English Literature in 2000 from Kenyon College. Previously, I worked as an in-house editor at Media Communications Publications. I was quickly named Head of Acquisitions, overseeing the work of four editors. In that capacity, I developed strong leadership, time management, organizational, and teamwork skills, which are all characteristics I can use in the classroom.

I am currently student teaching in an eighth grade English classroom at Fox Run Middle School in Paradise, California. I am an enthusiastic, organized, and highly motivated teacher. I want to encourage students to grow academically, extending their diverse personal limits. During my two student teaching experiences, it has been my focus to instill a love of learning, as well as teaching my students to be respectful and responsible.

My previous student teaching experience was in an urban district. I have enjoyed the rewards and challenges of both settings. In particular, it has been greatly rewarding to work with "at-risk" students, who need adapted lessons that break down complicated concepts to simple examples. Involving parents through routine communication has taught me the value of this relationship and its connection to a successful classroom. In addition, I have worked well in both schools with the team of colleagues and administrators, receiving letters of recommendation from both principals and a number of teachers.

I will call your office early next week to schedule an interview, and I look forward to meeting you.

Yours truly,

Jennifer Johnson

Jennifer Johnson

Illegal Interview Questions

U.S. law makes it illegal to make hiring decisions based on an applicant's age, color, disability, gender, national origin, race, religion, or creed. Interview questions that are not job related and that attempt to ascertain any of the qualities listed are illegal and do not have to be answered.

What should you do if an interview asks a question such as, "What an interesting accent! Where are you from?" One possibility is to answer the question, knowing that you might jeopardize your chances of landing the job. Another is to refuse to answer. However, it's almost impossible to do so without appearing negative or confrontational.

The third possibility is to answer the motive of the question without divulging the specific information illegally asked for. If an interviewer asks, "Where are you from?" you could interpret his or her motive as trying to determine whether you have a visa that allows you to work in the United States legally. You might answer, "I am legally authorized to work in the United States."

THE INTERVIEW

You're probably not going to get an interview if your résumé and cover letter are weak, but, with that said, the interview is the make-it-or-break-it component of job seeking. Making a favorable impression in person is *critical*. But how can you be relaxed enough to let your personality come through, remain professional, and answer questions thoroughly and thoughtfully? The key is preparation. You need to know the kinds of questions principals ask, and how to answer them. Then, you need to practice.

Interview Basics

These points apply to any interview situation, and are worth repeating:

- Look the part. Dress conservatively and professionally.
- Do your homework. Read everything you can about the school and its district. Prepare specific questions for your interviewer that makes your knowledge of the school obvious.

- Take a trial run. Get good directions, and travel to the school a week before your interview at the same time you'll be traveling on the day of the interview. If there is traffic, you'll be able to adjust your plans to ensure that you arrive on time. If you get lost, you've got plenty of time to figure out where you need to be.
- Prepare your paperwork. Neatness counts! Your application should be flawlessly filled out, résumé proofread and corrected, and portfolio ready to show. If other documentation is requested, have it ready.
- Determine who is conducting the interview. The hiring principal typically does the interviewing, but some larger school districts have human resource departments that conduct preliminary interviews. If you "pass" this interview, you are recommended to the principal. Other schools use administrators other than the principal for interviews. If it isn't clear who will be interviewing you, ask. You don't want any surprises the day of the interview. The more information you have ahead of time as you formulate questions and create expectations, the less nervous you'll be.

Questions: Theirs

New-teacher interviews differ from those for other professions in that they aim to assess performance skills that they can't witness and that you have had limited experience using. Therefore, in addition to the traditional, expected questions ("Why do you want to be a teacher?"), you will probably be asked a number of experience- or performance-based questions. These questions ask you to give the background of a situation, describe the actions you took, and the results you achieved. Interviewers don't focus these types of questions solely on your successes—they're interested in conflict management ("Tell me about a time when you disagreed with your cooperating teacher") and how you handled situations that didn't have positive results. You may be asked as a follow-up, "What would you do differently if you had a chance to do this over again?" This type of question gives the interviewer a sense of how well you reflect upon and learn from your experiences.

Traditional questions are typically centered on these common subjects: strengths and weaknesses, classroom management, student teaching experiences, teaching philosophy and style, future plans, motivational theories, employment history, salary, college course of study and GPA, lesson planning, curriculum, extracurricular interests, volunteering, and community activities. You may also be asked, "What will your classroom be like?" For this question, the interviewer wants you to describe how it looks and sounds, and what it feels like.

Traditional Interview Questions:

- How would you (or someone else) describe yourself, using five adjectives?
- What are your strengths and weaknesses?
- Why did you decide to major in ___?
- What has been your greatest accomplishment so far?
- What is your style of classroom management?
- Describe your teaching style.
- Do you want students to like you?
- Tell me about yourself.
- What have been your experiences with diversity?
- What is your philosophy of education?
- What is the role of the principal?

Experience-based questions (usually with a lead-in of "Tell me about...") may include the following

- How you adapted lessons to meet the needs of different types of learners in your classroom
- A time when you had to make an unpopular decision
- The most difficult obstacle you've had to overcome in your teaching
- How you would set up a program in your teaching area
- Being unable to complete a project on schedule in spite of your best effort
- How you handle discipline in your classroom
- A time when you had to contact a parent about a student's behavior
- A time when you worked collaboratively with other teachers
- An example of how you achieved a great deal in a short amount of time
- A time when you worked effectively under a great deal of pressure
- How you were especially creative in solving a problem
- When your flexibility was put to the test
- A disappointing performance in the classroom
- When you didn't handle a stressful situation well
- A lesson that you taught in detail

The Answers: What Do They Want to Hear?

Principals are in agreement about one of the most important qualities they look for: common sense. You can have an outstanding education, have read all of the top teaching manuals, and have learned what it takes to succeed from highly successful teachers. But if you don't have the common sense to be able to apply what you've learned right from the start, those credentials don't matter. Teachers are "on" all day, from the minute their students begin filing in until that last bell rings for dismissal. On other jobs, you can work your way in slowly, learning the ropes week by week. In the classroom, 100 percent is required on day one.

They also agree about another quality: Principals hire candidates who can articulate a clear classroom management plan and can present evidence that they can enforce it. The last thing any administrator wants is more work, which is what you'll provide if your discipline strategy is to send students to the office for every conflict, major and minor. Be prepared to discuss your plan, breaking it down into steps and showing that different behaviors call for different solutions. Discipline isn't a one-size-fits-all endeavor.

Interviewers want to hear that you will be a team player. The better the faculty works together, the stronger the school. If you project a willingness to embrace the school philosophy and participate in the life of the school, you will score points. That means sharing your talents freely, whether, for example, by covering for another teacher in a crisis, playing the piano for a school production, or volunteering as a cafeteria monitor.

While you need to be confident and enthusiastic about your abilities, don't overstate them. Overconfidence will probably turn off your interviewer. Administrators and veteran teachers know that the field of education is large and complex. No one person, no matter how much experience they have, knows it all. In particular, new teachers are better off being confident enough to ask for help, welcome mentoring, and, above all, be willing to constantly learn more.

Interviewers want to experience your enthusiasm and passion for working with children. They look for candidates who will love their job. The best way to express your emotions is through anecdotes. When you use an interview question to tell a personal story about an experience with a child or a class of young people, your enthusiasm will show. Be sure to include pictures of you working with children in your portfolio to reinforce the interview.

Questions: Yours

Your questions should be specific enough to indicate that you are well informed about the school or district. Remember that when asking, your tone must remain positive and enthusiastic. Don't ask questions that seem confrontational or negative.

Questions will vary by school, but may include the following:

- Are extracurricular assignments available?
- How many students participate in extracurricular activities?
- Do you offer faculty in-service training during the school year?
- What reading series do you use? If you already know, ask a specific question about it.
- What is your average faculty turnover rate?
- What would be my budget for supplies I need to purchase during the school year?
- Do you subscribe to one curriculum theory?
- Do you have an active parent-teacher organization?
- What percentage of your graduates continues on with their education?
- Are there opportunities for team teaching or team planning?

Practice, Practice, Practice

It makes sense to write your answers to the sample interview questions listed above. Take your time to create thoughtful, thorough answers, keeping in mind the qualities interviewers are looking for ("What They Want to Hear"). But you also need to practice giving those answers to another person. Enlist the help of a friend, or ask your Career Services Center about interview practice. They may work with you and even, in some cases, videotape you in a mock interview session to help you correct any errors.

You can also "practice" interviewing online. Many websites offer interactive interview tools that let you type answers to typical interview questions and then compare your answers to ones prepared by job search experts. The questions are not specifically geared toward the teaching profession, but they include many common questions you'll probably be asked.

Here are a few to try:

1. Quintessential Careers (*www.quintcareers.com/interview_question_database/*)
2. Western State College of Colorado's Virtual Interview (*www.western.edu/ career/interview_virtual/virtual_interview.htm*)
3. Monster (*http://tools.monster.com/archives/virtualinterviews/*)
4. Minnesota Jobs (*http://minnesotajobs.com/info/intprac.html*)

As you practice, aim for the following:

- Fully answer the question that was asked
- Don't go off topic
- Speak clearly
- Be enthusiastic
- Use positive body language (firm handshake, upright posture, eye contact, smile)
- Explain why you want to be a teacher
- Ask good questions of your interviewer
- Describe your theory of classroom management
- Include a discussion of diversity (relating to learning styles, socioeconomics, race, religion, etc.)
- Demonstrate your knowledge of state teaching standards
- Talk about your student teaching experience(s) in ways that make you stand out from other candidates (refer to your portfolio)

Follow Up

After every interview, send a thank-you note to your interviewer within 24 hours. It is a small step that many job seekers fail to take, often to great disadvantage. Sending a note will not only keep your name fresh in the administrator's mind, but will also show that you have good follow-up skills, and that you're genuinely interested in the job.

You may choose to use a standard business letter format, typing the note on personal stationary. Or handwrite the note on a professional-looking note card. Thank the interviewer for taking the time to meet with you and for considering you for the job vacancy. Mention the exact position you applied for. In one or two sentences, highlight any important details you discussed. You want the interviewer to remember you. Finally, reaffirm your interest in the position and close confidently with a sentence such as "I look forward to hearing from you soon."

16 West End Avenue
Atlanta, Georgia 30315
123-555-4567

Mrs. Lenore Ferraro
Lakeview School District
314 Southern Blvd.
Atlanta, GA 30313

Dear Mrs. Ferraro,

Thank you for meeting with me at the Atlanta Educator's Association Career Fair today. I appreciate your time and attention in the midst of so many education students seeking jobs.

Your description of Big Lake High School, its philosophy, and programs helped me to realize that not only would I be an asset to the school, but that the school would provide me with the right environment to grow as a professional.

My 17 years of experience as a media consultant have allowed me to develop many skills that will translate well to the classroom, as my student teaching experience at Peachtree High School confirmed. I recently passed the GACE History 6–12 exam, and I have enclosed my results with a copy of my résumé.

Thank you again for your time and consideration; I enjoyed meeting you.

Sincerely,

Jonathan Pratt

Jonathan Pratt

EVALUATING A JOB OFFER

The job search process isn't easy, and you've already accomplished many steps by the time you get a job offer. But it's not over quite yet. Not every offer is worth taking, so you'll need to consider many issues before making a decision. Unlike other professionals, teachers are rarely able to negotiate the terms of the offer. Salary, vacations, and benefits are all typically used as "bargaining chips" by employers and potential employees. But for educators, these are set by the local school board and the hiring district, which means instead of negotiating for the right deal, you need to figure out some of your priorities, and do some research, to make your decision.

Here are some important things to consider:

- *Are you really a good fit?* You know more now than you did when you first drew up a list of schools you'd like to work at. What was the principal really like? Did he live up to your expectations? If not, why? Was the school atmosphere welcoming? Would you be happy teaching there?
- Did the interviewer make a hard sell? Was she trying too hard to convince you to work at the school? Consider whether the position is difficult to fill, and if it is, why?
- *Is the salary reasonable for your area?* School and District report cards will tell you what their teachers are earning, but how does it compare? Check the charts in Figures 11.1 and 11.2 to make some comparisons.
- *What hours are required?* Some schools expect teachers to volunteer to help with or run extracurricular activities that can add hours to your day. Are in-service programs held during the school year, during school breaks, or near vacations?
- *How will you be compensated for advanced coursework or degrees?* Does the school help with tuition?
- *What are the opportunities for professional development?* Does the principal value development and provide access to many opportunities? Are continuing education requirements fulfilled though the principal's offerings?
- *What kinds of benefits are offered?* They are non-negotiable, but they can vary greatly from district to district. How much of the cost must you bear for medical or life insurance? What is the pension plan?

Figures 11.1 and 11.2 show the most recent surveys on Teacher Salary Trends from 2003–2004.

FIGURE 11.1—Average Teacher Salary in 2003–2004, State Rankings

Rank	State	2003-04 Average Salary		2003-04 FTE* Teachers	Percent of U.S. Average
1	Connecticut	$56,516		42,003	121.3%
2	California	56,444	a.	303,968	121.1%
3	New York	55,181	b.	219,335	118.4%
4	Rhode Island	54,809	c.	10,042	117.6%
5	Michigan	54,474	c.	78,734 d.	116.9%
6	Illinois	53,820	a.e.	129,964	115.5%
7	New Jersey	53,663		107,643	115.2%
8	Massachusetts	53,274		73,441	114.3%
9	Pennsylvania	52,640		119,889	113.0%
10	Alaska	51,136		7,858	109.7%
11	Delaware	51,122		6,722	109.7%
12	Maryland	50,303		73,049	108.0%
13	Oregon	47,829		26,731	102.6%
14	Ohio	47,791		114,943	102.6%
15	Georgia	45,848		103,106	98.4%
16	Indiana	45,791		59,833	98.3%
17	Hawaii	45,456	a.f.	12,954	97.6%
18	Washington	45,437		52,892	97.5%
19	Minnesota	45,010	a.	52,311	96.6%
20	Virginia	43,936		95,365	94.3%
21	Colorado	43,318		44,904	93.0%
22	Nevada	43,211		20,015	92.7%
23	North Carolina	43,211	a.	87,947	92.7%
24	Vermont	43,009	a.	8,693	92.3%
25	New Hampshire	42,689		15,110	91.6%
26	Arizona	42,324	c.	47,396	90.8%
27	Wisconsin	41,687		59,405	89.5%
28	South Carolina	41,162		45,830	88.3%
29	Florida	40,598		165,607	87.1%
30	Texas	40,476		289,481	86.9%
31	Tennessee	40,318	a.	58,577	86.5%
32	Idaho	40,111		16,374	86.1%
33	Maine	39,864		17,153	85.6%
34	Kentucky	39,831		41,053	85.5%
35	Nebraska	39,635		20,784	85.1%
36	Wyoming	39,537		6,503	84.8%
37	Arkansas	39,226	a.	31,662	84.2%
38	Utah	38,976		21,660	83.6%
39	Kansas	38,622		35,430	82.9%
40	West Virginia	38,496		20,287	82.6%
41	New Mexico	38,469		21,224	82.6%
42	Iowa	38,381		34,754	82.4%
43	Alabama	38,282		45,920	82.2%
44	Missouri	38,247		65,003	82.1%
45	Montana	37,184		10,330	79.8%
46	Louisiana	37,123		50,495	79.7%
47	Mississippi	36,217		31,611	77.7%
48	North Dakota	35,411		8,720	76.0%
49	Oklahoma	35,061	e.f.	39,218	75.2%
50	South Dakota	33,236		9,031	71.3%
	U.S. Average 2003-04	**$46,597**			
	U.S. Average 2002-03	$45,578			
	Change in Current Dollars	$1,019			
	Percent Change	**2.2%**			
	American Samoa	$17,000		1,020	
	Guam	34,326	a.f.	2,093	
	District of Columbia	62,909		5,704	
	Puerto Rico	24,700		n/a	
	Virgin Islands	n/a		n/a	

* Full-time equivalent.
a. includes extra-duty pay; b. median; c. AFT estimate; d. 2002-03 data; e. includes employer pick-up of employee pension contributions where applicable; f. includes fringe benefits such as healthcare where applicable.
Source: American Federation of Teachers, annual survey of state departments of education.

Source: "Average Teacher Salary in 2003–2004, State Rankings" from Annual Salary & Analysis of Teacher Salary Trends. American Federation of Teachers, Washington, DC 2004. Retrieved July 28, 2006, from *http://www.aft.org/salary/2004/download/2004AFTSalarySurvey.pdf* .

FIGURE 11.2—Actual Average Beginning Teacher Salaries, 2002–2003 and 2003–2004

Rank	State	Beginning Teacher Salary	Beginning Teacher Salary	Average Teacher Salary	Salary as Percentage of Average
1	Alaska	$ 40,027	$ 37,401	$ 51,136	78%
2	Hawaii	37,615	34,549	45,456 a.e.	83%
3	New Jersey	37,061 c.	35,673 c.	53,663	69%
4	New York	36,400	35,259	55,181 b.	66%
5	California	35,135	34,805	56,444 a.	62%
6	Georgia	35,116	33,919	45,848	77%
7	Illinois	35,114	34,522	53,820 a.d.	65%
8	Delaware	34,566	33,811	51,122	68%
9	Connecticut	34,462	33,270	56,516	61%
10	Michigan	34,377 c.	33,596	54,474 c.	63%
11	Pennsylvania	34,140	32,897	52,640	65%
12	Massachusetts	34,041 c.	33,168 c.	53,274	64%
13	Maryland	33,760	32,939	50,303	67%
14	Oregon	33,396	32,804	47,829	70%
15	Rhode Island	32,902 c.	31,025 c.	54,809 c.	60%
16	Texas	32,741	31,874	40,476 a.	81%
17	Virginia	32,437 c.	31,414 c.	43,936	74%
18	New Mexico	31,920	28,120	38,469	83%
19	Colorado	31,296	32,063	43,318	72%
20	Alabama	30,973	30,927	38,282	81%
21	Minnesota	30,772	30,587	45,010 a.	68%
22	Florida	30,696	30,491	40,598	76%
23	Tennessee	30,449	29,275	40,318	76%
24	Washington	30,159	29,118	45,437	66%
25	Indiana	29,784	29,213	45,791	65%
26	Louisiana	29,655	28,812	37,123	80%
27	Oklahoma	29,473	29,451	35,061 d.e.	84%
28	Missouri	28,938	28,102	38,247	76%
29	Wyoming	28,900	27,596	39,537 a.	73%
30	Ohio	28,692	27,688	47,791	60%
31	Kansas	28,530	26,855	38,622	74%
32	Nebraska	28,527	27,127	39,635	72%
33	Kentucky	28,416	27,331	39,831	71%
34	Arizona	28,236	28,916	42,324	67%
35	Mississippi	28,106	25,347	36,217	78%
36	Nevada	27,942	27,434	43,211	65%
37	South Carolina	27,883	27,668	41,162	68%
38	North Carolina	27,572	27,572	43,211 a.	64%
39	New Hampshire	27,367	26,479	42,689	64%
40	Iowa	26,967	26,893	38,381	70%
41	West Virginia	26,692	26,692	38,496	69%
42	Utah	26,130 c.	26,534 c.	38,976	67%
43	Arkansas	26,129	25,459 c.	39,226	67%
44	Idaho	25,908	26,091	40,111	65%
45	Maine	25,901	24,631	39,864	65%
46	Vermont	25,819 c.	25,240 c.	43,009 a.	60%
47	South Dakota	25,504	24,311	33,236	77%
48	North Dakota	24,108	23,591	35,411	68%
49	Montana	24,032	23,088	37,184	65%
50	Wisconsin	23,952	27,277	41,687	57%
	U.S. Average	**$ 31,704**	**$ 31,351**	**$ 46,597**	**68%**
	American Samoa	$ 9,272	$ 8,215	$ 17,000	n/a
	Guam	28,410	28,789	34,326	n/a
	District of Columbia	38,566	40,085	62,909	n/a
	Puerto Rico	18,000	18,000	24,700	n/a
	Virgin Islands	26,563	n/a	n/a	n/a

a. includes extra-duty pay; b. median; c. AFT estimate; d. includes employer pick-up of employee pension contributions where applicable; e. includes fringe benefits such as healthcare where applicable.

Sources: National Occupational Employment and Wage Estimates, U.S. Department of Labor, Bureau of Labor Statistics, November 2003, May 2003. Civilian Personnel Management Service, Wage and Salary Division of the U.S. Department of Defense, List of School District Minimums, Maximums and Steps, Arlington, Va. May 2002. American Federation of Teachers, annual survey of state departments of education.

Source: "Actual Beginning Teacher Salaries, 2002–03, Estimated 2004" from Annual Salary & Analysis of Teacher Salary Trends. American Federation of Teachers, Washington, DC 2004. Retrieved July 28, 2006, from *http://www.aft.org/research/downloads/2004beginning.pdf*.

CHAPTER 12

Succeeding in the Classroom

Every teacher we interviewed mentioned the same thing: Coursework, student teaching, and substitute teaching don't completely prepare a teacher for his first classroom. The responsibilities; the challenges; and the relationships with students, parents, colleagues, and administrators are all new experiences. What do you need to know to succeed in the classroom? Veteran teachers share their wisdom here, offering ideas and tips to help you navigate your first year.

BEFORE THE FIRST DAY

To start the year off right, you'll need to get to work while your students are still at the beach. Weeks before the first bell rings, there are steps you can take to ensure a great experience for your students on the first day and throughout the year.

Reaching Out to Parents

The parents of your students are an important part of your success as a teacher. Parents who support their child's academic growth and your role in it are an asset that cannot be replicated. Establishing a positive relationship with those parents from the start is critical; you want them to understand your positive, professional approach to learning and your concern for their child—well before any problems might arise. A pro-active approach with parents makes it much easier to handle negative issues later in the year.

One of the best ways to establish this relationship early is to send a letter home before the school year starts. You can include a list of supplies and the dates of any upcoming events. Introduce yourself, emphasize how important parents are to their child's education, and tell them that you are looking forward to working with them. Explain that you will keep them in the loop with regular communication, not only when something goes wrong, but also to share their child's successes.

You could also schedule an open house for students and their parents. Open houses are typically held a few weeks into the school year, but because they help ease the anxiety of younger students, it makes sense to hold one before school starts. Invite students and their parents to visit the classroom a few days before school begins. They can explore the environment you've created, get an overview of the year (describe some of the units you'll be teaching, field trips, and other special activities), and, for young students, perhaps hear a story. You might choose to take pictures of the children (or request a picture in the letter you send to their homes) for display in the classroom.

The Name Game

By writing letters and holding an open house, you will quietly be working on another important goal: learning the name of each student. Another way to learn these names is by compiling a class list. Once the school year begins, the list will help you keep track of each student. If you use a spreadsheet program, you can expand the list to store parent names and home addresses, as well as to print labels and compose student letters. The process of creating the list will teach you your students' names even before you have faces to match them with. If you ask parents to send pictures, you can create nametags and place cards with them. Any project that involves names (and faces, if possible) will make it easier for you to quickly learn those names. Experienced teachers point out that referring to students by name as quickly as possible is one of the best ways to engage them and earn their respect.

Arranging Your Room

It seems simple: Place desks in orderly rows, create some eye-catching bulletin boards, and set up materials within easy reach of your students. But what if you knew that *how* you do those things affects not only how effective your lessons are, but also how well you are able to manage your class's behavior? You'd probably give it more thought. In this section, we'll explore some of the important considerations of room arrangement.

Placing desks in orderly rows makes it difficult to walk among them. Teachers who frequently move around the room to check students' work have found that they have better behaved classes. Kids won't misbehave, or stop working, if they know at any minute you'll be looking over their shoulder. Strolling also ensures that you can make eye contact with every student. Your goal should be to create wide walkways between rows and in the front and back of the class so you can constantly "work the room" with ease.

Consider the dimensions of your classroom and the number of students you have when arranging desks. Your own desk, if placed at the front of the room, will put you about eight feet away from the nearest student and will block the walkway in front of the chalkboard. Try placing it in the back of the room, or in a corner instead. Next, place the student desks. They don't need to be in straight rows; it might work best in your classroom to angle desks on the side so they face slightly toward the center. You'll be able to fit more desks in a row that way. They also don't need to be placed singly. Side-by-side placement of two to four desks works well and can facilitate cooperative learning as well as create wider walkways.

For older students, consider the semicircle, with one row of desks arcing around yours in the center. This arrangement facilitates discussion and allows you to make frequent eye contact with each student. No matter how you arrange the desks, though, remember that you're not setting them in concrete. If an arrangement isn't working, or a new unit calls for different seating, change it.

Younger students typically work independently and in small or large groups within the course of a school day. That means arranging a room that can physically accommodate those different work modes. Desks or small tables work well for independent endeavors, and bigger tables or open spaces provide space for large-group projects. Quiet activities should be placed away from noisy activities. Messy activities, such as water tables and easels, need to be separated from activities that could easily be damaged (books, paper, puzzles, etc.).

Divide your space into smaller areas by arranging shelving units, tables, and desks. If possible, vary the lighting in these areas. Some students work best in bright lighting, while others become overstimulated and work better when lights are dimmer. Keep in mind that the more you are able to separate the areas you create, the easier students will be able to concentrate without distractions from students in other activities. Some teachers who are particularly handy (or can enlist the help of someone who is) build structures such as lofts, specially designed storage units, and even theater areas for their classrooms.

Arrange supplies to make them easily accessible. When needed materials are quickly within reach, you eliminate delays—delays that can cause bored students to misbehave. You might choose to store frequently used items (markers, scissors, glue) in more than one area. Grouping like materials together makes them easier to find. Consistency is important, too. Students should be able to find worksheets, dictionaries, and homework assignments in the same place every day. Labeling shelves (use pictures for younger children) makes it easy to maintain your organization system throughout the year.

Beyond the furniture, arranging your classroom should involve creativity and personalization. Plants, posters, bulletin boards, mobiles, floor pillows, and other objects help make your room your own and make it more inviting for your students. A stereo with classical CDs can also add to the environment. Think about ways to eliminate the rigid, austere feeling by adding interesting, comfortable objects.

Assigned Seats: Should You or Shouldn't You?

The debate over assigned seating can get heated. Some teachers believe it's too controlling, insisting you can encourage good behavior without it. Proponents of assigned seating cite a variety of reasons for their preference. Some teachers like assigned seats because it makes taking attendance and learning names easier. Others do it to send a message that they, and they alone, are in control. These teachers see assigned seating as a form of discipline; if they don't set the rules, their students will by choosing seats that put the teacher at a disadvantage.

Is it true that disruptive students, who tend to be weak learners, sit in the back, while stronger, better-behaved students sit in the front? A study by the American Association of Physics Teachers *(http://scitation.aip.org/journals/doc/PHTEAH-ft/vol_43/iss_1/30_1.html)* came to a different conclusion. Researchers noted that when seats were assigned randomly, those in the back of the room were almost six times more likely to receive an F as students who sat in the front of the room.

Some teachers who prefer assigned seats for consistency reasons use an approach that straddles the line between student choice and strict rule imposition. They invite students on the first day of class to choose their seats, then announce that that seat will be their assigned seat for the rest of the year.

(continued)

Assigned Seats: Should You or Shouldn't You? *(continued)*

Another reason you might want to assign seats, especially if you group desks together and plan to assign plenty of group work, is that it keeps students from being left out. Once you know your students better, you can change the arrangement periodically to keep groups balanced from a skills perspective. In addition, older students may appreciate not having to collaborate with friends who aren't easy to work with.

Whatever you decide, let a few weeks go by and then reflect on the seating arrangement. As with the desks in your room, your seating arrangement isn't set in concrete. If it's not working, make a change.

What's in Your Backpack?

Students aren't the only ones who need to come to school prepared. After you've set up your classroom, you'll know what's missing, what you can and can't find in the supply closet, and what you'll need to bring with you. Here are some ideas from veteran teachers about what you need to start the year:

- Chalk and an eraser; even if your classroom starts out well equipped, these items tend to "walk away." Play it safe by keeping your own supply.
- Miscellaneous stationary items (if they're not already in your classroom): rubber bands; pens (including one red); one highlighter; mechanical pencils; scissors; paper clips; magic markers; stapler
- List of supplies your students will need, with enough copies for each student
- Post-it notes™
- Calculators
- Extra batteries
- Posters and/or maps
- 3 × 5 index cards
- Wet wipes for cleanups
- Appointment book or PDA with space to keep a to-do list
- Cell phone
- Grade book (or PDA) with attendance list, homework assignments, etc.
- Aspirin or the like
- Sense of humor!

What's in That Closet?

Your school will provide many supplies that won't be permanently located in your room. Overhead projectors, copy machines, televisions, DVD and video players, stereos, and other equipment are stored around the school with access by all teachers. You'll need to know not only where to find these supplies, but what procedures are in place for their use. Do you need to sign them out a day or more ahead of time? If you need copies made, must you fill out a request, or can you use the machine before or after school on your own? Having this information before the first day will ensure fewer hassles and help you begin to build positive relationships with the support staff at your school (see the section on work relationships later in this chapter for more ideas about strengthening these important ties).

Create a Website

Most schools and districts maintain websites that provide general information, access to faculty and administrators, and school report cards and testing results. Many are more elaborate, providing space for individual teachers or teams of teachers to publish their own pages. If your school's site doesn't allow teacher pages, consider another host for a site, such as your Internet provider. Sites such as *www.teacherwebsite.com* and *http://teacherweb.com* offer free hosting services, as well as templates that make publishing and updating your site simple.

Schools that have websites with teacher pages may require every teacher to get online. They typically offer training sessions and technical support to make it easy. If you create a site on your own, your Internet provider probably offers guidance and support. With the range of easy-to-use software available, creating a website is possible even for the most technologically challenged teacher.

Why should you put your class online? A website allows you to publicize students' work and achievements, sharing them with parents and other relatives. Homework assignments and long-term project dates can be posted and checked by both parents and students (this is particularly useful for students who have been absent). The routine of creating and updating this information can help you stay organized and think ahead. Contact with parents can be maintained through periodic newsletters that inform them about classroom activities. And a website is a great antidote to the "missing flyer" syndrome, in which half of the announcements you send home mysteriously never make it into parents' hands.

THE FIRST DAY

No matter how much you prepare during the days and weeks before the first day, you'll probably be nervous as you wait for your students to arrive. Even experienced teachers report feeling the jitters as they meet a new class. Detailed planning for the day can help calm your nerves and produce the two results you're looking for: getting to know your students as they get to know you and establishing classroom rules.

Ice Breakers and Team Builders

Whether you're teaching 1st grade or 11th grade chemistry, the first day isn't for jumping quickly into the curriculum. At the very least, most high school teachers provide an overview of the class and explain their grading system, rules, and other information. For younger students, a day or two of getting-to-know you activities, familiarizing them with the classroom and your expectations and easing into the school year, are in order.

The activities described here are all teacher tested and approved. They'll help you learn your students' names as well as something about them as you build "team" spirit and have fun together. In addition, you'll be able to watch students interact with their peers. You'll see who the leaders are, who prefers to work alone, and whose self-confidence could use a boost.

- *Two Truths and a Lie.* Ask older students to think about their summer vacation, then write two truths and one lie about what they did. After a student reads her three items to the class, the class votes on which one is the lie. The student who stumps the most classmates wins. In an alternate version, keep it noncompetitive by not keeping track of the scores or declaring a winner.
- *Class Bulletin Board.* Using a spotlight, have the students trace around each other's heads, or have the students trace their feet (whichever option you choose, create one of your own before the first day as a sample). Cut out the tracings, and instruct them to write about themselves on them. They might write a list of likes and dislikes, places they've been or would like to go, favorite music groups or books, etc.
  Attach the heads or feet to a bulletin board (get creative with a caption—"Heads Up" or "Stepping Out"). Then have students guess whose is whose. After school, be sure to read the descriptions; the more you know about your students, the easier it will be to relate to them and choose activities, especially "reward" activities, that they will enjoy.
- *Crystal Ball.* Younger students will appreciate the fact that this activity doesn't require writing, although older elementary classes might enjoy it, too. Hand

each child a drawing of a large circle on a pedestal-type base. Ask them what they are looking forward to doing or learning in school this year. They can draw pictures or use short descriptions to share their wishes for the future. You might choose to display the crystal balls for a while, and then save them for the end of the year, when your students can find out if their "predictions" came true.

- *What's in Common?* For this activity, you need to create Venn diagram sheets (two large circles with approximately 20 percent overlapping) and copy one for each pair of students. Ask them to choose partners and write one name above each circle on their diagram. Have students take turns saying a word or phrase that describes themselves. If their partner has that quality in common, they write the word or phrase in the middle. If it's unique to that child, they write it under his or her name. For example, if Student #1 says "I live with my grandmother," and Student #2 lives with his father, Student #1 writes, "I live with my grandmother" under her name in the circle. If Student #2 also lives with his grandmother, Student #1 writes it in the overlapping portion of the circles.

- *Class PowerPoint Presentation.* Older elementary and middle school students will enjoy using their technology skills to create a multimedia presentation. You will need a digital camera and access to the Internet in the classroom (alternatively, use a number of baby name books). As you, or one of your students, takes a digital picture of each student, have the students look up the origin of their names, either online or in baby name books, and write them down. Ask them to include meaning, where they originated, and whether the name belonged to a relative, friend of the family, or other special person.

  Upload the digital pictures, and use each one as the first slide in a four- or five-slide presentation on each student. On the second slide, ask the student to describe his family, home, or even his room. The next one or two slides can display something about the student—something he enjoys, a hobby, a trip he took, his favorite book or music group, etc. On the fourth or fifth slide, the student should list his academic goals for the year.

  The more technologically advanced your students are, the more complicated your presentation can be. The class might want to select music, animation, backgrounds, transitions, and other PowerPoint features. They might also want to update the presentation during the year. You could make it available on your website, at parent-teacher conferences, and/or at an open house.

- *Census Taking.* Before you begin, create a census form for your class that asks for about ten pieces of information, including name, date of birth, favorite color, type of pet owned, etc. Younger students will need to learn what a census is before you begin this activity. Note that *www.census.gov* has sample census forms and other information to help you introduce the theme.

Have older students tally the responses, and create a graph or chart. You can get elaborate and turn this into a math activity, or simply make a bar graph and have them fill it out. As with the bulletin board activity, use the information in the weeks and months to come by planning suitable reward activities, assigning seats or chores, and applying it to lessons (math, science, and writing could all work).

- *Scavenger Hunt.* There are two ways to play this familiar game in the classroom. One teacher uses it to help students become familiar with their surroundings. They race around the classroom of their team trying to find specific supplies, equipment, and designated areas. Another uses it to get to know her students and help them get to know one another.

For either game, create a 4×4 grid on a sheet of paper, and write 16 items or descriptions in the boxes. Give students a grid, and tell them they must either find the 16 items and record their locations, or find 16 people who match the descriptions and have those people sign their name in the appropriate box. Descriptions will vary with the age of the students, but here are some ideas:

- Read at least five library books over the summer
- Has a pet with scales
- Favorite color is orange
- Has a brother or sister in the same school
- Has a cell phone
- Has a brother or sister over 16 years old
- Has no relatives living in this state
- Has a birthday on the 15th
- Has more than 10 letters in his or her last name
- Favorite subject is science
- Loves cafeteria food
- Knows at least 10 state capitals
- Has a house with one story
- Was born in a month ending in -ary
- Is wearing a red shirt
- Lived in at least three states
- Plays more than one musical instrument
- Went to a summer camp
- Plays on more than one sports team
- Took a family summer vacation in the state
- Likes comic books
- Rode his or her bike to school

Setting Expectations

The first day of school is when you'll begin using your classroom management techniques. Students behave with respect for you and each other when you set clear policies from the start (maintaining consistency, and other techniques for successful classroom management, are dealt with later in this chapter).

To set policies, you must first decide on the classroom climate you want. Some teachers don't mind a high noise level or being interrupted. Others need quiet and an orderly form of communication. When you know what you want, you can create policies to help you achieve your goals. How much noise can you tolerate? Do you want students to turn in homework in the same place every day, such as an inbox, or can they just leave it on your desk? Would a messy room drive you crazy?

Once you've decided what is important, come up with a list of expectations that will communicate those goals to your students. For example, if you need quiet, you might think about setting a policy that they must raise their hand and wait to be recognized before speaking out. Some teachers print their policies on a poster for their room or on a handout that they distribute the first day. Others prefer to have a class discussion to include student input in the policy-setting process.

If you choose to include students in the process, ask them what kinds of rules they think would be appropriate. You'll probably get answers such as the Golden Rule (treat others they way you would like to be treated), "don't interrupt the teacher or other students," "keep your hands to yourself," "treat the things in the classroom with respect." Write their ideas on the blackboard so you can discuss them and come to a consensus about which are the most important.

Very young students will respond well to written rules. Even if their reading skills aren't strong, you can point out the rule when it has been broken—they'll understand quickly. Older students might respond better to a set of general expectations calling for respect for you, each other, and everyone else in the school.

During a discussion of rules and expectations, you may want to bring up the subject of rewards and consequences for breaking the rules. Rewards must be age appropriate and might include extra recess time; being first in line; not having to do a chore; getting a "good citizen" award to bring home to parents; or performing a "prestigious" classroom job such as collecting papers, distributing snacks, etc.

BEYOND THE FIRST DAY

What are the essential skills and traits you'll need to get through your first year of teaching? Staying organized, working well with colleagues, and maintaining consistency with classroom management are at the top of the list.

Lesson Planning

Lesson plans are specific, detailed maps that provide structure not only for your students, but for you as well. Successful teachers prepare lesson plans for every day (although they might be a little less detailed the more practice they have). In fact, some schools require all teachers (or just new teachers) to turn in weekly lesson plans every Monday or Friday. But even if they aren't required, lesson plans should be an integral part of your plan for success.

Lesson plans aren't just "roadmaps"; their creation helps you better organize the content of your classes, thinking through the methods and materials you can use to teach most effectively. There are other benefits, too: Students who are involved in engaging lessons are less likely to misbehave; there is less stress for you because you don't have to "wing it"; if there is a disruption in your classroom, it will be easier to stay focused; and you'll impress your principal by covering the assigned curriculum in a highly organized, planned way.

> **Is Strict the Only Way to Go?**
>
> What about the rule "no smiling until Thanksgiving (or even Christmas)"? To get your class to behave, do you have to behave like a drill sergeant? While there are successful teachers who swear by this rule, many others find it unnecessary. These teachers cite a sense of humor as an essential tool of the trade. Good-natured bantering, respectful language, and props make learning fun. Allowing students to see you as a human being who doesn't take herself too seriously models the kind of behavior you'd like from them.

There are hundreds of lesson plan formats you can use, including computer and PDA software; printed record books; and downloadable, printable forms. But there are four common components found in each (although they might have different names or be broken down into steps or parts). A good lesson plan involves the following:

- *An objective.* What do you want your students to know or be able to do at the end of the lesson?
- *Prerequisites.* What do your students need to already know in order to understand the new lesson?
- *Procedures.* Exactly what will you and your students do? Specifically, how will you teach the content of the lesson? Describe the examples, problems, projects, materials, and activities you will use.
- *Assessment.* How can you measure the success of the lesson? For example, if you're teaching subtraction, the accuracy of your students' answers to given problems is an assessment.

Avoiding a Common Lesson Plan Mistake

Great lesson plans deliver content to your students in the most efficient way possible. How can you achieve efficiency? By choosing the best teaching methods and materials for the lesson. Poor lesson plans often incorporate materials that aren't necessary or directly related to the lesson. They also engage students in activities that aren't directly related to the lesson. These ill-chosen materials and activities are "fillers"; they take up time in an unconstructive way. The less the materials and activities appropriately relate to the lesson, the more your students will lose interest (and probably fail to achieve the objective). Before you bring a lesson plan into the classroom, evaluate your choice of materials and activities. Do they support and/or reinforce the lesson, or could they be replaced with better choices?

In addition to these four components, warm-up or "bell ringer" activities should be a part of your lesson planning. These activities quiet and focus students during the first few minutes of class. Puzzles, math problems, and short writing activities are all great examples.

Bell ringers can be directly relevant to the day's lesson or instead reinforce a more general skill. For example, some math teachers use a warm-up problem that they write on the board each morning. The problem is of a type the students have already learned how to solve. Other teachers create warm-ups for each class that act as an introduction to the day's lesson. If they're going to present a lesson on Shakespeare's sonnets, they might hand out a puzzle such as a word search that includes titles of Shakespeare's plays. Remember that great lesson plans are specific. They don't indicate "warm-up activity"; they describe the activity and include any handouts, transparencies, or blackboard content needed.

The actual teaching time of your lessons can be unpredictable—some days, you'll whiz through a complex lesson with 15 minutes to spare, and other days you won't be able to finish a lesson on time. For this reason, it also makes sense to plan for extra activities to use at the end of class on those days when your plan seems too short. Think of them as "wind-downs" rather than fillers; they still need to be relevant to the lesson or unit. Aim for about five a week—if they're general enough and you don't use them one day, you can use them on the next.

FIGURE 12.1—Lesson Plan

Lesson Title:	Date:	Class:

Objective:

Prerequisites:

Procedures:

Materials:

Assessment:

Lesson Outline / Notes:

Here are some ideas for warm-ups and wind-downs:

1. *Journaling.* Have each student keep a journal; write a prompt on the board that's relevant to your lesson, and have them write a few sentences at the beginning of each class.
2. *Puzzles.* Word searches, crosswords, Sudokus, etc.
3. *Quiz.* Ask students to answer questions that assess the prerequisites for the day's lesson or get them thinking about the topic (not for a grade).
4. *Review.* Recall previous lessons for review.
5. *Dictionary games.* Depending on the class level, ask them to look up words or determine which word would be on a certain page (choose one of three).
6. *Vocabulary.* Guess the correct definition for words, formulas, scientific prefixes, etc., to be used in day's lesson.
7. *Either/Or.* Provide a list of items that must be identified as one thing or another (acid or base, noun or pronoun, etc.).
8. *Matching.* Draw a line between the famous person (writer, scientist, leader) and the event or achievement for which they are famous.

The Supply Closet

Another common theme brought up by veteran teachers is the fact that they need to purchase supplies for their classroom continuously throughout the school year. Even in very well funded districts, the protocol for getting money for supplies, or the supplies themselves, can be time consuming. Expect a request to take between two and six weeks at most schools. Science teachers in particular point out that the items they need for labs and experiments can be unpredictable, and they often buy them themselves rather than skip a lesson or wait for the school to decide whether to fund it.

One teacher noted that it was not uncommon to spend more than $1,500 a year on supplies. Although she plans her lessons in advance, she maintains there must be flexibility because students learn at different rates, get excited about a particular topic and want to explore it further, or get excited about an offshoot of a topic and want to explore something new. Here is her list from the 2005–2006 school year:

The more detailed your lesson plans, and the further ahead you write them, the better you can anticipate the things you'll need and put in requests for them. But be prepared: you will, at least occasionally, need to adjust your plans, and that could entail a shopping trip.

Lesson Planning Resources

Writing your own lesson plans is a skill that you will develop over the course of your career. But in the beginning, you might need to rely on examples developed by other teachers, if only to provide a starting point. Here are some great resources:

Education World: lessons for every subject, teacher-submitted lessons, five-minute fillers, and more. *(www.educationworld.com/#LessonPlanning)*

Lesson Plans 4 Teachers: links to hundreds of lesson plans online, organized by subject. *(www.lessonplans4teachers.com)*

The Teacher's Corner: lesson plans, units, online forums for teachers' idea exchange. *(www.theteacherscorner.net)*

Lesson Planet: bills itself as a "searchable guide to over 75,000 lesson plans." Each plan is rated and reviewed. A one-year subscription costs $19.95. *(www.lessonplanet.com)*

---

posters

computer printer paper

printer cartridges

book shelves

art supplies

comfortable desk chair

packing tape (lots of it)

binders for students who don't have them

pencils

glue sticks

CLASSROOM MANAGEMENT

Principals look for them when they're hiring, weak teachers seek their advice, and parents shake their heads in awe saying, "How do they do it?" Successful educators work amidst a large group of children, maintaining order, teaching curriculum, and side-stepping distractions. What they do isn't magic, and it's not a secret. Classroom management begins with setting policies and expectations and continues with consistency and reinforcement. It might not be easy, but it can be learned!

These approaches are all part of effective class management (note that many of them have been discussed earlier in this chapter):

- Base daily lesson planning on unit and long-term goals.
- Create a place for everything and a consistent method for how materials are distributed and collected.
- Learn student names quickly.
- Use a technique for gaining students' attention (hand raised, dimmed lights, whistle, clap, finger snap, etc.). Don't try to talk over them.
- Once you assign a task, don't interrupt your students while they are working on it.
- Don't introduce too many topics simultaneously. Think through the delivery of content before you get to the classroom.
- Think through directions you will give students (write them down, if that helps, before giving them verbally). Directions should be brief, and as the word implies, *direct*.
- Don't play favorites. If you are perceived as being unfair, you'll have a difficult time gaining your students' trust and respect.
- Be consistent in everything you say and do.

Look on the Bright Side

Your sense of humor is an important component of your management techniques. It can eliminate disruptions by relieving tense classroom situations. It will make your class more enjoyable, which in turn will command better attention and respect from your students. Your sense of humor will help you maintain a balanced picture of your work and career, alleviating stress and keeping you from taking yourself, and day-to-day dilemmas, too seriously.

Organization also helps students gain control over their own work. Even young students can understand what you expect and what good effort looks like. Once children begin receiving letter grades, consider letting them keep track in a journal or log book. Give them a copy of your grading scale for the inside front page of their book and have them title each page with one subject. When you return an assignment, ask them to take out their books and record the name of the assignment, the date, and the grade. If they did not turn in the assignment, they record a zero. During math class, you might ask students to average their grades. This exercise helps them monitor their progress and feel more in control.

The students who will potentially give you the most trouble will be the ones you're not reaching. If they think you don't believe they can achieve, they'll tune you out. To avoid this misperception, highlight achievements, spending more time focusing on positives than negatives. Allow students to see your

Eliminate Dead Space

As one veteran teacher put it, "Ten minutes of dead space can equal chaos for hours." What does she mean? If your lesson plan runs short, or you need to stop teaching to find something or someone, and your class has nothing to do for ten minutes, beware! You can "lose" your students for the rest of the class period, or in the case of younger children, have to spend an hour or more reinstating order.

How do you eliminate dead space? Plan for more each day than you think you need. Have plenty of relevant warm-ups and wind-downs ready to go. Stretching out time for an activity is a sure way to bore them! Be organized. Have all materials for a lesson ready and easy to access.

To become adept at classroom management, you'll need to conduct your class in an organized way. Procedures and expectations should be clearly stated. Use routines and patterns that help students know what's coming. The more organized and efficient you are, the better students can focus on the task at hand, and the better they'll behave.

fun side, and take the time to interact with all of your students.

Another technique for holding your students' interest is to deliver lessons in a variety of ways. Walk around the room, making eye contact with them, rather than always standing at the board or at your desk. You could use a high stool and a chair placed in different parts of the room when you need a break from standing. Speak loudly enough so that every student can hear you clearly; if you're too quiet, students may lose interest. Monotony is another cause of disinterest. No matter how interesting your lesson, if you deliver it like a robot, students won't pay attention for long. Smiles, gestures, movement, and props all help to add animation and variety to your lessons.

What other techniques do successful teachers use in managing their classrooms? Here are more ideas:

- Keep it interesting by varying your teaching strategies.
- Give students a chance to answer your questions by using wait-time (see sidebar "Using Wait-Time").

- Reinforce positive behavior appropriately. If you say "great job" every time a student lifts a pencil, she won't believe you.
- If one student needs a lot of personal attention, monopolizing class time, consider helping him before or after school. Don't allow the entire class to wait for long periods of time while you focus on one of them.
- Intermittently assess comprehension. Don't move forward with a lesson until the class "gets it."
- Don't threaten unless you are prepared to carry out the threat. Hollow or meaningless threats will tell your students they can get away with bad behavior.
- Don't allow behavior problems to escalate. If you address them immediately, they're easier to solve.
- After reprimanding a student (preferably one-on-one rather than in front of the whole class), move on. Don't dwell on the behavior.
- Again, be fair. Inappropriate punishments or showing favoritism by choosing whom to punish will cost you respect.

WORK RELATIONSHIPS

If you thought that by leaving your desk job for the classroom you'd be leaving behind office politics…think again. Even though you'll spend most of the day alone, the only adult in a sea of children, your relationships with fellow teachers, administrators, and support staff are vital to your success.

The dynamics between coworkers are no different in a school than they are in business. That's the good news—you probably already know plenty about how to work these relationships. But how does it work when you spend most of the day in your "office," with little or no interaction with fellow teachers? You need to make the most of the opportunities you'll have to mingle with colleagues.

Almost every school has a faculty lounge where teachers spend free periods, eat lunch, or grab a cup of coffee. It's common for teachers to organize the simple tasks of managing the lounge, including supplying coffee and bagels or other snacks. At some schools, teachers also hold collections for birthday cakes, baby gifts, and other remembrances. Take advantage of the lounge by spending some time there at least a few times a week. When you're getting a coffee, make a point of talking with the other teachers. Volunteer to provide drinks or snacks.

If you're employed at a school in which committees do much of the work, you'll probably be assigned to one or more, even if you're a first-year teacher. Committee work will take time, but think of your commitment in terms of relationship building. Even if your teaching skills are in their infancy, you are probably already adept at committee work. Serving on one gives you the opportunity to interact positively with colleagues, showing competency and professionalism.

Faculty meetings and in-service days are other times when you'll get a chance to spend time with other teachers as well as your administrators. Some new teachers have reported an interesting dilemma regarding these gatherings. When career changers begin teaching, they're typically the same age as colleagues who've been teaching for decades. The veteran educators can easily "forget" that they're new because (age-wise) they are peers. If you're involved in a discussion and realize it is assumed you have more experience than you do, don't be afraid to gently remind other teachers that you're new. You could miss out on an opportunity to learn something if you go along with the crowd. Ask for help when you need it.

Here are a few other rules of "office" politics:

- *Build sharing rather than competitive relationships.* If you read an interesting article in an educator's newsletter or organization's publication, share it with your colleagues. A gesture like this not only enhances your reputation, but also helps with team building. There is no reason for teachers to be competitive with one another. Even if an award or other incentive is up for grabs, the teacher who has positive relationships with others and who has a reputation for sharing and adding to a professional work environment will shine over competitors.
- *Become known as a team player.* Hard work, sincerity, honesty, and sharing will add to your reputation as a teacher who is a vital part of the school community.

Using Wait-Time

Since 1972, when Mary Budd Rowe invented the idea of "wait-time" as an educational variable, its effectiveness has been proven by numerous studies. What is wait-time? It is the seconds of quiet period between a teacher's question and her student's responses. In most classrooms, that time is about 1.5 seconds. Rowe found that if students were given at least 3 seconds to answer, they were able to come up with more correct and complete responses. In addition, wait-time increases the number of students who formulate an answer and volunteer to share it.

Teachers who practice wait-time use a greater variety of questioning techniques and have a higher quality of questions. They also tend to expect more of their students by asking more complex follow-up questions.

■ *Keep a distance from difficult colleagues.* Spending time with teachers who engage in negative behaviors will cause others to assume you're negative, too. If you get involved in backstabbing and gossip, you'll alienate other teachers and appear petty and vindictive. These behaviors also have a tendency to come back to haunt you.

■ *Choose your battles wisely.* Even when you know you're right, there may at times be other teachers or administrators who think you're wrong. Does it make sense to stand firm and state your position until everyone agrees with you? Sometimes (e.g., when doing it your way will prevent a catastrophe). If the disagreement concerns an issue of taste, opinion, or preference, you may want to leave the situation alone or accept the decisions of others. State your case, but be willing to let it go or suggest a compromise. Build a reputation as someone who will listen to and consider the options and ideas of others.

Your relationships with administrators, whether your principal, department chairperson, curriculum director, or district manager, will be similar to those you've had with superiors in an office situation. They have significant leverage in your career, so you'll need to use a positive, professional approach with them. That doesn't mean pretending you have all the answers—principals know as a beginner you will need support and advice.

When you seek help from an administrator, you need to be calm and professional. If that means waiting a few hours, or a day or two, and a delay won't negatively affect

Criticism 101

During the course of a workday, teachers interact with students, fellow teachers, administrators, and parents. At some point, someone is going to express his disappointment or even anger over something you've done. When someone criticizes your job performance, you need to do three things. The first is to remain calm. You need to hear what is being said, and that is nearly impossible when you're upset. Listen and understand the criticism without trying to defend yourself or correcting the person who has a problem with your work.

Second, ask for clarification and concrete help to rectify the situation. If you've been told that you need to work on your classroom management skills, find out exactly what the problem is. If you're sending too many students to the office for misbehavior, get advice on how better to deal with those students in the classroom.

(continued)

Criticism 101 *(continued)*

Other teachers are a great resource; you can also check out the books, websites, and other resources listed in Chapter 13. When you know exactly what the problem is, you can find a solution.

Third, follow any advice given, and ask the person who's critiquing you for help in the future. By maintaining your composure and behaving nondefensively, you can walk away from criticism looking professional and eager to grow, turning a negative into an opportunity for positive change.

---

the situation, take the time to get some perspective. Don't display irrational, self-defensive behavior. When you're calm, think through the situation. Exactly what are you looking for? A solution to a problem? A new approach? A day off? Be specific. Then, think about the issue from the point of view of the administrator. Frame the issue in a way that will engage her. Trying to get pity or arouse anger toward a student or parent probably won't work. Describe the issue in terms that will get a positive response. Chances are she will be more than willing to help you.

The rest of the staff deserves your attention, too. The administrative assistants not only control access to the principals, but they may handle requests for things, such as supplies, copies, and field trips. Guidance counselors can be your bridge between an unruly or troubled student and his parents. The custodial staff handles not only routine tasks but emergencies as well. When you need them, chances are you'll need them right away. People are always more apt to help someone who treats them with respect and kindness. In general, you want to build positive relationships with all of these people. They are all part of the school community, and as such, you'll need to work with or request something from them all at some point.

Mentors

Finding and learning from a mentor can be an essential element in your early success. It's probably one of the best ways to continue your education on the job, giving you a professional "coach" who can observe your classroom performance and teach you how to improve it. As a growing amount of research overwhelmingly confirms the positive effects of teacher mentoring, more schools are providing this service to new teachers.

California has a statewide teacher mentor program, Beginning Teacher Support and Assessment (BTSA). It provides every new teacher with individualized support and assessment from an experienced teacher. The University of Texas at Austin provides its apprentice, first-, and second-year teachers with mentors through its WINGS (Welcoming Interns and Novices with Guidance and Support) program. Experienced mentor educators work on-on-one with new teachers through a telementoring service. But even if your school, state, or college has no official mentoring program, you can find your own mentor and create your own mentoring experience.

Locating a mentor in your school shouldn't be difficult. Most teachers will be flattered that you have singled them out as great educators and will be willing to share their knowledge. Visit several classrooms to watch teachers in action, and ask around. Which teachers get the most placement requests (who do parents want their children taught by)? Who has won an outstanding teacher award?

If you can't find a mentor in your school, check the Internet. Some mentors provide their services for a fee to teachers in their area and for a reduced fee to distant teachers who want to correspond via email. A search with the terms "teacher mentor" will get you started.

What should you expect from a mentor? Mentoring can be as casual as an occasional question-and-answer session with a teacher you admire, or it can be highly structured, using standard assessments and scheduled observations. Ask questions to determine whether the mentor is willing to provide the kind of relationship you are looking for. Do you want to be able to call her at night when you're in a panic over a lesson plan? Are you looking for immediate aid such as intervention with classroom management issues (such as from a teacher on your hall)? Would you prefer to learn how to improve your skills through observation and discussion? The more clear you are about your expectations, the better chance you'll have finding the mentor who can meet them.

Spend time listening to what others have to say about your potential mentor. Professional reputations can help you to narrow down your search. If you have difficulty dealing with parents, find a teacher who cultivates and enjoys relationships with her students' parents. If your lesson planning needs work, discover who's known for turning in excellent plans, week after week.

Once you've found a mentor, expect your relationship to progress from more practical matters to deeper concerns of the teaching profession. During your first weeks and months, you will probably need help with basic tasks such as ordering supplies, organizing your classroom, and learning the culture of your school. As the year progresses, you may seek advice on classroom management and lesson planning and delivery. As your relationship with your mentor and teaching experience grows, your concerns may shift to long-term goals and strategies and professional development. A mentor can help you through all of these stages; don't limit the relationship by believing that once you've survived a few months, and can handle the basics, you don't still have much to learn from a mentor.

Final Ideas

Here are a few additional considerations to guide you successfully through your first year in the classroom.

- *Maintain your health and your sanity.* Your first year of teaching can be stressful. In other jobs, you can hide in your office for a few minutes to come up with the solution to a problem, cool down if you're angry, or rest if you're tired. When you're a teacher, you are "on" almost all day, and the energy demand is great. And in what other job can you come into close contact with dozens of coughing, sneezing children most days? Managing stress will not only improve job performance—it's critical to your health.

  Experienced teachers emphasize the need to take care of yourself. Being healthy is part of being a good teacher. Let off steam and share your problems with empathetic friends and family. Eat well and exercise. Seek help from mentors or other teachers. Go easy on yourself, too. There are some students you simply won't be able to help, and after you've tried your best, you'll need to let go of guilt.
- *Consider extracurriculars.* Another pointer from successful teachers is to get involved in after-school activities. You'll get to know your students better outside the classroom, and the more you get to know them, the better the experience in the classroom will be. In addition, you'll be seen as a team player and a more integral part of the school community.

- If there are no opportunities at your school, create your own. Do you have a skill or hobby you could share with your students? Some towns run Parks and Recreation programs through local schools. You could teach a class in cooking, yoga, or even Legos. Get creative!

- *Be flexible.* You know the importance of planning and setting clear expectations. But you should also plan for and expect constant change. Your lessons will be interrupted and disrupted often. If you're flexible, you will be able to handle situations as they arise, stay in control, and therefore experience less stress.

  If something isn't working, don't be afraid to change it. You might even involve students in a discussion of the kinds of improvements that could be made. Even young children can brainstorm ways to keep noisy activities from disrupting quieter ones or how to reward students who follow class rules.

PART FIVE

Resources

CHAPTER 13

Useful Services, Websites, and Print Resources

WEBSITES

http://philville.com/agencies.html
This is a comprehensive list of websites that contains various organizations for teachers and administrators.

Art Teaching Ideas: www.teachingideas.co.uk/art/contents.htm
This site contains ideas on how to teach art in elementary school. There are links to different topics in art such as color mixing, watercolors, and stained glass windows.

The Math Forum @ Drexel: *http://mathforum.org/teachers*
This site contains a multitude of lesson plans and lists links for different resources on teaching math. It ranges from pre-kindergarten up through college. There are links for summer programs, adult education, and more.

The Music Education Madness Site: *www.musiceducationmadness.com/contributions. shtml*
This is a website created for teachers by teachers. This site offers suggestions for lesson plans at the elementary and secondary levels.

The Sourcebook for Teaching Science: *www.csun.edu/~vceed002*
This site gives strategies and ideas for teaching to science teachers of all experience levels. It contains curriculum standards; lesson plan ideas; and reference data for physics, biology, chemistry, and geoscience.

Lesson Plans and Resources for Social Studies Teachers: *www.csun.edu/~hcedu013*
This site, developed by a professor emeritus of secondary education from California State University, contains teaching strategies, newsgroups, and mailing lists for social studies teachers. Also included are online activities and curriculum frameworks.

Technology in Education Resource Center: *www.rtec.org*
This website is devoted to the integration of technology within the curriculum. It provides a variety of tools and Web-based materials in each subject for grades K–12, higher education, and adult education as well.

Sites for Teachers: *www.sitesforteachers.com*
This page contains a list of websites with books and activities for teachers to use in the classroom. These sources can be helpful in creating lesson plans and assignments.

Teachers First: *www.teachersfirst.com/matrix.cfm*
This site contains a list of teaching resources, both professional and in the classroom. The "In the Classroom" resources are divided up by subject and grade level.

Apples 4 the Teacher: *www.apples4theteacher.com*
This site contains games and quizzes as well as tools for creating worksheets. These tools vary in subject from the core curriculum to foreign language, the creative arts, and more.

Gander Academy's Theme-Related Resources on the World Wide Web: *www.cdli .ca/CITE*
This site contains pages of links based on themes taught in primary/elementary school by a fifth grade teacher in Canada.

Hazel's Home Page: *www.marshall-es.marshall.k12.tn.us/jobe*
This is a must-visit site for K–6 teachers. Hazel, a first and second grade teacher in Tennessee, has posted classroom-tested online projects, links, and interactive games.

Integrating Technology in the Classroom: *www.siec.k12.in.us/~west/slides/integrate*
A slide presentation developed by a first grade teacher in Indiana gives tips on how to integrate technology into the elementary classroom. Included are management tips for a centers approach to teaching.

NewsQuiz: *www.ket.org/cgi/foxweb.exe/db/ket/dmps/Programs?id=NEWQ/newsquiz/ do=overview/newsquiz/template=index*
This site contains a listing of Kentucky Educational Television's (KET) weekly 15-minute current events television program for grades 4–8. The program consists of news segments, a current events quiz, "Letters to News Quiz," and periodic "News Kids" features, which may include reports submitted by students.

The MSN Lesson Collection: *www.microsoft.com/education/LessonPlans.mspx*
This is a growing archive of lesson plans and student activity sheets designed by teachers. U.S. teachers who submit their favorite original lesson plan are eligible to win a computer or other prizes.

Playground Pals: *www.richardsonps.act.edu.au/pals*
This is an Australian project that aims to develop positive playground environments. Through mailing lists and class collaboration, students can teach others their favorite

games, and teachers can share successful strategies for peer mediation and playground programs.

Teacher's Edition Online: *www.teachnet.com*

This fabulous K–12 site offers a "Lesson Plan of the Day," a lesson plan archive, bulletin board tips, and "Take 5" activities—ideas to use in the few minutes of dead time when a lesson finishes up early.

Tapped In[TM]**:** *http://tappedin.org/tappedin*

This is a growing community of K–16 teachers, staff members, and researchers engaged in professional development programs and informal collaborative activities with colleagues.

www.salem.k12.va.us/south/teacher/index.htm

This site contains general resources for elementary school teachers along with resources dealing with the core curriculum of English, math, science, and social studies.

AskERIC Lesson Plans: *www.eduref.org/Virtual/Lessons*

Contains more than 2,000 unique lesson plans written and submitted to AskERIC by teachers from all over the United States.

The Missouri Botanical Garden: *www.mbgnet.net*

Contains four videos about the environment for primary through grade 8. Lesson plans and Web-based activities enhance the curriculum and complement the videos.

TeachNow: *www.teachnow.org*

Offers customizable teacher resources for those who want to find an alternate way to obtain certification.

TeacherSource: *www.pbs.org/teachersource/thismonth/index.shtm*

A collection of Public Broadcasting System (PBS) resources for teachers.

The World of Puppets: *www.itdc.k12.ca.us/curriculum/puppetry.html*

In this webquest, K–2 students create their own puppets and explore world cultures through their puppetry. Internet experiences are designed to be teacher-directed, whole-class experiences. A computer hooked to a TV or other presentation system is recommended.

www.middleweb.com

MiddleWeb provides a wealth of resources for schools, districts, educators, parents, and public school advocates working to raise achievement for all students in the middle grades. Established in 1996 with grant support from the Edna McConnell Clark Foundation's Program for Student Achievement, it focuses its grant-making on middle school improvement. In July 2003, MiddleWeb's grant support ended and is now supported by a single advertiser and by the volunteer efforts of members of the MiddleWeb Community.

High School Chemistry Teacher Support Group: *www.csun.edu/chemteach*
This is the California State University Northridge website for high school chemistry teachers in the area. The site allows teachers to network and to share resources.

Teachers of Psychology in Secondary Schools (TOPSS) (division of the American Psychological Association): *www.apa.org/ed/topss/homepage.html*
This site contains information about teaching high school psychology. There is information about the curricula standards and about workshops and conferences; a collection of teaching resources is included.

Teachers Count: *www.teacherscount.org*
This is a list of different websites devoted to teaching. There are sites for teachers, those studying to become teachers, those who are considering it, and others who want to support teachers.

Teachers Network: *www.teachnet.org*
This site contains links to lesson plans, discussion lists, and information on online courses, grants, and teacher research. Their core purpose is to empower, recognize, and connect teachers to improve student learning and to advocate for teacher leadership, all for the public good.

University of San Diego's Continuing Education Department: *www.usd-online.org/seriescourses.aspx?id=2*
This site lists online courses and other resources for teachers.

ONLINE PERIODICALS

Education News: *www.educationnews.org*
Updated daily, this site provides summaries and links to the top news articles and commentaries on education from newspapers across the country and the world. A free online subscription allows you to receive a daily email news update.

Education Week: *www.edweek.org*
This online edition of America's top educational newspaper features daily news and current and archived issues of *Education Week* and *Teacher Magazine.*

ORGANIZATIONS

The Core Knowledge Foundation: *www.coreknowledge.org*
This is an independent, nonprofit, nonpartisan organization founded in 1986 by E. D. Hirsch, Jr., professor emeritus at the University of Virginia. The Foundation conducts research on curricula, develops books and other materials for parents and teachers, and offers workshops for teachers as well.

Educational Resources Information Center (ERIC): *www.eric.ed.gov*
ERIC, a national information system supported by the U.S. Department of Education's

Office of Educational Research and Improvement, provides a variety of services and products covering a broad range of education-related issues.

The Exploratorium Teacher Institute (TI): *www.exploratorium.edu/ti/index.html*
TI is a professional home for middle and high school science teachers. It offers a rich mix of hands-on activities based on Exploratorium exhibits, content-based discussions, classroom materials, Web-based teaching resources, and machine shop experiences. TI offers Summer Institutes and districtwide in-services for both new and experienced teachers. Saturday workshops are also available. All program participants are provided with stipends for attending institutes and workshops.

The Gateway to 21st Century SkillsSM **(GEM):** *www.thegateway.org*
GEM is a 700-member consortium effort to provide educators with quick and easy access to thousands of educational resources found on various federal, state, university, nonprofit, and commercial Internet sites. With NEA at its side, GEM is prepared to move forward in bringing the nation's teachers the classroom resources necessary to meet the challenges of education in the 21st century. New resources include the following:

- Educational resources correlated to state academic standards
- Expert ratings of educational resources
- Teacher comments on educational resources including "best practices" and new uses

Learning First Alliance: *www.learningfirst.org*
The Learning First Alliance is a partnership of 12 educational associations that have come together to improve student learning in America's public elementary and secondary schools. Through the website, visitors may download Every Child Reading: An Action Plan, and Every Child Reading: A Professional Development Guide, which provide reading tips for parents, teachers, and schools.

National Association for the Education of Young Children (NAEYC): *www.naeyc.org*
NAEYC is an organization of early childhood professionals and others dedicated to improving the quality of early childhood education programs for children from infancy to age 8. A variety of resources and publications are available, including NAEYC and IRA's 1998 joint position statement, "Learning to Read and Write: Developmentally Appropriate Practices for Young Children."

National Board for Professional Teaching Standards: *www.nbpts.org*
NBPTS is an independent, nonprofit, nonpartisan organization governed by a board of directors, the majority of whom are classroom teachers. Other members include school administrators, school board leaders, governors and state legislators, higher education officials, teacher union leaders, and business and community leaders. NBPTS is leading the way in making teaching a profession that is dedicated to student learning, while upholding high standards for professional performance. They have raised the standards

for teachers, strengthened their educational preparation, and created performance-based assessments that demonstrate accomplished application of the standards.

National Center for Alternative Certification: *www.teach-now.org*
Established in September 2003 with a discretionary grant from the U.S. Department of Education, the National Center for Alternative Certification is a one-stop, comprehensive clearinghouse for information about alternative routes to certification in the United States. The Center, through a toll-free call center and a major interactive website, provides immediate answers to questions and guidance for individuals interested in becoming teachers, as well as for policymakers, legislators, educators, researchers, and members of the public.

National Council for Accreditation of Teacher Education (NCATE): *www.ncate.org*
NCATE is a national accrediting body for schools, colleges, and departments of education authorized by the U.S. Department of Education. It determines which schools, colleges, and departments of education meet national standards in preparing teachers and other school specialists for the classroom.

National Education Association: *www.nea.org/index.html*
NEA is the nation's largest professional employee organization and is committed to advancing the cause of public education.

National Head Start Association (NHSA): *www.nhsa.org*
NHSA is a private, nonprofit organization that provides a national forum for the continued enhancement of Head Start services for poor children, from birth to age 5, and their families. The website offers online publications, an update on government affairs, a virtual community, and a schedule of upcoming meetings and events.

National Staff Development Council (NSDC): *www.nsdc.org*
NSDC is the largest nonprofit association committed to ensuring success for all students through the development of staff and improvement of schools.

National Teacher Recruitment Clearinghouse: *www.rnt.org*
This is a national nonprofit organization. Its mission is to increase respect for teaching and improve the nation's teacher recruitment, development, and diversity policies and practices. It pursues this by conducting innovative public service outreach, action-oriented research, and national conferences.

Teaching Matters: *www.teachingmatters.org*
This is a nonprofit professional development organization that partners with educators to improve public schools. They use technology in the classroom to prepare teachers and their students for 21st-century learning and achievement.

U.S. Department of Education: *www.ed.gov*
This site contains resources to help teachers get better at teaching. There are tools to assist with development of teaching skills and lesson plans. There are summer workshops that teachers can register for, which are targeted to specific grades and subject areas. Other

teachers share their strategies for raising student achievement and informing teachers of the latest, most successful research-based practices.

BOOKS

First-Year Teacher's Survival Kit: Ready-to-Use Strategies, Tools & Activities for Meeting the Challenges of Each School Day
By Julia G. Thompson, published by Jossey-Bass, 2002.

How to Become a Teacher : A Complete Guide (Paperback)
By David Haselkorn, published by Recruiting New Teachers, 2000.

How to Get the Teaching Job You Want: The Complete Guide for College Graduates, Teachers Changing Schools, Returning Teachers and Career Changers (Paperback)
By Robert Feirsen and Seth Weitzman, published by Stylus Publishing, 2nd ed., 2004.

Inside Secrets of Finding a Teaching Job: The Most Effective Search Methods for Both New and Experienced Educators
By Jack Warner, Clyde Bryan, and Diane Warner, published by JIST Works, 2nd ed., 2003.

New Teacher's Complete Sourcebook/Middle School: A Success Guide That Takes You Through Your First Year in the Classroom (Paperback)
By Paula Naegle, published by Scholastic, 2002.

TEACHER RECOMMENDED BOOKS ON CLASSROOM MANAGEMENT

Cooperative Discipline (Paperback)
By Linda Albert published by AGS Publications, 1996.

Punished by Rewards: The Trouble with Gold Stars, Incentive Plans, A's, Praise, and Other Bribes
By Alfie Kohn, published by Mariner Books, new ed. 1999.

The First Days of School: How to Be an Effective Teacher (Paperback)
By Harry K. Wong and Rosemary T. Wong, published by Harry K. Wong Publications, 2004.

FINANCIAL AID RESOURCES

Telephone Numbers

Federal Student Aid Information Center (U.S. Department of Education)

Hotline. 800-4-FED-AID, 800-433-3243

TDD Number for Hearing-Impaired.............................800-730-8913

For suspicion of fraud or abuse of federal aid
....800-MIS-USED (800-647-8733)

Selective Service...847-688-6888

Immigration and Naturalization (INS) 415-705-4205

Internal Revenue Service (IRS) 800-829-1040

Social Security Administration 800-772-1213

National Merit Scholarship Corporation.........................708-866-5100

Sallie Mae's College Answer^{SM} Service 800-222-7183

Career College Association 202-336-6828

ACT: American College Testing Program.........................916-361-0656

(about forms submitted to the need analysis servicer)

College Scholarship Service (CSS) 609-771-7725

TDD...609-883-7051

Need Access/Need Analysis Service 800-282-1550

FAFSA on the WEB Processing/Software Problems 800-801-0576

Websites

www.career.org
This is the website of the Career College Association (CCA). It offers a limited number of scholarships for attendance at private proprietary schools. You can also contact CCA at 750 First Street NE, Suite 900, Washington, DC 20002-4242.

www.fafsa.ed.gov/fotw0607/fslookup.htm
This site offers a list of Title IV school codes that you may need to complete the FAFSA.

www.fafsa.ed.gov/FOTWWebApp/complete013.jsp
These sites enable you to fill out and submit the FAFSA online. You'll need to print out, sign, and send in the release and signature pages.

www.salliemae.com
Official website for Sallie Mae that contains information about loan programs.

http://studentaid.ed.gov/students/publications/student_guide/index.htm
The Student Guide is a free informative brochure about financial aid and is available online at the Department of Education's Web address listed here.

http://studentaid.ed.gov/students/publications/completing_fafsa
This site offers students help in completing the FAFSA.

Software Programs

Cash for Class
Tel: 800-205-9581
FAX: 714-673-9039
Email: cashclass@aol.com

This is a program that allows homeowners to sell their houses and upon doing so, donations are made to the school program's general or classroom funds.

C-LECT Financial Aid Module
Tel: 800-622-7284 or 315-497-0330
FAX: 315-497-3359
Chronicle Guidance Publications
66 Aurora Street
P.O. Box 1190
Moravia, NY 13118-1190

This financial aid database contains a database of more than 1,360 scholarships, grants, loans, and work/study programs. It is available for the PC in disk or CD-ROM versions and is updated annually.

Peterson's Award Search
Tel: 800-338-3282 or 609-243-9111
Peterson's
P.O. Box 2123
Princeton, NJ 08543-2123
Email: custsvc@petersons.com

This is the largest college scholarship database (1,900 sources) and most heavily traveled education resource. It contains books, websites, online products, and admissions services.

Pinnacle Peak Solutions (Scholarships 101)
Tel: 800-762-7101 or 602-951-9377
FAX: 602-948-7603
Pinnacle Peak Solutions
7735 East Windrose Drive
Scottsdale, AZ 85260

This is a business that provides financial aid to high schools, colleges, and universities online and with software such as "Scholarships 101." This software contains information about 7,000+ sources of academic funding representing 400,000 college-controlled aid and government aid programs, individual scholarships, and private-sector scholarships. The database is updated continuously.

Redheads Software, Inc.
Tel: 714-673-9039
FAX: 714-673-9039
3334 East Coast Highway #216
Corona del Mar, CA 92625

This is a private company that sells prepackaged software in both the standard and North American industrial classifications.

TP Software—Student Financial Aid Search Software
Tel: 800-791-7791 or 619-496-8673
TP Software
P.O. Box 532

Bonita, CA 91908-0532
Email: mail@tpsoftware.com

This is a company that specializes in student financial aid software, most notably *College Funding Finder* and *The Hypertext Student Guide to Financial Aid from the US Department of Education*. Downloadable versions of their software are available online.

Books and Pamphlets

College Costs & Financial Aid Handbook, 18th ed.
By the College School Service, published by The College Entrance Examination Board (NY), 1998.

College Financial Aid for Dummies
By Davis Hern and Joyce Lain Kennedy, published by IDG Books Worldwide, 1999.

College Scholarships and Financial Aid
By John Schwartz, published by Simon & Schuster, Macmillan (NY), 1995.

College Student's Handbook to Financial Assistance and Planning
By Melissa L. Cook, published by Moonbeam Publications, 1991.

Financing College: How to Use Savings, Financial Aid, Scholarships, and Loans to Afford the School of Your Choice
By Kristen Davis, published by Random House (Washington, D.C.),1996.

How Can I Receive Financial Aid for College?
Published from the Parent Brochures ACCESS ERIC website. Order a printed copy by calling 800-LET-ERIC or write to ACCESS ERIC, Research Blvd-MS 5F, Rockville, MD 20850-3172.

Looking for Student Aid
Published by the U.S. Department of Education; this is an overview of sources of information about financial aid. To get a printed copy, call 1-800-4-FED-AID.

Peterson's Scholarships, Grants and Prizes 2000
By Peterson's Guides, published by Peterson's (Princeton, NJ), 1999.

Scholarships 2000
By Gail Schlacter and R. David Weber, published by Kaplan (NY), 1999.

The Scholarship Book 2000: The Complete Guide to Private-Sector Scholarships, Fellowships, Grants, and Loans for the Undergraduate
By Daniel J. Cassidy, published by Prentice Hall (Englewood Cliffs, NJ), 1999.

Scholarships, Grants & Prizes: Guide to College Financial Aid from Private Sources
By Peterson's Guides, published by Peterson's (Princeton, NJ), 1998.

Student Advantage Guide to Paying for College, 1997 Edition
By Kalman A. Chany and Geoff Martz, published by Random House, The Princeton Review (NY), 1997.

The Student Guide
Published by the U.S. Department of Education; this is the handbook about federal aid programs. To get a printed copy, call 1-800-4-FED-AID.

Winning Scholarships for College: An Insider's Guide
By Marianne Ragins, published by Henry Holt & Co. (NY), 1994.

Other Related Financial Aid Books

Annual Register of Grant Support
Chicago: Marquis, annual.

A's and B's of Academic Scholarships
Alexandria, VA: Octameron, annual.

Chronicle Student Aid Annual
Moravia, NY: Chronicle Guidance, annual.

College Blue Book: Scholarships, Fellowships, Grants, and Loans
New York: Macmillan, annual.

College Financial Aid Annual
New York: Prentice-Hall, annual.

Directory of Financial Aids for Minorities
San Carlos, CA: Reference Service Press, biennial.

Directory of Financial Aids for Women
San Carlos, CA: Reference Service Press, biennial.

Don't Miss Out: The Ambitious Student's Guide to Financial Aid
Robert and Ann Leider. Alexandria, VA: Octameron, annual.

Financial Aids for Higher Education
Dubuque: Wm. C. Brown, biennial.

Financial Aid for the Disabled and Their Families
San Carlos, CA: Reference Service Press, biennial.

Paying Less for College
Princeton: Peterson's Guides, annual.

ADULT STUDENT SITES AND BOOKS

www.adultstudent.com
Companion site for the book *The Adult Student's Guide to Survival & Success*, 5th ed., by Al Siebert, Ph.D., and Mary Karr, M.S., published by Practical Psychology Press, 2003.

www.adultstudentcenter.com
This is a resource for adults looking to go back to college or looking to go for the first time. It provides information on how to get into schools, how to pay, and how to make it through.

Back to College: *www.back2college.com/connection.htm*
Find fully accredited distance degree programs that offer American Council on Education credit for life experience (prior learning or portfolio credit), business and military credit, and other accelerated options. Profiles the top distance degree programs in a wide range of disciplines offered through the Internet, correspondence, multimedia, or broadcast/video. Includes distance education opportunities by state.

College Credit Without Classes: How to Obtain Academic Credit for What You Already Know **(Paperback)**
By James L. Carroll, published by Ferguson Publishing Company, 1996.

Getting a College Degree Fast
By Joanne Aber, Ph.D., published by Prometheus Books, 1996.

CHAPTER 14

Professional Affiliations, Unions, and Organizations, Including National Teaching Associations

The American Federation of Teachers: *www.aft.org*
Founded in 1916 to represent the economic, social, and professional interests of classroom teachers, it is an affiliated international union of the AFL-CIO. It has more than 3,000 local affiliates nationwide, 43 state affiliates, and more than 1.3 million members. There are five divisions within the organization: teachers; paraprofessionals and school-related personnel (PSRP); local, state and federal employees; higher education faculty and staff; and nurses and other health care professionals. In addition, the union includes more than 170,000 retiree members.

The AFT advocates thorough public education policies, including high academic and conduct standards for students and greater professionalism for teachers and school staff; excellence in public service through problem-solving and workplace innovations; and high-quality health care provided by qualified professionals.

The National Education Association (NEA): *www.nea.org/aboutnea/affiliates.html*
The nation's largest professional employee organization is committed to advancing the cause of public education. NEA's 2.8 million members work at every level of education—from preschool to university graduate programs. NEA has affiliate organizations in every state and in more than 14,000 communities across the United States. NEA is a volunteer-based organization supported by a network of staff at the local, state, and national levels.

At the local level, more than 14,000 NEA local affiliate organizations are active in a variety of activities as determined by the local members. These may range from raising funds for scholarship programs to conducting professional workshops on issues that affect faculty and school support staff to bargaining contracts for school district employees.

At the state level, NEA affiliate activities are equally wide-ranging. NEA state affiliates, for instance, regularly lobby legislators for the resources schools need, campaign for higher professional standards for the teaching profession, and file legal actions to protect academic freedom and the rights of school employees.

At the national level, from its headquarters in Washington, D.C., NEA lobbies Congress and federal agencies on behalf of its members and public schools, supports and coordinates innovative projects, works with other education organizations and friends of public education, provides training and assistance to its affiliates, and generally conducts activities consistent with the policies set by its elected governing bodies. At the international level, NEA is linking educators around the world in an ongoing dialogue dedicated to making schools as effective as they can be. To find out more information about NEA's international involvement, check out *www.nea.org/ international/index.html.*

PROFESSIONAL AFFILIATIONS BY SUBJECT

Art

National Art Education Association: *www.naea-reston.org*
This site has information about art education and award programs. The goal of the association is to promote art education.

Curriculum Development

Association for Supervision and Curriculum Development: *www.ascd.org/portal/ site/ascd/index.jsp*
This site has research-based resources for principals. Theses resources are to help principals improve their schools.

Early Childhood

National Association for the Education of Young Children: *www.naeyc.org*
This is the world's largest association for improving the education and programs of children up through the age of 8.

English Literature

American Classical League (ACL): *http://aclclassics.org*
This league is devoted to teaching classical languages such as Latin and Greek. There are resources for teaching these languages for elementary, secondary, and college levels of education.

International Reading Association: *www.ira.org*
This is an association dedicated to teaching people of all ages how to read and encourage people to keep reading.

National Council of Teachers of English: *www.ncte.org*
This site is about improving English education. There are also some helpful resources for teachers of ESL.

National Council of Teachers of English: *www.ncte.org*
This group provides resources for improving English and language arts education. There are also award programs to promote the advancement of student achievement.

ESL

California Association of Teachers of English to Speakers of Other Languages (CATESOL): *www.catesol.org*
This site has publications and journals as well as other resources for teachers of English as a second language. It also has information on what is required to become an ESL teacher.

Teachers of English to Speakers of Other Languages (TESOL): *www.tesol.org*
This is the site for the international professional association of ESL teachers. TESOL has been around for 40 years and has several publications as well as a multitude of other resources for ESL teachers.

Foreign Language

American Association of Teachers of French (AATF): *www.frenchteachers.org*
The mission of the association is to encourage and assist in the study of French. The site includes a "What's New" section, links to other Web resources and information on how to study and travel in France.

American Association of Teachers of German (AATG): *www.aatg.org*
AATG offers teachers links to relevant Web resources, monthly job postings, summer session offerings, a materials center, and a mailing list to share ideas and experiences via email.

American Association of University Supervisors and Coordinators of Foreign Language Programs (AAUSC): *http://darkwing.uoregon.edu/~rldavis/aausc*
AAUSC contains information of interest to language program coordinators including an archive of relevant materials, publications, and links to Web resources for a variety of languages.

American Council of Teachers of Russian (ACTR): *www.councilnet.org/pages/ CNet_Members_ACTR.html*
ACTR is a professional organization of university and secondary school educators and

specialists in Russian language and area studies. The site is operated in conjunction with the American Council for Collaboration in Education and Language Study (ACCELS). It is a private, nonprofit educational association devoted to improving education, professional training, and research within and about the Russian-speaking world including the many score of non-Russian cultures and populations of Eastern and Central Europe and Eurasia.

American Council on the Teaching of Foreign Languages (ACTFL): *www.actfl.org/ i4a/pages/index.cfm?pageid=1*
This professional association represents teachers of all languages at all educational levels. The site contains links to related organizations of interest.

Computer Assisted Language Instruction Consortium (CALICO): *http://calico.org*
CALICO, the Computer Assisted Language Instruction Consortium, is a professional organization that has an emphasis on modern language teaching and learning, but it reaches out to all areas that employ the languages of the world to instruct and to learn.

Mathematics

National Council of Teachers of Mathematics: *www.nctm.org*
Founded in 1920, this council provides leadership and support to teachers of mathematics and has several publications and resources to aid them.

Music

Music Educators National Conference: *www.menc.org*
This association was formed in 1996 to promote music education, diversity in school music programs, and teacher recruitment. There are a number of links for resources, as well as a job-listing page.

Science

National Science Teachers Association (NSTA): *www.nsta.org*
NSTA is devoted to providing and expanding development, support, and interest for science education. The site contains a job bank and page where teachers can post announcements.

Social Studies

National Council for the Social Studies: *www.socialstudies.org*
Founded in 1921, this is the largest association devoted to social studies. It provides leadership and support for social studies teachers.

Technology

International Society for Technology in Education: *www.iste.org*
This is a nonprofit organization for advancing the use of technology, such as the Internet in K–12 education.

ORGANIZATIONS FOR RETURNING ADULT STUDENTS

Adult Student Center: *www.adultstudentcenter.com/index.htm*
This website is a source of inspiration and information on returning to college. You can find resources to help you get started, explore your options, develop good study habits, and make career transitions.

American Association for Adult and Continuing Education: *www.aaace.org*
The American Association for Adult and Continuing Education is the nation's premier organization dedicated to enhancing the field of adult learning. With members from 60 affiliates and 40 nations, the Association represents its members from secondary and post-secondary education, business and labor, military and government, and from community-based organizations. AAACE publishes three of the nation's leading periodicals in education and training topics.

American Council on Education Center for Adult Learning Educational Credentials (CALC): *www.acenet.edu/Content/NavigationMenu/ProgramsServices/Adults/adults11.htm*
ACE's Center for Adult Learning and Educational Credentials has championed lifelong learning for more than 50 years. The Center serves adult learners through three main programming activities: corporate programs, military programs, and the GED testing service.

Association for Non-Traditional Students in Higher Education: *www.antshe.org*
ANTSHE is an international partnership of students, academic professionals, institutions, and organizations whose mission is to encourage and coordinate support, education, and advocacy for the adult learning community.

California Advocates for Re-Entry Education (CARE): *http://stars.ucsc.edu/Care*
This active statewide organization holds an annual Southern California Fall Workshop. This year it will be held at Orange Coast College on November 16. Check out their website for details.

Counsel on Adult and Experiential Learning (CAEL): *www.cael.org*
CAEL is a national organization dedicated to expanding lifelong learning opportunities for adults. Through collaboration with educational institutions, industry, government, and labor, CAEL promotes learning as a tool to empower people and organizations. In addition to offering services, they have published resources to assist adult learners. Some of their titles include *Prior Learning Assessment: A Guidebook to American Institutional Practices*; *Assessing Learning: A CAEL Handbook for Faculty*; *Assessing Learning:*

Standards, Principles, and Procedures; Earn College Credit for What You Know; and Portfolio Development and Adult Learning: Purposes and Strategies.

The National Clearinghouse for Commuter Programs: *www.nccp.umd.edu*
This is the only national organization that exists solely to provide information, consultation, and assistance to professionals who work for, with, and on behalf of commuter students. It offers professional assistance in meeting the challenges of working with commuter students in all types of colleges and universities.

Non-Traditional Student Organizations (by state): *www.antshe.org*
This is a great resource that links to nontraditional student services sections of university websites. It can be a great assistance to advisors looking to establish services for adult learners.

Prior Learning Portfolio Development:

- Alverno College: *www.alverno.edu/prospective_students/credit_pl_major_elementary_ed.html*
- LaGuardia Community College ePortfolio: *www.eportfolio.lagcc.cuny.edu/*
- Linfield Credit for Prior Learning: *www.linfield.edu/dce/prospective_students/credit.php*
- University of Massachusetts Amherst University Without Walls: *www.umass.edu/uww*

University Continuing Education Association (UCEA): *www.ucea.edu*

UCEA seeks to "promote expanded opportunities and high quality in continuing higher education," which is defined as programs or courses offered by colleges or universities to students with at least a high school diploma attending on a part-time basis.

State Listings, Including Alternative Route Options and Financial Aid Contacts

CONTACT INFORMATION FOR STATE DEPARTMENTS OF EDUCATION

Alabama
Alabama Department of
Education
5201 Gordon Persons Building
50 North Ripley Street
P.O. Box 302101
Montgomery, AL 36130-2101
334-242-9977
www.alsde.edu

Alternative Routes:
Fifth Year Masters Program (E)
Alternative Baccalaureate-Level
Approach (C)
Preliminary Certificate Approach
(H)
334-242-9977

Financial Aid:
Alabama Commission on Higher
Education
100 North Union Street, 7th Floor
Montgomery, AL 36130
334-242-1998
www.ache.state.al.us/

Alaska
Alaska Department of Education,
Teacher Education & Certification
Attn: Assessment Center
801 West 10th Street, Suite 200
P.O. Box 110500
Juneau, AK 99801-1894
907-465-2831
*www.eed.state.ak.us/
TeacherCertification/*

Financial Aid:
Alaska Commission on
Postsecondary Education
3030 Vintage Boulevard
Juneau, AK 99801-7100
907-465-6740
http://alaskaadvantage.state.ak.us/

American Samoa
American Samoa Department of
Education
Pago Pago, American Samoa
96799
011-684-633-5237
www.doe.as/

Financial Aid:
American Samoa Community
College Board of Higher
Education
c/o American Samoa Government
P.O. Box 3389
Pago Pago, American Samoa
96799-2609
011-684-699-9155

Arizona
Arizona Department of Education,
Teacher Certification Unit
1535 West Jefferson
P.O. Box 6490
Phoenix, AZ 85005
602-542-4367
www.ade.state.az.us/certification/

Alternative Routes:
Emergency Certificate (F)
602-542-4367

Financial Aid:
Arizona Commission for
Postsecondary Education

2020 North Central Avenue, Suite 550
Phoenix, AZ 85004-4503
602-258-2435
www.azhighered.gov/home.aspx

Arkansas

Arkansas Department of Education, Teacher Education/ Licensure
Arch Ford Building, No. 4 State Capitol Mall, Room 106B
Little Rock, AR 72201
501-682-4342
http://arkansased.org/

Alternative Routes:
Alternative Certification Program (B)
Probationary Provisional Certificate (D)
501-371-1580

Financial Aid:
Arkansas Department of Higher Education
114 East Capitol
Little Rock, AR 72201
501-371-2000
www.arkansashighered.com

California

California Commission on Teacher Credentialing
1900 Capital Avenue
Sacramento, CA 95814
916-445-8778
www.ctc.ca.gov

Alternative Routes:
District Intern Certificate (A)
University Intern Credential (D)
Pre-Internship Teaching Certificate (J)
Emergency Teaching Permit (F)

Eminence Credential (H)
Sojourn Credential (H)
SB 57 Intern-Early Completion Option (K)
Pre-Internship Teaching Certificate (J)
Sojourn Credential (H)
916-445-4438
www.cde.ca.gov

Financial Aid:
California Student Aid Commission
P.O. Box 419026
Rancho Cordova, CA 95741-9026
916-445-7274
www.csac.ca.gov

Colorado

Colorado Department of Education, Educator Licensing
201 East Colfax Avenue, Room 105
Denver, CO 80203
303-866-6628
www.cde.state.co.us/index_license .htm

Alternative Routes:
Alternative Teacher Program (A)
Teacher in Residence (A)
303-866-6932

Financial Aid:
College Access Network
999 18th Street, Ste. 425
Denver, CO 80202-2471
303-305-3000
www.cslp.org/

Connecticut

Connecticut Department of Education,
Bureau of Certification and Professional Development

P.O. Box 150471, Room 243
Hartford, CT 06115-0471
860-713-6969
www.state.ct.us/sde

Alternative Routes:
Alternative Route to Teacher Certification (A)
Postbaccalaureate Certification (E)
Cross Endorsement (G)
860-947-1300

Financial Aid:
Connecticut Department of Higher Education
61 Woodland Street
Hartford, CT 06105-2326
860-947-1855
www.ctdhe.org/SFA/sfa.HTM

Delaware

Delaware Department of Education, Office of Certification
P.O. Box 1402
Townsend Building
Dover, DE 19903-1402
302-739-4686
www.doe.k12.de.us/

Alternative Routes:
Delaware Alternative Route to Certification / Secondary Education (B)
Special Institute for Teacher Certification (E)
Master's in Primary / K-4 or Middle Level / 5-8 Education (E)
Master's in Secondary Education with Initial Certification (E)
302-831-4598
www.udel.edu/artc/

Financial Aid:
Delaware Higher Education Commission

Carvel State Office Building
820 North French Street, 4th Floor
Wilmington, DE 19801
302-577-3240
www.doe.state.de.us/high-ed

District of Columbia
District of Columbia Public
Schools
The Presidential Building
825 North Capitol Street NE
Washington, DC 20002
202-724-4222
www.k12.dc.us

Alternative Routes:
D.C. Teaching Fellows (A)
Provisional Teacher Program (B)
Teach for America (B)
202-442-5377

Financial Aid:
District of Columbia Office
of Postsecondary Education
Research, and Assistance
2100 Martin Luther King, Jr.,
Avenue SE, Suite 401
Washington, DC 20020-5732
202-727-3685

Florida
Florida Department of Education,
Bureau of Educators Certification
Suite 201, Turlington Building
325 West Gaines Street
Tallahassee, FL 32399-0400
850-488-2317
www.fldoe.org

Alternative Routes:
Alternative Certification Program
(C)
Add-On Programs (G)
Temporary Certificate (includes
older Alternate Route) (J)

850-488-2317
www.altcertflorida.org

Financial Aid:
Florida Department of Education
Office of Student Financial
Assistance
1940 North Monroe Street,
Suite 70
Tallahassee, FL 32309-4759
888-827-2004
*www.floridastudentfinancialaid.
org/osfahomepg.htm*

Georgia
Georgia Professional Standards
Commission
2 Peachtree Street, Suite 6000
Atlanta, GA 30303
404-657-9000
www.gapsc.com

Alternative Routes:
Georgia Teacher Alternative
Preparation Program (TAPP) (B)
Teach for America (B1)
Postbaccalaureate Non-Degree
Preparation Programs (D)
PostBaccalaureate Non-Degree
Preparation Programs for
Transitioning Military
Personnel (D)
Master's Degree Level Initial
Preparation (E)
Provisional Certification (F)
Probationary Certification (G)
Permitted Personnel (H)
404-232-2500
*www.gapsc.com/
TeacherCertification/Documents/
alt_routes.asp*

Financial Aid:
Georgia Student Finance
Commission

2082 East Exchange Place
Tucker, GA 30084
770-724-9000
www.gsfc.org

Guam
Guam Department of Education
P.O. Box DE
Agana, Guam 96932
671-475-0461
www.guam.net/pub/fpd/

Alternative Routes:
Georgia Teacher Alternative
Preparation Program (TAPP) (B)
Teach for America (B1)
Postbaccalaureate Non-Degree
Preparation Programs (D)
Postbaccalaureate Non-Degree
Preparation Programs for
Transitioning Military
Personnel (D)
Master's Degree Level Initial
Preparation (E)
Provisional Certification (F)
Probationary Certification (G)
Permitted Personnel (H)

Financial Aid:
University of Guam Financial Aid
Office
40G Station
Mangilao, Guam 96923
671-734-4469

Hawaii
Hawaii Teacher Standards Board
650 Iwilei Road, Suite #201
Honolulu, HI 96817
808-586-2616
http://doe.k12.hi.us

Alternative Routes:
Alternative Program for Shortage
Areas (E)

269

Respecialization in Special Education (RISE) Program-Alternative Certification Program for Special Education (G) Alternative Licensing Program in Special Education (ABC-SE) (E)
808-586-2616

Financial Aid:
Hawaii State Postsecondary Education Commission
244 Dole Street, Room 202
Honolulu, HI 96822-2394

Idaho

Idaho Department of Education, Teacher Certification
P.O. Box 83720
Boise, ID 83720-0027
208-332-6800
www.sde.state.id.us/certification

Alternative Routes:
Secondary Field Centered Teacher Training Program: An Alternate Route to Certification (B)
208-332-6800

Financial Aid:
Idaho State Board of Education
650 West State Street, Room 307
P.O. Box 83270, Boise, ID 83720-0037
208-334-2270
www.boardofed.idaho.gov/

Illinois

Illinois State Board of Education, Teacher Certification
100 North 1st Street
Springfield, IL 68777
866-262-6633
www.isbe.state.il.us/teachers/Default.htm

Alternative Routes:

Alternative Route to Teacher Certification (A)
Alternative Teacher Certification (A)
800-845-8749

Financial Aid:
Illinois Student Assistance Commission
1755 Lake Cook Road
Deerfield, IL 60015-5209
800-899-4722
www.collegezone.com

Indiana

Indiana Professional Standards Board, Division of Teacher Licensing
101 West Ohio Street, Suite 300
Indianapolis, IN 46204
866-542-3672
www.doe.state.in.us/dps/

Financial Aid:
Indiana State Student Assistance Commission
150 Market Street, Suite 500
Indianapolis, IN 46204
888-528-4719
www.in.gov/ssaci/

Iowa

Iowa Board of Educational Examiners
Grimes State Office Building
Des Moines, IA 50319-0146
515-281-3245
www.state.ia.us/boee

Alternative Route:
Teacher Intern License (A)
www.state.ia.us/boee/tilal.html

Financial Aid:
Iowa College Student Aid Commission

200 10th Street, 4th Floor
Des Moines, IA 50309-2036
515-281-3501
www.Iowacollegeaid.org

Kansas

Kansas Department of Education
Teacher Education and Licensure
120 SE 10th Avenue
Topeka, KS 66612-1182
785-296-4318
www.ksde.org

Alternative Routes:
Restricted Teaching License (B)
Postbaccalaureate Program to Alternative Certification (D)
Master of Science in Teaching: Certification Emphasis (D)
785-291-3678

Financial Aid:
Kansas Board of Regents
1000 SW Jackson Street, Suite 520
Topeka, KS 66612-1368
785-296-3421
www.kansasregents.org

Kentucky

Education Professional Standards Board
1024 Capital Center Drive, Suite 225
Frankfort, KY 40601
502-573-4606
www.kyepsb.net

Alternative Routes:
Local District Certification Option (A)
Exceptional Experience Option (B)
College Faculty Certification Option (H)

Adjunct Instructor Certification Option (H)
Minority Recruitment (E)
Veterans of the Armed Forces (H)
University Based Alternative Teacher Certification (H)
502-573-1610

Financial Aid:
Kentucky Higher Education Assistance Authority
P.O. Box 798
Frankfort, KY 40602-0798
800-928-8926
www.kheaa.com

Louisiana

Louisiana Department of Education
Division of Teacher Standards, Assessment, and Certification
P.O. Box 94064
Baton Rouge, LA 70804-9064
225-342-3490
www.louisianaschools.net

Alternative Routes:
Practitioner Teacher Program (A)
Master's Degree Program (D)
Non-Master's/Certification-Only Program (D)
Alternate Postbaccalaureate Certification Program—Secondary (E)
Alternate Postbaccalaureate Certification Lower Elementary (E)
Alternate Postbaccalaureate Certification Program—Upper Elementary (E)
Alternate Postbaccalaureate Certification Program—Special Education (E)
504-342-3490
www.louisianaschools.net/lde/

tsac/614.html

Financial Aid:
Louisiana Student Financial Assistance Commission
P.O. Box 91202
Baton Rouge, LA 70821-9202
800-259-5626
www.osfa.state.la.us

Maine

Maine Department of Education, Certification and Placement
23 State House Station,
Augusta, ME 04333-0023
207-624-6603
www.state.me.us/education/

Alternative Routes:
Transcript Analysis (D)
207-624-6603

Financial Aid:
Finance Authority of Maine
5 Community Drive
P.O. Box 949
Augusta, ME 04332-0949
800-228-3734
www.famemaine.com

Maryland

Maryland Department of Education, Certification Branch
200 West Baltimore Street
Baltimore, MD 21201
410-767-0412
www.marylandpublicschools.org/ MSDE/divisions/certification

Alternative Routes:
Resident Teacher Certificate (A)
410-767-0406

Financial Aid:
Maryland Higher Education Commission
Jeffrey Building

16 Francis Street
Annapolis, MD 21401
410-974-5370
www.mhec.state.md.us/ financialAid/index.asp

Massachusetts

Massachusetts Department of Education, Teacher Certification Center
350 Main Street
Malden, MA 02148
781-338-3000
www.doe.mass.edu

Alternative Routes:
Massachusetts Institute for New Teachers (MINT) (A)
Certification Review Panel-Alternative Route to Certification (C)
Waiver (F)
Internship (G)
781-388-3300

Financial Aid:
Massachusetts Educational Financing Authority
125 Summer Street, 3rd Floor
Boston, MA 02110
800-449-6332
www.mefa.org

Michigan

Michigan Department of Education
Office of Professional Preparation and Services
P.O. Box 30008
Lansing, MI 48909
517-373-3310
www.michigan.gov/mde

Alternative Routes:
Michigan's Alternative Routes to Teacher Certification

(MARTC) (D)
Limited License to Instruct (Mid-Career Model) (D)
Limited License to Instruct (General Model) (D)
Emergency Permit (F)
517-373-3310

Financial Aid:
Bureau of Student Financial Aid
Office of Information and Resources
P.O. Box 30466
Lansing, MI 48909-7966
877-323-2287
www.michigan.gov/mistudentaid

Minnesota

Minnesota Department of Children
Personnel Licensing Division
1500 Highway 36 West
Roseville, MN 55113-4266
651-582-8691
http://education.state.mn.us

Alternative Routes:
Alternative Preparation to Teacher Licensure Program (B)
651-582-8833

Financial Aid:
Minnesota Higher Education Services Office
1450 Energy Park Drive, Suite 350
St. Paul, MN 55108-5227
651-642-0567
www.mheso.state.mn.us

Mississippi

Mississippi Department of Education, Educator Licensure
P.O. Box 771
Jackson, MS 39205
601-359-3483

www.mde.k12.ms.us

Alternative Routes:
Teacher Mississippi Program (B)
Mississippi Alternate Path to Quality Teachers (B)
Alternate Route License (D)
601-359-3483
www.mde.k12.ms.us/ed_licensure/alternate_path.html

Financial Aid:
Postsecondary Education Financial Assistance Board
3825 Ridgewood Road
Jackson, MS 39211-6453
601-982-6663

Missouri

Missouri Department of Elementary & Secondary Education
Division of Teacher Quality & Urban Education, Educators Certification
P.O. Box 480
Jefferson City, MO 65102-0480
573-751-0051
http://dese.mo.gov/divteachqual/teachcert/

Alternative Routes:
An Alternative Certification Program (D)
573-751-0051

Financial Aid:
Missouri Department of Higher Education
3515 Amazonas Drive
Jefferson City, MO 65109-5717
573-751-3940
www.dhe.mo.gov

Montana

Montana Office of Public

Instruction, Teacher Educator Licensure
P.O. Box 202501
Helena, MT 59620-2501
406-444-3150
www.opi.state.mt.us

Alternative Routes:
Class 5 (Provisional) Teaching Certificate [redefined as an Alternate Route (G)]
www.montana.edu/nptt/

Financial Aid:
Montana University System
P.O. Box 203171
2500 Broadway
Helena, MT 59620-3103
406-444-6594
www.montana.edu/wwwbor/

Nebraska

Nebraska Department of Education, Teacher Certification
P.O. Box 94987
301 Centennial Mall South
Lincoln, NE 68509
402-471-2496 or 471-0739
www.nde.state.ne.us

Alternative Routes:
Provisional Commitment Teaching Certificate (G)
Provisional Re-Entry Teaching Certificate (G)
Provisional Trades Teaching Certificate (G)
402-471-2496 or 402-471-0739
www.nde.state.ne.us/TCERT/Htchcert.html

Financial Aid:
Nebraska Coordinating Commission for Postsecondary Education

P.O. Box 95005
Lincoln, NE 68509-5005
402-471-2847
www.ccpe.state.ne.us

Nevada

Nevada Department of Education,
Teacher Licensing Office
1820 East Sahara, Suite 205
Las Vegas, NV 89104-3746
702-486-6458
www.doe.nv.gov/

Alternative Routes:
Nonrenewable License (G)
702-486-6457

Financial Aid:
Nevada Department of Education
Capitol Complex
400 West King Street
Carson City, NV 89710
775-687-9200
www.doe.nv.gov/

New Hampshire

New Hampshire Department of
Education
Bureau of Credentialing
101 Pleasant Street
Concord, NH 03301-3860
603-271-3873
www.ed.state.nh.us/education/

Alternative Routes:
Alternative 5: Site-Based
Certification Plan (C)
Alternative 4: Individual
Professional Development Plan
(Restricted) (C)
Conversion Programs (E)
Emergency Permission to Employ
(F)
Alternative 3: Demonstrated
Competencies and Equivalent

Experiences (H)
603-271-2408

Financial Aid:
New Hampshire Postsecondary
Education Commission
3 Barrell Court, Suite 300
Concord, NH, 03301-8543
603-271-2555
www.nh.gov/postsecondary/

New Jersey

New Jersey Department of
Education
Office of Licensing and
Credentials
100 Riverview Plaza
P.O. Box 500
Trenton, NJ 08625-0500
609-292-2070
www.state.nj.us/education/

Alternative Routes:
Provisional Teacher Program (A)
609-292-2070

Financial Aid:
Higher Education Student
Assistance Authority
4 Quakerbridge Plaza
P.O. Box 540
Trenton, NJ 08625
800-792-8670
www.hesaa.org

New Mexico

New Mexico Department of
Education
Professional Licensure Unit
Education Building
Santa Fe, NM 87501-2786
505-827-6587
www.sde.state.nm.us

Alternative Routes:
Alternative Licensure (A)
505-827-6587

Financial Aid:
New Mexico Commission on
Higher Education
1068 Cerrillos Road
Santa Fe, NM 87505
505-476-6500
*http://hed.state.nm.us/default
.asp?CustComKey=193313&Catego
ryKey=&pn=&DomName=hed
.state.nm.us*

New York

New York State Education
Department, Office of Teaching
5 N. Education Building
Albany, NY 12234
518-474-3901
www.nysed.gov

Alternative Routes:
Alternative Teacher Certification—
Transitional B (A)
Internship Certificate (E)
Temporary License (E)
Alternative Completion of
Requirements (formerly Transcript
Analysis) (G)
Visiting Lecturer (H)
518-474-3901

Financial Aid:
New York State Higher Education
Services Corporation
99 Washington Avenue
Albany, NY 12255
888-697-4372
www.hesc.com

North Carolina

North Carolina Department of

Public Instruction, Licensure Section
301 North Wilmington Street
Raleigh, NC 27601-2825
919-807-3300
www.ncpublicschools.org

Alternative Routes:
Lateral Entry Provisional License (D)
Alternative Entry Licensure (C)
919-807-3300

Financial Aid:
North Carolina State Education Assistance Authority
P.O. Box 141-3
Research Triangle Park, NC 27709
919-549-8614
www.ncseaa.edu

North Dakota
North Dakota Educational Standards and Practices Board
Teacher Licensure Office
600 East Boulevard Avenue, Dept. 202
Bismarck, ND 58505-0440
701-328-2264
www.state.nd.us/espb/

Alternative Routes:
Emergency (Interim) License (F)
701-328-1659

Financial Aid:
North Dakota University Systems Office
North Dakota Student Financial Assistance Program
600 East Boulevard Avenue
Bismarck, ND 58505-0230
701-328-4114

Ohio
Ohio Department of Education,

Office of Certification/Licensure
25 South Front Street
Mailstop 105
Columbus, OH 43215-4183
614-466-3593
www.ode.state.oh.us

Alternative Routes:
Internship Certification Program (B)
Alternative Educator License (A)
Conditional Teaching Permit for Intervention Specialist (K-12) (C)
Conditional Teaching Permit for Adolescence to Young Adult (7-12) (C)
614-466-3593

Financial Aid:
Ohio Board of Regents
State Grants and Scholarships Department
P.O. Box 182452
Columbus, OH 43218-2452
614-466-7420
www.okhighered.org/student-center/financial-aid/

Oklahoma
Oklahoma State Department of Education
Professional Standards Section, Teacher Certification
2500 North Lincoln Boulevard, Room 212
Oklahoma City, OK 73105-4599
405-521-3337
http://sde.state.ok.us

Alternative Routes:
Alternative Placement Program (C)
Teacher Competency Review Panel (C)
405-521-3337

Financial Aid:
Oklahoma State Regents for Higher Education
655 Research Parkway, Suite 200
Oklahoma City, OK 73104
405-225-9100
www.okhighered.org/student-center/financial-aid/

Oregon
Oregon Teacher Standards and Practices Commission
465 Commercial Street NE
Salem, OR 97310
503-378-3586
www.tspc.state.or.us/

Alternative Routes:
Restricted Transitional License (B)
Teaching Associate License (D)
Limited Teaching License (H)
503-378-3757

Financial Aid:
Oregon State Student Assistance Commission
1500 Valley River Drive, Suite 100
Eugene, OR 97401
800-452-8807
www.ossc.state.or.us

Pennsylvania
Pennsylvania Department of Education
Bureau of Teacher Certification and Preparation
333 Market Street
Harrisburg, PA 17126-0333
717-787-3356
www.teaching.state.pa.us

Alternative Routes:
Alternative Candidate Certification (B)

Teacher Intern Program (D)
717-787-3356

Financial Aid:
Pennsylvania Higher Education
Assistance Agency
1200 North 7th Street
Harrisburg, PA 17102-1444
800-692-7392
www.pheaa.org

Puerto Rico

Puerto Rico Department of
Education
P.O. Box 19900
San Juan, Puerto Rico 00910-1900
787-724-7100
*http://de.gobierno.pr/dePortal/
Inicio/Inicio.aspx*

Financial Aid:
Council on Higher Education
P.O. Box 19900
San Juan, PR 00910-1900
787-724-7100

Rhode Island

Rhode Island Department of
Elementary and Secondary
Education
Office of Teacher Certification
255 Westminster Street, 4th Floor
Providence, RI 02903
401-222-4600
www.ridoe.net

Financial Aid:
Rhode Island Higher Education
Assistance Authority
560 Jefferson Boulevard
Warwick, RI 02886
401-736-1100
www.riheaa.org

South Carolina

South Carolina Department of

Education, Teacher Certification
1600 Gervais Street
Columbia, SC 29201
803-734-5280
www.myscschools.com/

Alternative Routes:
Alternative Certification for
Educators (C)

Financial Aid:
South Carolina Commission on
Higher Education
133 Main Street, Suite 200
Columbia, SC 29201
803-737-2260
www.che400.state.sc.us

South Dakota

South Dakota Department of
Education and Cultural Affairs,
Office of Policy and Account
Certification
Kniep Building, 3rd Floor
700 Governors Drive
Pierre, SD 57501-2291
605-773-5470
http://doe.sd.gov/

Alternative Routes:
Alternative Certification (D)
605-773-4771

Financial Aid:
South Dakota Board of Regents
306 E. Capitol Ave., Suite 200
Pierre, SD 57501-2545
605-773-3455
*www.sdbor.edu/student/cost/
paying_for_college.htm*

Tennessee

Tennessee Department of
Education, Office of Teacher
Licensing
Andrew Johnson Tower, 5th Floor

Nashville, TN 37243-0377
615-532-4873
www.state.tn.us/education/

Alternative Routes:
Interim License Type E—
Alternative licensure for persons
not completing college
programs (D)
Interim License Type C—
Alternative Preparation for
Licensure (D)
Interim License Type D—
Alternative Preparation for
Licensure (D)
Interim License Type A (G)
Interim License Type B (G)
Permit to Teach (F)
615-532-4880;
www.state.tn.us/education/lic/

Financial Aid:
Tennessee Student Assistance
Corporation
Parkway Towers, Suite 1950
404 James Robertson Parkway
Nashville, TN 37243
615-741-1346
www.state.tn.us/tsac/

Texas

Texas State Board for Educator
Certification
4616 West Howard Lane, Suite 120
Austin, TX 78701-2603
512-238-3200
www.sbec.state.tx.us

Alternative Routes:
Alternative Teacher
Certification (A)
512-469-3000

Financial Aid:
Texas Higher Education

Coordinating Board
P.O. Box 12788
Austin, TX 78711-2788
512-427-6340
www.thecb.state.tx.us/SBECOnline/
default.asp

Utah

Utah State Office of Education,
Educator Licensing
250 East 500th South
P.O. Box 144200
Salt Lake City, UT 84111-2400
801-538-7741
www.usoe.k12.ut.us

Alternative Routes:
Alternative Preparation for
Teaching Program (C)
Letter of Authorization (G)
Eminence or Special Qualification
Authorization (H)
801-538-7978

Financial Aid:
Utah Higher Education Assistance
Authority
Board of Regents Building
The Gateway, 60 South 400 West
Salt Lake City, UT 84101-1284
801-321-7200
www.uheaa.org

Vermont

Vermont Department of
Education, Licensing Office
120 State Street
Montpelier, VT 05620-2501
802-828-2445
www.state.vt.us/educ/

Alternative Routes:
License by Evaluation (C)
Transcript Analysis (G)
802-828-2445

Financial Aid:
Vermont Student Assistance
Corporation
Champlain Hill, 4th Floor
P.O. Box 2000
Winooski, VT 05404
802-655-9602
http://services.vsac.org/ilwwcm/
connect/VSAC

Virginia

Virginia Department of Education
Division of Teacher Education and
Licensure
P.O. Box 2120
Richmond, VA 23218-2120
804-225-2022
www.pen.k12.va.us

Alternative Routes:
Career Switcher Alternative Route
to Licensure Pilot Programs for
Career Professions (D)
Provisional Licensure (G)
804-225-2022

Financial Aid:
State Council of Higher Education
for Virginia
James Monroe Building
101 North 14th Street, 9th Floor
Richmond, VA 23219
804-225-2632
www.schev.edu

Virgin Islands

Virgin Islands Department of
Education
44-46 Kongens Gade
St. Thomas, VI 00802
340-774-3156
www.doe.vi/

Financial Aid:
Virgin Islands Board of Education

P.O. Box 11900
St. Thomas, VI 00801
809-774-4546

Washington

Washington Office of the
Superintendent of Public
Instruction Professional
Certification
Old Capitol Building
P.O. Box 47200
Olympia, WA 98504-7200
360-725-6400
www.k12.wa.us

Alternative Routes:
Alternative Routes One, Two, and
Three under Partnership Grants
Program (B)
Troops to Teachers Program (B)
Conditional Certificate (H)
360-725-6275

Financial Aid:
Washington State Higher
Education Coordinating Board
917 Lakeridge Way
P.O. Box 43430
Olympia, WA 98504-3430
360-753-7800
www.hecb.wa.gov

West Virginia

West Virginia Department of
Education, Teacher Certification
1900 Kanawha Boulevard East
Charleston, WV 25305
800-982-2378
http://wvde.state.wv.us

Alternative Routes:
Alternative Program for the
Education of Teachers (APET) (A)
Permit for Full-Time Teaching (an
Emergency License) (F)
304-558-7010

Financial Aid:
West Virginia Higher Education Policy Commission
1018 Kanawha Boulevard East, Suite 700
Charleston, WV 25301
304-558-2101
www.hepc.wvnet.edu/students/index.html

Wisconsin
Wisconsin Department of Public Instruction
Teacher Education Professional Development and Licensing
P.O. Box 7841
Madison, WI 53707-7841
608-266-3390
www.dpi.state.wi.us

Alternative Routes:
Experimental and Innovative Teacher Education Programs (D)
Permits (F)
Compton Fellows (F)
608-266-1027

Financial Aid:
Higher Education Aids Board
P.O. Box 7885, Madison, WI 53707
608-267-2206
www.heab.state.wi.us

Wyoming
Wyoming Department of Education, Cheyenne Office
2300 Capitol Avenue
Hathaway Building, 2nd Floor
Cheyenne, WY 82002-0050
307-777-7690
www.k12.wy.us/index.asp

Alternative Routes:
Portfolio Certification (C)
Temporary Employment Permit (F)

307-777-6261
http://ptsb.state.wy.us/altCert.asp

Financial Aid:
Wyoming State Department of Education
Hathaway Building
2300 Capitol Avenue, 2nd Floor
Cheyenne, WY 82002-0190
307-777-6265
www.k12.wy.us

Key to Alternative Licensure Programs
Use the following classification system to learn what each state in the directory offers in the way of "alternative licensure" programs.

Class A:
This category is reserved for those programs that meet the following criteria:

- The program has been designed for the explicit purpose of attracting talented individuals who already have at least a bachelor's degree in a field other than education into elementary and secondary school teaching.

- The program is not restricted to shortages, secondary grade levels, or subject areas.

- The alternative teacher certification programs in these states involve teaching with a trained mentor, and formal instruction that deals with the theory and practice of teaching during the school

year—and sometimes in the summer before and/or after.

Class B:
Teacher certification routes that have been designed specifically to bring talented individuals who already have at least a bachelor's degree into teaching. These programs involve specially designed mentoring and formal instruction. However, these states either restrict the program to shortages and/or secondary grade levels and/or subject areas.

Class C:
These routes entail review of academic and professional background, and transcript analysis. They involve specially (individually) designed in-service and course-taking necessary to reach competencies required for certification, if applicable. The state and/or local school district have major responsibility for program design.

Class D:
These routes entail review of academic and professional background, transcript analysis. They involve specially (individually) designed in-service and course-taking necessary to reach competencies required for certification, if applicable. An institution of higher education has major responsibility for program design.

Class E:
These post-baccalaureate programs are based at an institution of higher education.

Class F:
These programs are basically emergency routes. The prospective teacher is issued some type of emergency certificate or waiver that allows the individual to teach, usually without any on-site support or supervision, while taking the traditional teacher education courses requisite for full certification.

Class G:
Programs in this class are for persons who have very few requirements left to fulfill before becoming certified through the traditional approved college teacher education program route, e.g., persons certified in one state moving to another; persons certified in one endorsement area seeking to become certified in another.

Class H:
This class includes those routes that enable a person who has some "special" qualifications, such as a well-known author or Nobel Prize winner, to teach certain subjects.

Class I:
These states reported in 1999 that they were not implementing alternatives to the approved college teacher education program route for licensing teachers.

Class J:
These programs are designed to eliminate emergency routes. They prepare individuals who do not meet basic requirements to become qualified to enter an alternative route or a traditional route for teacher licensing.

Reprinted with permission from Recruiting New Teachers, Inc. *www.recruitingteachers.org/channels/clearinghouse/*

ALTERNATIVE ROUTES TO CERTIFICATION INFORMATION

Alabama

Degree or Previous Education Required:

Alternative Class A Program: Candidates shall have completed a baccalaureate degree at a regionally accredited college or university. In extenuating circumstances, the head of the program may request a waiver of admission requirements from the state superintendent of education.

Grade Point Average (GPA) Required for Admission:
Baccalaureate or higher degree grade point average of 2.50.

Program Admissions Test:
Submission of the score made on the basic portion of the Graduate Record Examination (GRE) or a score on the Miller Analogies Test (MAT).

Notes:
Undergraduate level is a Class B certificate.

In extenuating circumstances, the head of the program may request a waiver of admission requirements from the state superintendent of education.

Other Admissions Requirements:
Under Unconditional Admission, each institution is required to establish and enforce a policy that specifies when admission criteria must be met by the student prior to admittance to the program.

A person who wishes to earn certification in a teaching field listed below is required to have completed, prior to unconditional admission, a specific number of coursework hours indicated for each field.

- Early Childhood or Elementary Education
- Single Teaching Field for Middle Level or Secondary
- Comprehensive Middle Level or Secondary Teaching Fields, including English language arts, general science, general social science and career/technical education
- P–12 Programs

Alaska

There are currently no alternative route programs to teacher certification in Alaska.

American Samoa

There are currently no alternative route programs to teacher certification in American Samoa.

Arizona

Degree or Previous Education Required:

Alternative Secondary Preparation Program:

Bachelor's degree or higher from an accredited institution.

Grade Point Average (GPA) Required for Admission:

A cumulative grade point average of at least a 3.0 based on a 4.0 scale.

Program Admissions Test:

A passing score on the subject portion of the Arizona Educator Proficiency Assessment or a minimum of 24 semester hours of courses in the subject area.

Notes:

The Alternative Secondary Professional Preparation Program is a Pilot Program under the State Board of Education beginning with the 2005–2006 school year and ending on June 30, 2007.

Other Admissions Requirements:

- A "Letter of Intent" to hire from a participating school district

- Successful completion of the initial summer training program
- Demonstration of writing competence
- Valid fingerprint clearance card

Arkansas

Degree or Previous Education Required:

Candidates must hold a bachelor's degree or higher.

Grade Point Average (GPA) Required for Admission:

Pending state board of education approval, candidates will be required to provide documentation of a cumulative undergraduate or graduate grade point average (GPA) of 2.50 or higher, or a minimum of 2.75 on their last 60 credit hours of coursework.

Program Admissions Test:

PRAXIS I Score Report—The original ETS score report for passed PRAXIS I: Basic Skills Assessment

PRAXIS II Score Report—The original ETS score report for passed PRAXIS II: Content Knowledge Assessments

Applicants with a master's degree may substitute scores from GRE, GMAT, LSAT, MAT, or MCAT for the PRAXIS I.

Notes:

The Arkansas Department of Education Non-Traditional Licensure Program (NTLP) is a progressive and innovative program designed to prepare eligible candidates to enter the classroom as teacher-of-record while earning an Arkansas teaching license.

TeachArkansas is an Arkansas Department of Education program/site.

There was no state policy found regarding specific Teacher Preparation Program.

The state defers to NCATE for standards.

Other Admissions Requirements:

- Official transcript(s) from each accredited institution of higher education documenting degree(s) awarded.
- Out-of-country transcripts must be evaluated prior to application by an independent in-country evaluation agency. Academic credentials must be documented as being equal to a bachelor's degree or higher from an accredited U.S. college or university.
- Criminal Background—A copy of the fingerprint card is required as documentation of the

background check process. A teaching license will not be issued until the applicant has cleared background checks.

- Program Fee of $1,200 is required along with the online application. The electronic program fee must be paid at time of application.
- Online Application— Electronic NTL application to be submitted with electronic payment.

California
Degree or Previous Education Required:

For admission to all teaching internship programs, an applicant shall have a baccalaureate or higher degree from a regionally accredited institution of postsecondary education.

Applicants who will teach in departmentalized classes in grades 6 to 12 (including bilingual) must have completed an undergraduate academic major or minor in the subjects(s) to be taught. Applicants who will teach in self-contained classes in kindergarten or grades 1 to 8 (including bilingual) must have completed an undergraduate degree with an academic major or minor, or a diversified or liberal arts program. The diversified or liberal arts subject matter program must include a minimum of 84 semester units, or equivalent

quarter units, in the following subject matter coursework:

- Language studies
- Literature
- Mathematics
- Science
- Social science
- History
- Humanities
- The arts
- Physical education
- Human development

Grade Point Average (GPA) Required for Admission:

No state policy found.

Program Admissions Test:

Each intern admitted into the program has passed the California Basic Educational Skills Test (CBEST) in the areas of reading, writing and mathematics. In order to pass CBEST, a score of 41 or higher must be obtained in each of the three sections (reading, writing, and mathematics). However, a section score of 37 is acceptable if the total score is at least 123.

District Intern:
Each Multiple Subject intern admitted into the program has passed the Commission-approved subject matter examinations(s) for the subject area(s) in which the District Intern is authorized to teach, and each Single Subject intern admitted into the program has passed the Commission-approved subject matter examination(s) or completed

the subject matter program for the subject areas(s) in which the District Intern is authorized to teach.

The California Subject Examinations for Teachers (CSET) is a series of subject matter examinations for prospective teachers who choose to meet the subject matter competence requirement by taking examinations. CSET replaces the Single Subject Assessments for Teaching (SSAT) and the Single Subject and Multiple Subject Assessments for Teachers (MSAT), titled PRAXIS II Series, as the required subject matter examinations for Multiple Subject, Single Subject and Education Specialist Credentials.

Until a CSET examination is available in a specific subject area, candidates may continue to demonstrate their subject matter competence by completing the required SSAT or PRAXIS II examinations for their teaching credential subject area.

In a given subject area, a minimum scaled score of 220 must be achieved on each subtest.

Other Admissions Requirements:
Internship Programs:
Each intern admitted into the program must have a Certificate of Clearance verifying the intern's personal identification and good moral character.

Each intern who is authorized to teach in bilingual classrooms has passed the oral language component (speaking only) of the Commission-approved assessment program leading to the Bilingual Crosscultural Language and Academic Development Certificate.

Additional entry requirements for admission to the program:

- Complete a course or examination in the provisions and principles of the U.S. Constitution
- Offer of employment as a teacher of record.

Colorado

Degree or Previous Education Required:

Alternative Teacher Licensing Program:
Hold a bachelor's degree from a regionally accredited institution of higher education.

The Teacher in Residence Program:
At least a baccalaureate degree from an accepted institution of higher education.

For participation in either program, the candidate must have completed the necessary coursework required for teaching in the endorsement area. Generally, you must have 30+ semester hours of coursework that corresponds closely to one of the endorsement areas listed. The 30 semester hours must have been completed in areas to meet Colorado State Standards.

Candidates for Early Childhood Education, Elementary Education and Special Education should have broad liberal arts preparation in the content areas of Science, Social Studies, Math, and English.

Grade Point Average (GPA) Required for Admission:
No state policy found.

Program Admissions Test:
Alternative Teacher Licensing Program and The Teacher in Residence Program:
For participation in either program, candidates must pass the appropriate content assessment exam prior to finding employment. Colorado accepts PRAXIS II test scores in some endorsement areas. Candidates may also select to take the PLACE® exam.

Notes:
There are two separate programs: the Alternative Teacher Licensure Program (one-year) and the Teacher In Residence Program (two-year).

Connecticut

Degree or Previous Education Required:
A minimum of a bachelor's degree from an accredited institution with a major in, or closely related to, the subject the applicant wants to teach. Applicants must also meet any specific course requirements for certification in their subject area as established by the department of education.

Grade Point Average (GPA) Required for Admission:
A minimum grade point average of "B" (3.0 on a 4.0 scale) in the undergraduate program or the same minimum average in 24 semester hours of graduate study. Waivers may be granted in extenuating circumstances.

Program Admissions Test:
Applicants must have a passing score on the PRAXIS I examination or a waiver from the state department of education based on SAT scores.

Notes:
No specific program for graduate/post-baccalaureate—follow the general teacher preparation program requirements.

The Alternate Route to Teacher Certification (ARC I & ARC II) is an innovative program conducted by the Connecticut Department of Higher Education to attract mid-career professionals into teaching. ARC is intended for persons from diverse fields such as industry, government, the military or human services who wish to change careers or those who want to reenter the work force. Individuals who have worked as substitutes, or who have experience as independent school teachers, are encouraged to apply.

Other Admissions Requirements:
World language applicants may also be required to take the Oral Proficiency Interview (OPI) from the American Council on the

Teaching of Foreign Languages (ACTFL) as a requirement for eligibility.

Teacher preparation programs identify the "dispositions for teaching" that will be the foundation for all aspects of their programs. According to the National Council for Accreditation of Teacher Education, dispositions for teaching are "those values, commitments, and professional ethics that influence behaviors toward students, families, colleagues, and communities and affect student learning, motivation, and development as well as the educator's own professional growth." A teacher preparation program should reflect these dispositions.

During the admission process, the Alternate Route to Certification Program (ARC) looks for applicants who most strongly reflect its six dispositions for teaching, which are:

- Effective teachers have a passion for teaching that makes them committed to being the best teachers possible
- Effective teachers believe that all children can learn and thus a quality education should be accessible to all children
- Effective teachers possess a positive, caring attitude toward all children and recognize that children learn in many different ways

- Effective teachers respect and appreciate diversity among their students, colleagues, and the community at large
- Effective teachers are committed to their own continued learning so that they can become even more effective teachers
- Effective teachers believe that educators must be committed to and exhibit the highest levels of moral and ethical behavior.

In addition, application requirements include:

- Completed application form
- Current résumé
- Three sealed letters of recommendation
- College transcripts
- Application fee
- Working with youth waiver, if required

A review of applicants includes an interview of the highest rated applicants by subject area faculty members. The focus is on determining which of the applicants have the strongest potential to become effective teachers.

Delaware
Degree or Previous Education Required:
Alternative Route to Certification: Requires a bachelor's degree from a regionally accredited college or university in a coherent major or its equivalent, which shall

be no less than 30 credit hours appropriate to the instructional field.

The Special Institute for Teacher Licensure and Certification: Must have received a bachelor's degree, other than in Education, from a regionally accredited four-year program. The major field of study must be in a content area that has been designated as a critical needs area by the department of education.

Grade Point Average (GPA) Required for Admission:
No state policy found.

The Special Institute for Teacher Licensure and Certification: Must have a grade point index in the major field of the bachelor's degree which is two-tenths of a point higher than the grade point index required for students entering regular teacher education programs at the teacher education institution(s).

Program Admissions Test:
Alternative Route to Certification: Requires passage of the state basic skills test, such as PRAXIS I, and a state test of subject matter knowledge for fields of teaching specialization, such as PRAXIS II, within the period of time from the date of hire to the end of the next consecutive fiscal year.

The Special Institute for Teacher Licensure and Certification: Must meet the state standards on the pre-professional skills tests.

Other Admissions Requirements:
Alternative Route to Certification:
Requires the candidate to obtain an acceptable health clearance as per the department of education regulations and a acceptable criminal background check clearance and obtain and accept an offer of employment in a position that requires licensure and certification.

The Special Institute for Teacher Licensure and Certification:
Must agree to teach at least one year in a Delaware public school for each year the individual receives funding. Such service is to be completed within five years of the successful completion of the Special Institute for Teacher Licensure and Certification program.

District of Columbia
Degree or Previous Education Required:
A bachelor's degree is required for admission to the DC Teaching Fellows program.

Grade Point Average (GPA) Required for Admission:
No state policy found.

Program Admissions Test:
No state policy found.

Notes:
DC Teaching Fellows, www.dcteachingfellows.org/

District of Columbia Title II Report (2001), Certification/Licensure, Alternative Routes, www.title2.org/scripts/statereports/choosestate.asp

Other Admissions Requirements:
Candidates for the DC Teaching Fellows program must submit the following:
- Résumé
- Cover letter
- Completed application form

Those applicants selected are then invited to participate in a daylong interview consisting of:
- A sample teaching presentation
- A group discussion
- A one-on-one interview

Candidates are evaluated based on all components of the application process.

Florida
Degree or Previous Education Required:
Educator Preparation Institutes:
At least a bachelor's degree from an accredited institution of higher learning is required for admission.

School District Alternative Certification and Education Competency Programs:
No state policy found.

Grade Point Average (GPA) Required for Admission:
Educator Preparation Institutes:
Each applicant must have attained at least a 2.5 overall grade point average on a 4.0 scale in the applicant's major field of study.

School District Alternative Certification and Education Competency Programs:
No state policy found.

Program Admissions Test:
Educator Preparation Institutes:
Must demonstrate mastery of general knowledge by achieving passing scores on basic skills examination or on the College Level Academic Skills Test and for subject area knowledge by achieving a passing score on the professional education competency examination required by state board rule.

School District Alternative Certification and Education Competency Programs:
No state policy found.

Other Admissions Requirements:
Educator Preparation Institutes:
- Must submit to background screening and be of good moral character.
- Must be competent and capable of performing the duties, functions, and responsibilities of an educator.

School District Alternative Certification and Education Competency Programs:
- Must hold a temporary certificate, which requires holding a valid Official Statement of Eligibility that reflects that the applicant has satisfied specialization requirements for the subject requested.
- Must obtain full-time employment in a position for which a Florida educator's certificate is required and satisfy the fingerprint requirement.

Georgia
Degree or Previous Education Required:
Teacher Alternative Preparation Program (TAPP):
Bachelor's degree or higher in an appropriate field from a Professional Standards Commission accepted college.

Grade Point Average (GPA) Required for Admission:
Teacher Alternative Preparation Program (TAPP):
A minimum grade point average of 2.5 in all completed college-level work is required for admission.

Program Admissions Test:
Teacher Alternative Preparation Program (TAPP):
A passing score on PRAXIS I (or SAT, ACT, or GRE scores high enough to exempt this requirement) is required for admission.

In August 2005, the Professional Standards Commission changed the entrance requirements for the following TAPP candidates:

All Early Childhood Education candidates:
- Special education candidates who are assigned to teach core academic content as the teacher of record
- Any middle grades and secondary teachers who do not have a concentration or major in the subject area(s) they are assigned to teach.
- Candidates are required to have passing scores on the PRAXIS II assessments. TAPP candidates who do not have a passing score on the appropriate PRAXIS II test cannot be designated as highly qualified.

Notes:
The Georgia Teacher Alternative Preparation Program (TAPP) is a classroom-based teacher preparation option for individuals who have the basic qualifications to teach early childhood, middle-grades, secondary or P–12 education but have not completed a teacher preparation program. In addition there are two other routes but they are not necessarily programs:
- Non-Renewable Certificate-Based Option—Under specific situations, candidates with a current job offer may, at the discretion of the employing school system, obtain a Non-Renewable certificate.
- Non-Renewable Test-Based Option—Under specific situations, candidates holding a PSC-accepted college degree with appropriate GPA and a current job offer may, at the request of the employing school system, obtain a Non-Renewable certificate.

Other Admissions Requirements:
Teacher Alternative Preparation Program (TAPP):
- A satisfactory criminal background check and an offer of a full-time teaching position by a participating school system are required for admission to the program.
- At the request of an employing school system, an Intern Certificate may be issued to individuals accepted into TAPP.

Hawaii
There are currently no alternative route programs to teacher certification in Hawaii.

Idaho
Degree or Previous Education Required:
Alternative Authorization Teacher to New Certification:
Bachelor's degree.

Alternative Authorization Content Specialist:
Bachelor's degree.

Computer-Based Alternative Route to Teacher Certification:
Bachelor's degree or higher from an institution of higher education.

Paraeducator to Teacher:
Candidate must hold an associate of arts degree or an associate of applied science degree.

Grade Point Average (GPA) Required for Admission:
Alternative Authorization Teacher to New Certification:
Candidate will work toward completion of the alternative route preparation program through a participating college/university

and the employing school district. The participating college/university shall provide procedures to assess and credit equivalent knowledge, dispositions, and relevant life/work experiences.

Alternative Authorization Content Specialist:
The candidate will work toward completion of the alternative preparation program through a participating college/university and the employing school district. The participating college/university shall provide procedures to assess and credit equivalent knowledge, dispositions, and relevant life/work experiences.

Paraeducator to Teacher:
Candidate must be employed as a paraeducator. The candidate will work toward completion of the alternative preparation program through a participating college/university and the employing school district. The participating college/university shall provide procedures to assess and credit equivalent knowledge, dispositions, and relevant life/work experiences.

Computer-Based Alternative Route to Teacher Certification:
No state policy found.

Program Admissions Test:
Alternative Authorization Teacher to New Certification:
Candidate will work toward completion of the alternative route preparation program through a participating college/university and the employing school

district. The participating college/university shall provide procedures to assess and credit equivalent knowledge, dispositions, and relevant life/work experiences.

Alternative Authorization Content Specialist:
The candidate will work toward completion of the alternative preparation program through a participating college/university and the employing school district. The participating college/university shall provide procedures to assess and credit equivalent knowledge, dispositions, and relevant life/work experiences.

Paraeducator to Teacher:
Candidate must be employed as a paraeducator. The candidate will work toward completion of the alternative preparation program through a participating college/university and the employing school district. The participating college/university shall provide procedures to assess and credit equivalent knowledge, dispositions, and relevant life/work experiences.

Computer-Based Alternative Route to Teacher Certification:
No state policy found.

Other Admissions Requirements:
Alternative Authorization Teacher to New Certification:
A valid Idaho teacher certificate without full endorsement in content area of need. The school district must declare an emergency and provide supportive information attesting to the ability of the candidate to fill the position.

Alternative Authorization Content Specialist:
The candidate shall meet enrollment qualifications of the alternative route preparation program, which includes a consortium of a designee from the college/university to be attended, a representative from the school district, and the candidate to determine preparation needed to meet the Idaho Standards for Initial Certification of Professional School Personnel.

Computer-Based Alternative Route to Teacher Certification:
The program must include, at a minimum, a pre-assessment of teaching and content knowledge.

Paraeducator to Teacher:
Candidate must meet state paraeducator standards.

Illinois
Degree or Previous Education Required:
Alternative Teacher Certification:
Alternative teacher candidates must hold a bachelor's or higher degree from an accredited institution of higher education.

Alternative Route to Teacher Certification:
Alternative teacher candidates must hold a bachelor's or higher degree from an accredited institution of higher education.

Grade Point Average (GPA) Required for Admission:
Alternative Teacher Certification:
No state policy found. The selection process is independently

developed and conducted by the program partners.

Alternative Route to Teacher Certification:
No state policy.

The selection process is independently developed and conducted by the program partners.

Program Admissions Test:
Alternative Teacher Certification:
Illinois Certification Testing System (ICTS) tests, including:
- ICTS Basic Skills test (required for program admission)
- Appropriate ICTS test of subject-matter knowledge (53 tests)

Illinois Certification Testing System's (ICTS) test of basic skills in the following areas:
- Reading: 70 out of 100
- Writing: 70 out of 100
- Grammar and language arts: 70 out of 100
- Mathematics: 70 out of 100

Teacher candidates must obtain a total test scaled score of 240 out of 300 on the test as a whole and at least the minimum acceptable score on each subject area.

ICTS: Subject Matter Knowledge Cut Score: 70 out of 100

Note:
A new state test, the Assessment of Professional Teaching, will be implemented in October 2003 to assess teacher candidate

knowledge of the Illinois Professional Teaching Standards, the core technology standards and the core language arts standards. Illinois State Board of Education, Illinois Certification Testing System Attention Basic Skills Examinees, *www.isbe.state. il.us/teachers/ICTS_Info/ bsscorereportinfo.htm*

Illinois State Board of Education, State Board Approves Enhanced Basic Skills Test for Future Teachers, *www.isbe.net/news/2001/ aug23-01.htm*

Illinois State Board of Education, Tests Required for Certification (August 2002), *www.isbe.net/ teachers/ICTS_Info/testreq.pdf*

Illinois Title II Report (2002), Assessments, Assessment Requirements, *www.title2.org/ title2dr/Requirements.asp*

Illinois State Board of Certification, Minimum Requirements for State Certificates, *www.isbe.state.il.us/ teachers/Documents/minreq.htm*

Illinois State Board of Education, Content-Area Standards for Educators (2nd ed., 2002), *www. isbe.net/profprep/Content%20Area %20Standards/Cover%20TofC%20I ntro%20FAQ.pdf*

Other Admissions Requirements:
Alternative Teacher Certification:
No state policy found. The selection process is independently developed and conducted by the program partners.

Alternative Route to Teacher Certification:
No state policy. The selection process is independently developed and conducted by the program partners.

Indiana
Degree or Previous Education Required:
Teacher candidates seeking to obtain a license to teach in grades K–6 must meet one of the following prerequisites:
- A bachelor's degree or equivalent with a grade point average of 3.0 from an accredited institution of higher education
- A bachelor's degree from an accredited institution of higher education with a grade point average of 2.5 and five years of professional experience in an education related field.

Teacher candidates seeking to obtain a license to teach in grades 6–12 must meet one of the following prerequisites:
- A bachelor's degree or equivalent with a grade point average of 3.0 from an accredited institution of higher education in the subject area they intend to teach
- A graduate degree from an accredited institution of higher education in the subject area they intend to teach

- A bachelor's degree from an accredited institution of higher education with a grade point average of 2.5 and five years of professional experience in the subject area they intend to teach.

Program Admissions Test:
No state policy found. However, the PRAXIS I: Pre-Professional Skills Test (PPST) in reading, writing and mathematics and the appropriate PRAXIS II: Subject Assessment(s) are required for Indiana licensing.

Institutions of higher education offering the Transition to Teaching program may choose to require the assessments as a prerequisite for admission.

Notes:
Indiana's Transition to Teaching program was established to:
- Facilitate the transition into the teaching profession of competent professionals in fields other than teaching
- Allow competent professionals not holding a teaching license to earn and be issued a teaching license through participation in and satisfactory completion of the program.
- The Indiana Professional Standards Board has the authority to establish any program details not currently articulated in state policy.

Each accredited state teacher education institution is required to offer a Transition to Teaching program either independently or in collaboration with other institutions.

Other Admissions Requirements:
No state policy found.

Iowa
Degree or Previous Education Required:
Teacher intern candidates must possess a bachelor's or higher degree from a regionally accredited institution and meet the subject matter coursework requirements for a secondary teaching endorsement.

Grade Point Average (GPA) Required for Admission:
Teacher intern candidates must have a cumulative 2.5 grade point average.

Program Admissions Test:
No state policy found.

Notes:
There are no state policies specific to graduate or post-baccalaureate teacher preparation programs.

Iowa Department of Education, Frequently Asked Questions, Teacher Intern License— Alternative Licensure, *www.state. ia.us/boee/Doc/tilal.html*

Iowa Department of Education, Requirements for Teaching Endorsements, *www.state.ia.us/ boee/addition.html*

Other Admissions Requirements:
- Transcript evaluation
- In-person interview
- References
- Impromptu writing sample

Kansas
Degree or Previous Education Required:
Restricted Teaching License:
The applicant must hold a degree in the content area they want to teach or they must have a degree that has content coursework equivalent to a Kansas institution's approved program for which the license is sought.

Grade Point Average (GPA) Required for Admission:
Restricted Teaching License:
The applicant must have a minimum 2.5 cumulative grade point average.

Program Admissions Test:
No state policy found.

Other Admissions Requirements:
An offer of a teaching job from a Kansas school district is required. The job must be a middle/ secondary position teaching the subject the applicant has the content knowledge in and for which the license would be issued.

Kentucky
Degree or Previous Education Required:
Option 1 and Option 2:
A bachelor's degree from a nationally or regionally accredited postsecondary institution.

Option 3:
A master's degree or doctoral degree in the academic content area for which certification is sought.

Option 4:
For elementary certification, applicant must have a bachelor's degree. For middle or secondary certification, degree is not specified; however, a major/minor or area of concentration in the subject to be taught is required. For vocational education certification, applicant must have a high school diploma and at least four years of appropriate occupational experience.

Option 5:
At least a bachelor's degree in the content area or closely related area for which certification is sought, issued by a regionally or nationally accredited institution of higher education.

Option 6:
A bachelor's or master's degree.

Option 7:
Currently no universities or other entities are offering this program option.

Bachelor's degree with a declared academic major in the area in which certification is sought or a professional or graduate degree in a field related to the area in which certification is sought.

Grade Point Average (GPA) Required for Admission:

Option 1:
Cumulative grade point average of 2.5 on a 4.0 scale or a grade point average of 3.0 on a 4.0 scale on the last 60 hours of credit completed, including undergraduate and graduate coursework from a nationally or regionally accredited postsecondary institution.

Option 2:
Grade point average of 2.5 on a 4.0 scale or, upon approval by the education professional standards board, at least a grade point average of 2.0 on a 4.0 scale if the candidate has exceptional life experience related to teaching and has completed the bachelor's degree at least five years prior to submitting an application to the program.

Option 3:
No state policy found.

Option 4:
For elementary certification, applicant must have an overall GPA of 2.5. For middle or secondary certification, applicant must have an overall GPA of 2.5 and have a GPA of 2.5 in the major/minor or area of concentration in the subject to be taught.

Option 5:
A grade point average of 2.5 on a 4.0 scale.

Option 6:
Must meet university admission standards.

Option 7:
Currently no universities or other entities are offering this program option.

A cumulative grade point average of 3.0 on a 4.0 scale.

Program Admissions Test:
Option 1:
An academic major or a passing score on the academic content assessment designated by the education professional standards board.

Option 2:
The candidate must pass written tests designated by the education professional standards board (EPSB) for content knowledge in the specific teaching field of the applicant with minimum scores in each test as set by the EPSB. To be eligible to take a subject field test, the applicant shall have completed a 30-hour major in the academic content area or five years of experience in the academic content area as approved by the EPSB.

Option 3:
No state policy found.

Option 4:
No state policy found.

Option 5:
A passing score on the written exit assessment examination designated by the education professional standards board for content knowledge.

Option 6:
Must meet university admission standards.

Option 7:
Currently no universities or other entities are offering this program option.

Must have a minimum score of 500 on the verbal section and a minimum score of four on the analytical writing section of the Graduate Record Examination (GRE). In addition, teachers of mathematics and physical and biological sciences shall have a minimum score of 450 on the quantitative section of the GRE. A candidate who has a professional degree shall be exempt from these requirements.

Must pass written tests designated by the education professional standards board for content knowledge in the specific teaching field of the applicant with minimum scores in each test as set by the board.

Notes:
There are seven alternative routes to certification:
Option 1: Exceptional Work Experience Certification
Option 2: Local District Training Program Certification
Option 3: College Faculty Certification
Option 4: Adjunct Instructor Certification
Option 5: Veterans of the Armed Forces

Option 6: University-Based Alternative Route to Certification
Option 7: University Institute Alternative Route to Certification—Currently no universities or other entities are offering this program option.

Other Admissions Requirements:
Option 1:
Candidate needs three to five recommendations from employers directly associated with their ten years of exceptional work experience all of which specifically support the exceptional aspects of their work experience and also need an offer of employment in a local school district.

Option 2:
Candidate has to have been offered employment in a school district which has a training program approved by the education professional standards board.

Option 4:
Candidate has to have an offer of employment.

Option 5:
Candidate must have been discharged or released from active duty under honorable conditions after six years of active duty immediately before the discharge or release.

Louisiana
Degree or Previous Education Required:
Practitioner Teacher Program, Master's Degree Program and Non-Master's/Certification-Only

Program:
Must possess a baccalaureate degree from a regionally accredited university.

Grade Point Average (GPA) Required for Admission:
Practitioner Teacher Program:
Minimum of 2.50 GPA on undergraduate work. (Appropriate work experience can substitute for required GPA at the discretion of the program provider, but the GPA may not be less than 2.20. State law requires teacher candidates to have a 2.50 GPA for certification upon program completion.)

Master's Degree Program:
Minimum of 2.50 GPA on undergraduate work. (State law requires teacher candidates to have a 2.50 GPA for certification upon program completion.)

Non-Master's/Certification-Only Program:
Minimum of 2.20 GPA on undergraduate work. (An overall 2.50 GPA is required for certification. If GPA is lower than 2.50, candidate may have to take additional courses in the program to achieve a 2.50 GPA.)

Program Admissions Test:
Practitioner Teacher Program, Master's Degree Program and Non-Master's/Certification-Only Program:
For each program, the applicant must pass the PRAXIS Pre-Professional Skills Test in reading, writing and mathematics (PRAXIS I). (Individuals with an earned

graduate degree from a regionally accredited institution may be exempted from this requirement.) Applicants must pass the PRAXIS content specific examination (PRAXIS II).

If Louisiana has not adopted an examination in the certification area, candidates must present a minimum of 31 semester hours of coursework specific to the content area.

Other Admissions Requirements:
Candidates with an earned master's degree from a regionally accredited institution may qualify for exemption of PPST admissions tests requirements.

All candidates entering an alternate certification program after May 1, 2004, must demonstrate proficiency in the Reading Competencies, as adopted by the state board of elementary and secondary education, through either of the following options:

Successfully complete the same number of semester hours in reading as required for undergraduate teacher preparation programs, as follows:

- Early Childhood PK–3 or Elementary 1–5 programs, nine hours
- Middle Grades 4–8 programs, six hours
- Secondary 6–12 or All-Level K–12 programs, three hours
- Pass a reading competency assessment.

Practitioner Teacher Program: Meet other noncourse requirements established by the college or university.

Non-Master's/Certification-Only Program: No state policy found.

Maine

There are currently no alternative route programs to teacher certification in Maine.

Maryland

Degree or Previous Education Required:
Secondary candidates for the Resident Teacher Certificate alternative program must hold a bachelor's degree or higher from an accredited college/university with an academic major or concentration in a discipline appropriate to an assignment in the secondary school curriculum. A secondary applicant who does not possess an appropriate academic major as defined by his or her institution of higher education (and so noted on the transcript), but does have a minimum of 30 semester hours of academic content in the certification area, may satisfy the intent of the regulation.

Candidates who seek a RTC in Elementary Education must possess 36 hours, including 6 in English grammar, composition and/or literature; 9 in easily identifiable mathematics courses; 6 in natural science; 6 in history,

political science, geography and/or economics; and, 9 from any core area above in any combination and/or fine arts and foreign language.

Grade Point Average (GPA) Required for Admission:
The secondary RTC applicant must have an average of B or better in the 30 semester hours. Applicants for a RTC at the elementary and early childhood levels must have an average of "B" or better in 36 semester hours of coursework.

Revised Resident Teacher Certificate Policy For Academic Course Requirements:
Teacher preparation programs are required by the state to establish requirements that are consistent with state-approved standards. Flexibility regarding alternative preparation program requirements is based on candidates' prior knowledge, skills, and experience.

Program Admissions Test:
The teacher certification tests needed prior to application for the RTC are PRAXIS I (Basic Skills) and the content area test of PRAXIS II in the area of certification. The pedagogy test of PRAXIS II is not required prior to the issuance of a RTC.

Revised Resident Teacher Certificate Policy For Academic Course Requirements:
Teacher preparation programs are required by the state to establish

requirements that are consistent with state-approved standards. Flexibility regarding alternative preparation program requirements is based on candidates' prior knowledge, skills, and experience.

Other Admissions Requirements:
RTC candidate must be enrolled in a Department-approved alternative preparation program and have completed an internship which was part of a Department-approved alternative preparation program.

Massachusetts
Degree or Previous Education Required:
All alternative programs require a bachelor's degree from an accredited institution of higher learning. Routes 3 and 4 also require a Preliminary Teaching License.

Grade Point Average (GPA) Required for Admission:
No state policy found.

Program Admissions Test:
Route 2 requires teacher candidates to have a passing score on the Communication and Literacy Skills test and on the subject matter knowledge test(s) appropriate to the license sought.

Routes 3 and 4 require candidates to have a Preliminary license, the requirements for which include passing the Communication and Literacy Skills test and on the subject matter knowledge test(s) appropriate to the license sought.

Other Admissions Requirements:
No state policy found.

Michigan
Degree or Previous Education Required:
A sponsoring institution recommending applicants for teachers' certificates shall establish selection techniques which ensure that only qualified students are admitted to the teacher education program and that only qualified students are sponsored for certification.

The state board at the request of an approved teacher education institution may waive for a specific time particular requirements of this code for experimental teacher education programs. A request for such a waiver shall provide sufficient detail as prescribed to allow the state board to approve such provisions in order that substantial experimentation with patterns of teacher education may be encouraged. Upon adequate evidence, the state board may give continuing status to an experimental teacher education program of demonstrated superiority.

Grade Point Average (GPA) Required for Admission:
A sponsoring institution recommending applicants for teachers' certificates shall establish selection techniques which ensure that only qualified students are admitted to the teacher education program and that only qualified

students are sponsored for certification.

The state board at the request of an approved teacher education institution may waive for a specific time particular requirements of this code for experimental teacher education programs. A request for such a waiver shall provide sufficient detail as prescribed to allow the state board to approve such provisions in order that substantial experimentation with patterns of teacher education may be encouraged. Upon adequate evidence, the state board may give continuing status to an experimental teacher education program of demonstrated superiority.

Program Admissions Test:
A sponsoring institution recommending applicants for teachers' certificates shall establish selection techniques which ensure that only qualified students are admitted to the teacher education program and that only qualified students are sponsored for certification.

The state board at the request of an approved teacher education institution may waive for a specific time particular requirements of this code for experimental teacher education programs. A request for such a waiver shall provide sufficient detail as prescribed to allow the state board to approve such provisions in order that substantial experimentation with patterns of teacher education may be encouraged. Upon adequate evidence, the state board may give continuing status to an experimental teacher education program of demonstrated superiority.

Other Admissions Requirements:
A sponsoring institution recommending applicants for teachers' certificates shall establish selection techniques which ensure that only qualified students are admitted to the teacher education program and that only qualified students are sponsored for certification.

The state board shall develop and approve, and advocate to state universities that they adopt, an expedited "fast-track" teacher preparation program to be available to individuals who have outstanding academic credentials, who are exceptionally gifted performers or artists, or who are outstanding professionals expert in their fields of endeavor.

Minnesota
Degree or Previous Education Required:
Bachelor's degree

Grade Point Average (GPA) Required for Admission:
No state policy found.

Program Admissions Test:
Candidates for an alternative route to certification are required to pass an examination of skills in reading, writing, and mathematics.

Other Admissions Requirements:
Candidates for an alternative route to certification must have been offered a job to teach in a school district, group of districts, or an education district approved by the Board of Teaching to offer an alternative preparation licensure program.

Mississippi
Degree or Previous Education Required:
Teach Mississippi Institute (TMI):
Alternative teacher candidates hold a bachelor's or higher degree, noneducation major from an accredited institution of higher education.

Mississippi Alternate Path to Quality Teachers:
Alternative teacher candidates hold a bachelor's or higher degree, noneducation major from an accredited institution of higher education.

Master of Arts in Teaching:
Alternative teacher candidates hold a bachelor's or higher degree, noneducation major from an accredited institution of higher education.

Grade Point Average (GPA) Required for Admission:
Teach Mississippi Institute (TMI):
No state policy found.

Mississippi Alternate Path to Quality Teachers:
Alternative teacher candidates who graduate more than seven years

prior to applying to the program must have an overall 2.0 grade point average. Candidates who graduated less than seven years prior to applying to the program must have an overall 2.5 grade point average.

Master of Arts in Teaching:
No state policy found.

Program Admissions Test:
All alternative pathways require that candidates successfully complete the PRAXIS I: Pre-Professional Skills Test (PPST) in reading, writing and mathematics and the appropriate PRAXIS II: Specialty Area Test.

PPST—Reading
Cut Score: 170 out of 190
National Median: 178

PPST—Writing
Cut Score: 172 out of 190
National Median: 175

PPST—Mathematics
Cut Score: 169 out of 190
National Median: 179

PRAXIS II: Subject Assessment(s)
Cut Score: Varies by test.
National Median: 179

Notes:
Mississippi Department of Education, Educator Licensure/Certification, *www.mde.k12.ms.us/license/index.htm*

Other Admissions Requirements:
No state policy found.

Missouri

Degree or Previous Education Required:

Innovative and Alternative Professional Preparation:
A bachelor's degree or higher is required for program admission.

Temporary Authorization Certificate:
A bachelor's or higher degree from an accredited college or university is required.

Grade Point Average (GPA) Required for Admission:

Innovative and Alternative Professional Preparation:
Alternative teacher candidates must have a grade point average of 2.5 or higher (on a 4.0 scale), both overall and in the major area of study.

Temporary Authorization Certificate:
Alternative teacher candidates must have a grade point average of 2.5 or higher (on a 4.0 scale), both overall and in the major area of study.

Program Admissions Test:

Innovative and Alternative Professional Preparation:
No state policy.

Temporary Authorization Certificate:
No state policy.

Other Admissions Requirements:

Innovative and Alternative Professional Preparation:
Alternative teacher candidate must present evidence of employment by a school district in Missouri prior to acceptance into an alternative certification program. In addition, candidates participate in a structured interview conducted by the teacher education institution to assess the candidate's beliefs about:

- Nature of students
- Mission and goals of education as a profession

This interview is used for screening, diagnostic, and advising purposes.

Temporary Authorization Certificate:
Alternative teacher candidates must submit:

- A joint application verifying contracted employment with a Missouri public school district or accredited nonpublic school
- Documentation of a plan of an academic program of study from a state-approved teacher preparation program

Montana

Degree or Previous Education Required:
No state policy found. However, the University of Montana at Bozeman offers the Northern Plains Transition to Teaching Program (NPTT) as an alternative route to certification. NPTT requires applicants to have a baccalaureate degree in a teachable subject area and presupposes satisfaction of the core requirements of a liberal arts education typical of most university baccalaureate degree programs, as well as completion of relevant content area course work.

Grade Point Average (GPA) Required for Admission:
No state policy found.

Program Admissions Test:
No state policy found.

Other Admissions Requirements:
No state policy found.

Nebraska

Degree or Previous Education Required:
The alternative certificate process in Nebraska, which results in a Transitional Teaching Certificate, requires the applicant to have at least a baccalaureate degree that includes at least three-fourths of the course requirements for preparation in the endorsement area required for the teaching position that is being filled by the applicant.

Grade Point Average (GPA) Required for Admission:
No state policy found.

Program Admissions Test:
Applicants to the alternative certificate process must provide evidence of basic skills competency.

Other Admissions Requirements:
Applicants to the alternative certificate process in Nebraska must have an offer for employment in a school district

that was unable to find a fully qualified teacher for the position.

Nevada
Degree or Previous Education Required:
Alternative teacher candidates must hold a bachelor's degree with a major in a field other than education from a regionally accredited postsecondary institution.

Grade Point Average (GPA) Required for Admission:
No state policy found.

Program Admissions Test:
Alternative teacher candidates complete the appropriate assessments, including:

- PRAXIS I: Pre-Professional Skills Test (PPST) in reading, writing, and mathematics
- PRAXIS II: Principles of Learning and Teaching (PLT)
- PRAXIS II: Subject Assessment(s)

PPST—Reading
Cut Score: 174
National Median: 178

PPST—Writing
Cut Score: 172
National Median: 175

PPST—Mathematics
Cut Score: 172
National Median: 179

PLT—Grades K–6
Cut Score: 169
National Median: 174

PLT—Grades 7–12
Cut Score: 161
National Median: 175

PRAXIS II: Subject Assessments:
Cut Score: Varies by test.
National Median: Varies by test.

Notes:
Nevada Department of Education, Licensing, Testing Requirements, *www.nde.state.nv.us/licensure/Test_requirements.pdf*

Educational Testing Service (ETS), PRAXIS Series, State Requirements, Nevada, *www.ets.org/praxis/prxnv.html*

Other Admissions Requirements:
A school district or private school must apply in writing to the department of state department of education before employing an individual who holds a conditional license.

The written application must include:

- Proof that the school district or private school has advertised in good faith its desire to fill a vacancy in the position of, as applicable, an unconditionally licensed teacher to teach elementary education to pupils who are enrolled in a program of bilingual education, an unconditionally licensed teacher to teach pupils in a program of early childhood education, an unconditionally licensed teacher to teach secondary education in the subject area and at the grade level in which there is a vacancy, or an unconditionally licensed teacher to teach pupils in kindergarten through grade 12 who have specific learning disabilities, emotional disturbances or mental retardation, and mild to moderate needs for assistance and intervention in their educational processes.

- An affidavit stating that despite the required advertisement the school district or private school was not successful in hiring, as applicable, an unconditionally licensed teacher to teach elementary education to pupils who are enrolled in a program of bilingual education, an unconditionally licensed teacher to teach a program of early childhood education, an unconditionally licensed teacher to teach secondary education in the subject area and at the grade level in which there is a vacancy, or an unconditionally licensed teacher to teach pupils in kindergarten through grade 12 who have specific learning disabilities, emotional disturbances or mental retardation, and mild to moderate needs for assistance and intervention in their educational processes.

- A written assurance that the school district or private school will, if required by statute or regulation, continue its efforts to hire unconditionally licensed educational personnel.

New Hampshire
Degree or Previous Education Required:
Alternative 3A:
An applicant shall hold a bachelor's degree

Alternative 3B:
A national level or regional certification which has been validated in the individual's endorsement area achieved by passing a national or regional examination designed to assess the individual's skills in the area in which the individual seeks certification; or

Proof of completion of a specialized program, such as, but not limited to, a bachelor's degree in social work, culminating in a bachelor's degree from a college or university accredited by a recognized national, regional, or state accrediting agency.

Alternative 4: Individualized Professional Development Plan (Restricted):
Hold at least a bachelor's degree prior to completion of the individualized professional

development plan.

Alternative 5: Site-Based Certification Plan:
The applicant shall possess a bachelor's degree from an institution approved by the New Hampshire Postsecondary Education Commission or equivalent regional accrediting agency such as but not limited to the Northeast Regional Association of Schools and Colleges.

The applicant shall meet one of the following criteria:

- For secondary education, the applicant shall possess at least 30 credit hours in the subject to be taught and an overall grade point average of at least 2.5, or equivalent;
- For elementary education, applicants shall have successfully completed courses in mathematics, English, social studies, and science with an overall grade point average of at least 2.5, or equivalent.

Grade Point Average (GPA) Required for Admission:
Alternative 2: States Other Than NH:
No state policy found.

Alternative 3: Demonstrated Competencies and Equivalent Experiences:
No state policy found.

Alternative 4: Individualized Professional Development Plan

(Restricted):
No state policy found.

Alternative 5: Site-Based Certification Plan:

- For secondary education, applicants shall possess at least 30 credit hours in the subject to be taught and an overall grade point average of at least 2.5, or equivalent;
- For elementary education, applicants shall have successfully completed courses in mathematics, English, social studies, and science with an overall grade point average of at least 2.5, or equivalent.

Program Admissions Test:
No state policy found.

Notes:
There are two versions of Alternative 3, both based on Demonstrated Competencies and Equivalent Experiences

Other Admissions Requirements:
Alternative 3A:
This alternative is relative to demonstrated competencies and equivalent experiences, and consists of 3 parts, a written application, submission of documentation that the applicant meets the required competencies in the area of endorsement, and an oral interview process as described below:

- An applicant for a credential who has acquired competencies, skills and knowledge through means other than Ed 505.01 or Ed 505.02 may request a credential on that basis;

- An applicant shall hold a bachelor's degree prior to submitting documentation that the applicant meets the required competencies, which may include, depending on the area of endorsement, documentation in the following forms:
  - o Written materials
  - o Videotapes
  - o Audiotapes
  - o Art portfolio

- To qualify, an applicant shall have at least 3 months of full-time continuous experience as an educator in the area of endorsement;
- Individuals seeking a credential through this part shall submit to the bureau:
  - o A completed application form required by Ed 508.03
  - o Official college or university transcript(s)
  - o A letter from the employer verifying that the applicant has completed at least 3 months full-time experience in the area of endorsement for which a credential is sought.

Alternative 3B:
This alternative is relative to demonstrated competencies and equivalent experiences, national or regional examination, and shall consist of the following:

Individuals shall be eligible for a New Hampshire credential who possess:

- A national level or regional certification that has been validated in the individual's endorsement area achieved by passing a national or regional examination designed to assess the individual's skills in the area in which the individual seeks certification; or
- Proof of completion of a specialized program, such as, but not limited to, a bachelor's degree in social work, culminating in a bachelor's degree from a college or university accredited by a recognized national, regional, or state accrediting agency;
- Applicants under this paragraph shall apply for a credential by submitting the scores along with an application for certification pursuant to Ed 508.03 to the bureau with the appropriate filing fees and accompanying documentation as required by Ed 508.

Alternative 4: Individualized Professional Development Plan (Restricted):

Alternative 4 shall be a qualifying method for certification limited to the following:

- Applicants recommended for employment under a critical staffing shortage who hold at least a bachelor's degree prior to completion of the individualized professional development plan;
- Applicants recommended for employment in the career and technical specialties pursuant to Ed 507.

Alternative 5: Site-Based Certification Plan:
The site-based certification plan shall be available in elementary and secondary teaching areas, excluding career and technical specialty certification under Ed 507.03 and special education, for those individuals who qualify under the following specific conditions:

The applicant shall possess a bachelor's degree from an institution approved by the New Hampshire postsecondary education commission or equivalent regional accrediting agency such as but not limited to the Northeast Regional Association of Schools and Colleges;

The applicant shall meet one of the following criteria:

- For secondary education, the applicant shall possess at

least 30 credit hours in the subject to be taught and an overall grade point average of at least 2.5, or equivalent;

- For elementary education, applicants shall have successfully completed courses in mathematics, English, social studies, and science with an overall grade point average of at least 2.5, or equivalent;
- An individual who fails to meet the grade point average requirement shall still qualify for the site-based certification plan provided that:
  o All other requirements are met;
  o Collegiate graduation occurred more than 5 years prior to application for the site-based plan; and
  o Occupational experience totaling 5 years directly related to the area to be taught is documented.

New Jersey
Degree or Previous Education Required:
Provisional Teacher Program: Bachelor's degree from an accredited institution.

For secondary candidates: a major in the subject teaching field (e.g., English, Mathematics); for elementary candidates: a major in the liberal arts or sciences.

Grade Point Average (GPA) Required for Admission:
Provisional Teacher Program: To meet the CE or CEAS requirements for admission to the Provisional Teacher program, candidates must have a cumulative GPA of at least 2.50 when a GPA of 4.00 equals an A grade for students graduating before September 1, 2004, in a baccalaureate degree program, higher degree program, or a state-approved post-baccalaureate certification program with a minimum of 13 semester-hour credits; for students graduating on or after September 1, 2004, achieve a cumulative GPA of at least 2.75 when a GPA of 4.00 equals an A grade in a baccalaureate degree program, higher degree program, or in a state-approved post-baccalaureate certification program with a minimum of 13 semester-hour credits.

Program Admissions Test:
Provisional Teacher Program: Applicants for certification in a subject teaching field must pass the appropriate PRAXIS II Subject Assessment/NTE Programs Specialty Area tests.

Applicants for certification in elementary education must pass the NTE General Knowledge test of the Core Battery. Candidates in the following subject teaching fields available through the Alternate Route are exempt from the test requirement:

foreign languages other than French, German, and Spanish; earth science; health education; psychology; and vocational education.

Other Admissions Requirements:
Requirements for the provisional certificate:
A candidate shall:
- Hold a CE or CEAS in the endorsement area required for the teaching assignment; and
- Obtain and accept an offer of employment in a position that requires instructional certification.

New Mexico
Degree or Previous Education Required:
Bachelor's degree including 30 credits that appertain to the licensure area sought; or Master's degree including 12 graduate credits that appertain to the licensure area sought; or Doctorate in a field that appertains to the licensure area sought.

Grade Point Average (GPA) Required for Admission:
No state policy found.

Program Admissions Test:
No state policy found.

Notes:
Alternative licensure candidates may be permitted to assume the functions of a teacher while pursuing an alternative route to licensure.

Other Admissions Requirements:
Submit an Application for Initial Licensure to the Professional Licensure Unit at the NM Department of Education and attach either a letter of acceptance in an alternative licensure program.

New York
Degree or Previous Education Required:
The Alternative Teacher Preparation Program (Transitional B):
The program requires candidates to hold a baccalaureate or graduate degree (with a major in the subject to be taught) from a regionally accredited institution of higher education or from an institution authorized by the Board of Regents to confer degrees.

Grade Point Average (GPA) Required for Admission:
A 3.0 cumulative grade point average. Candidates shall have achieved a 3.0 cumulative grade point average, or its equivalent, in the program leading to the baccalaureate or graduate degree, or shall have been found by an officer designated by the registered alternative teacher certification program to have the necessary knowledge and skills to successfully complete the program, which finding shall be in writing and include the basis for that finding.

Program Admissions Test:
No state policy found.

Notes:
At least 100 clock hours of field experiences related to coursework are to be completed prior to student teaching or practica.

North Carolina
Degree or Previous Education Required:
Lateral Entry Licensure Program:
Participants must hold at least a bachelor's degree from a regionally accredited college or university, and that degree must be directly related to the subject area you wish to teach.

Alternative Entry Licensure Program:
Alternative entry licenses are issued to individuals if requested by an employing LEA that has determined there is or anticipates there will be a shortage of qualified teachers available for specified subjects or grade levels. The LEA must have developed a plan to determine the individual's competence as a teacher, including review of the performance of students taught by the individual. The alternative entry license is a one-year temporary license.

This policy expires September 1, 2006, but remains in effect for any teacher employed by it prior to September 1, 2006.

Grade Point Average (GPA) Required for Admission:
All board approved teacher education preparation programs require at least a 2.50 grade point average on a 4.00 scale for formal admission of students into the program.

Lateral Entry Program:
You must have a minimum grade point average (GPA) of 2.5 (on a 4.0 scale) or have passed the PRAXIS I tests and have earned one of the following:

- GPA of 3.0 in major field of study
- GPA of 3.0 in all coursework completed in the senior year
- GPA of 3.0 on a minimum of 15 semester hours of coursework (related to teaching subject/areas of licensure) completed during the most recent five years

Program Admissions Test:
No state policy found.

Other Admissions Requirements:
Lateral Entry Licensure Program:
Employment by a North Carolina school system is required to participate in the Lateral Entry Licensure Program.

North Dakota
There are currently no alternative route programs to teacher certification in North Dakota.

Ohio
Degree or Previous Education Required:
Alternative teacher candidates must hold a bachelor's degree with a major in the content area to be taught or extensive work experience in a high school teaching area or special education.

Grade Point Average (GPA) Required for Admission:
Alternative teacher candidates must have a 2.5 or higher grade point average in the major and content area to be taught.

Program Admissions Test:
Alternative teacher candidates must successfully complete the appropriate PRAXIS II: Subject Assessment in the area in which they will be teaching.
Cut Score: Varies by test.
National Median: Varies by test.

For specific tests and scores, see *www.ode.state.oh.us/Teaching-Profession/Word/alt_praxis.doc.*

Ohio Department of Education, Ohio PRAXIS II Tests, Codes and Qualifying Scores for Alternate Educator License, *www.ode.state.oh.us/Teaching-Profession/Word/alt_praxis.doc*

Educational Testing Service (ETS), PRAXIS Series, State Requirements, Ohio, *www.ets.org/praxis/prxoh.html*

Ohio Title II Report (2002), Certification/Licensure, Alternative Routes, Description of Alternative Routes, *www.title2.org/title2dr/Description.asp*

Other Admissions Requirements:
Alternative teacher candidates complete six semester hours of professional education coursework, including:

- One course in teaching methods

- One course in adolescent development

Oklahoma
Degree or Previous Education Required:
Alternative teacher candidates must hold a bachelor's or higher degree from an institution whose accreditation is recognized by the Oklahoma State Regents for Higher Education.

In addition, the candidate must have completed a major in a field that corresponds to an area of specialization for an elementary-secondary certificate, a secondary certificate or a vocational-technical certificate.

Grade Point Average (GPA) Required for Admission:
No state policy found.

Program Admissions Test:
Alternative teacher candidates must pass the general education and subject area portion in the area of specialization for which certification is sought on following state mandated competency-based examination:

- The Oklahoma General Education Test (OGET)
- Oklahoma Subject Area Tests (OSAT).
- The cut score for both tests is 240 out of a possible 300

Notes:
Oklahoma Title II Report (2002), Certification/Licensure, Alternative Routes, *www.title2.org/title2dr/Description.asp*

Other Admissions Requirements:
Alternative teacher candidates must declare the intent to seek employment as a teacher at an accredited public school or have an offer of employment from a school district.

In addition, candidates must never have been denied admittance to a teacher education program approved by the Oklahoma State Regents for Higher Education, the North Central Association of Colleges and Schools and by the Oklahoma State Board of Education to offer teacher education programs, nor have enrolled in and subsequently failed courses necessary to successfully meet the minimum program requirements.

Oregon
Degree or Previous Education Required:
Oregon State University's (OSU) Career in Teaching Program requires alternative teacher candidates to complete an associate of general studies degree followed by completion of a bachelor's degree.

Grade Point Average (GPA) Required for Admission:
No state policy found.

Program Admissions Test:
Program provider(s) decision.

Notes:
Oregon State University, Career in Teaching, *www.ous.edu/aca/CIT.htm*

Other Admissions Requirements: Program provider(s) decision.

Pennsylvania
Degree or Previous Education Required:
Teacher intern candidates must hold a bachelor's degree related to the area of certification requested.

Grade Point Average (GPA) Required for Admission:
Teacher intern candidates must have a 3.0 grade point average.

Program Admissions Test:
Teacher intern candidates must successfully complete the PRAXIS I: Pre-Professional Skills Test (PPST) or Computerized PPST in reading, writing and mathematics and the appropriate PRAXIS II: Subject Assessment(s).

PPST/Computerized PPST—
Reading
Cut Score: 172 out of 190
National Median: 178

PPST/Computerized PPST—
Writing
Cut Score: 173 out of 190
National Median: 175

PPST/Computerized PPST—
Mathematics
Cut Score: 173 out of 190
National Median: 179

PRAXIS II: Subject Assessment(s)
Cut Score: Varies by test.
National Median: Varies by test.

Pennsylvania Department of Education, Testing Requirements, *www.teaching.state.pa.us/teaching/ cwp/view.asp?a=90&Q=32539&g=*

140&teachingNav=|93|87|&teachin gNav=|1904|

Educational Testing Service (ETS), PRAXIS Series, State Requirements, Pennsylvania, *www .ets.org/praxis/prxpa.html*

Pennsylvania Department of Education, PA Intern Certification Program, *www.teaching.state. pa.us/teaching/cwp/view.asp?a=6& Q=32343&teachingNav=|93|102|*

Pennsylvania Title II Report (2002), Certification/Licensure, Alternative Routes, Description of Alternative Routes, *www.title2 .org/title2dr/Description.asp*

Other Admissions Requirements: Teacher intern candidates must have completed the following coursework:

- College level mathematics, 6 credits
- College level English literature and composition, 6 credits

Candidates must also apply to and complete an approved institution of higher education's (IHE) preadmission screening and be accepted into the program. An offer of a teaching position is not a requirement for admission into a Teacher Intern Certification Program nor does it guarantee admission into a specific Teacher Intern Certification Program.

Puerto Rico
There are currently no alternative route programs to teacher certification in Puerto Rico.

Rhode Island
There are currently no alternative route programs to teacher certification in Rhode Island.

South Carolina
Degree or Previous Education Required:
Alternative teacher candidates must have a bachelor's or higher degree in a subject content area from a regionally or nationally accredited institution.

Grade Point Average (GPA) Required for Admission:
No state policy found.

Program Admissions Test:
Alternative teacher candidates must successfully complete the appropriate PRAXIS II: Subject Assessment(s).
Cut Score: Varies by test.
National Median: Varies by test.

South Carolina State Department of Education, The Division of Teacher Quality, Alternative Routes to Certification, *www. scteachers.org/cert/pace/overview. cfm*

Coastal Carolina University, Program of Alternative Certification for Educators (PACE), *www.coastal.edu/ criticalneeds/*

Educational Testing Service (ETS), PRAXIS Series, State Requirements, South Carolina, *www.ets.org/praxis/prxsc.html*

South Carolina State Board of Education regulations applicable to teacher education programs establish that graduate degrees acceptable for certification purposes include academic or professional degrees in the field of education or in an academic area for which the state board authorizes a corresponding or relevant teaching credential.

All credit at the graduate level must be earned through the graduate school of an institution of higher education accredited for general collegiate purposes by a regional or national accrediting agency.

Other Admissions Requirements:
Alternative teacher candidates must:

- Submit an application
- Submit transcripts
- Submit a fingerprint card
- Receive an offer of employment from a public school

The South Carolina State Department of Education, Division of Teacher Quality, Office of Teacher Certification handles all program admissions.

South Dakota
Degree or Previous Education Required:
Alternative teacher candidates hold a bachelor's or higher degree obtained at least two years prior to admittance into an alternative teacher preparation program.

Grade Point Average (GPA) Required for Admission:

Alternative teacher candidates must have maintained an overall grade point average of 2.5 on all undergraduate coursework.

Program Admissions Test:
Alternative teacher candidates must complete a state designated subject assessment or specialty area assessment only if they do not have a college major in the subject area to be taught and are admitted to an alternative program on the basis of five years' of experience in a related field.

Other Admissions Requirements:
No state policy found.

Tennessee
Degree or Previous Education Required:
Interim A Licensure:
Alternative teacher candidates must hold a bachelor's degree in a teaching field and an academic major or equivalent.

Interim C Licensure:
Alternative teacher candidates must hold a bachelor's degree in teaching or a related field and have completed the pre-service portion of an alternative preparation program approved by the Tennessee State Board of Education.

Interim E Licensure:
Alternative teacher candidates must hold:

- A bachelor's degree in the teaching field or pass the PRAXIS II: Subject

Assessment in the subject area to be taught
- An out-of-state license in a subject area of grade span that does not coincide with Tennessee's licenses

Tennessee State Board of Education, Alternative Preparation for Licensure Policy Revised (August 2002), *www.state.tn.us/ sbe/alternativepreplicpolicy.pdf*

Tennessee State Board of Education, Alternative Licensure, *www.state.tn.us/sbe/ alternativelicensure.htm*

Tennessee Department of Education, Interim Type A Teacher Licenses, *www.state.tn.us/ education/lic_ipta.htm*

Tennessee Department of Education, Interim Type C Teacher Licenses, *www.state.tn.us/ education/lic_altc.htm*

Tennessee Department of Education, Interim Type E Teacher Licenses, *www.state.tn.us/ education/lic_inte.htm*

Tennessee Title II Report (2002), Certification/Licensure, Alternative Routes, *www.title2.org/ title2dr/Description.asp*

Grade Point Average (GPA) Required for Admission:
No state policy found.

Program Admissions Test:
No state policy found.

Texas

Degree or Previous Education Required:
Alternative teacher candidates must hold a bachelor's or higher degree.

Grade Point Average (GPA) Required for Admission:
The entity delivering a teacher preparation program is required by state policy to establish policies for the following:

- Screening activities to determine the candidate's appropriateness for the certification sought Screening for admission to include but not limited to college level skills in reading, oral and written communication, critical thinking, and mathematics
- Academic criteria for admission that are published and applied consistently to all candidates.

Each preparation program must develop and implement specific criteria and procedures that allow admitted individuals to substitute experience and/or professional training directly related to the certificate being sought for part of the preparation requirements.

Program Admissions Test:
Same as above.

Note:
Preparation programs have the authority to adopt additional requirements in addition to those explicitly established by state policy.

Texas Title II Report (2002), Certification/Licensure, Alternative Routes, *www.title2.org/ title2dr/Description.asp*

Utah

Degree or Previous Education Required:
Licensing by Agreement:
Alternative teacher candidates must hold a bachelor's or higher from an accredited higher education institution in an area related to the teaching position sought.

Licensing by Competency:
Alternative teacher candidates must hold a bachelor's or higher from an accredited higher education institution in an area related to the teaching position sought.

Grade Point Average (GPA) Required for Admission:
No state policy found.

Program Admissions Test:
Licensing by Agreement:
No state policy.

Licensing by Competency:
Alternative teacher candidates must successfully complete a state-approved content knowledge and pedagogical knowledge examinations.

Other Admissions Requirements:
Licensing by Agreement:
Alternative teacher candidates have the skills, talents, or abilities, as evaluated by the employing institution, that qualify them for a teaching position.

Licensing by Competency:
Alternative teacher candidates have the skills, talents, or abilities, as evaluated by the employing institution, that qualify them for a teaching position.

Vermont

Degree or Previous Education Required:
There are currently no alternative route teacher preparation programs in Vermont.

However, license by evaluation (peer review) enables individuals who have acquired the knowledge and skills needed to meet the Principles for Vermont Educators and the endorsement competencies and requirements they seek through coursework and experiences, rather than through a preparation program.

For more information, see *www. state.vt.us/educ/license/alt_license. pdf.*

Grade Point Average (GPA) Required for Admission:
Not applicable.

Program Admissions Test:
Not applicable.

Notes:

- An "endorsement" establishes the grade level and field in which an educator is authorized to serve.

- "Liberal arts and sciences" coursework provides teacher candidates with a general knowledge in the arts, humanities, sciences, and mathematics, as opposed to professional and technical subjects.
- A "license" authorizes an individual to serve as an educator.
- A "minor" is granted as a part of a bachelor's degree by a state-approved institution or regionally accredited institution or a compilation of 18 credit hours (6 must be graduate level or advanced undergraduate courses) in the specified minor field from a state-approved institution or regionally accredited institution.
- "Student teaching" is the concentrated field experience required for initial licensure including student teaching, intern-ship, practicum, or other concentrated field experience.

For more information, see *www.state.vt.us/educ/new/pdfdoc/board/rules/5100.pdf.*

Other Admissions Requirements:
Not applicable.

Virgin Islands

There are currently no alternative route programs to teacher certification in the U.S. Virgin Islands.

Virginia
Degree or Previous Education Required:
Alternative teacher candidates must:

- Hold a bachelor's degree from an accredited institution of higher education
- Have completed requirements for an endorsement in a teaching area or equivalent

Note: Verifiable experience or academic study may be substituted for the completion of endorsement requirements.

Grade Point Average (GPA) Required for Admission:
No state policy found.

Program Admissions Test:
Alternative teacher candidates must successfully complete the appropriate assessments, including:

- PRAXIS I: Pre-Professional Skills Test in reading, writing and mathematics
- PRAXIS II: Subject Assessments (in certain areas).
- Teacher candidates may meet the PRAXIS I assessment requirements by achieving qualifying scores established by the state board on the three PRAXIS I tests, or by achieving the established composite score (523) on three tests. A minimum score on each

test is not required if the composite score is achieved.

PPST—Reading
Cut Score: 178 out of 190
National Median: 179

PPST—Writing
Cut Score: 178 out of 190
National Median: 176

PPST—Mathematics
Cut Score: 178 out of 190
National Median: 178

PRAXIS II: Subject Assessment
Cut Score: Varies by test.
National Median: Varies by test.

For specific information on required subject-area assessments, see *www.pen.k12.va.us/VDOE/newvdoe/CareerSwitcher/programdescription.html.*

Virginia Department of Education, Virginia's "Career Switcher" Alternative Route to Licensure Program for Career Professions, Fact Sheet, *www.pen.k12.va.us/VDOE/newvdoe/switcher_update.pdf*

Virginia Department of Education, Application for "Career Switcher" Alternative Route to Licensure Program for Career Professions, *www.pen.k12.va.us/VDOE/newvdoe/CareerSwitcher/programdescription.html*

Virginia Department of Education, Virginia's Career Switcher Altern-ative Route to Licensure Program for Career Professions, Fact Sheet, *www.pen.k12.va.us/VDOE/newvdoe/switcher_update.pdf*

Virginia Department of Education, Virginia Career Switcher Alternative Route to Licensure Program, Program Description, *www.pen.k12.va.us/VDOE/newvdoe/CareerSwitcher/programbackground.html*

Virginia Department of Education, Virginia Career Switcher Alternative Route to Licensure Program, Program Background, *www.pen.k12.va.us/VDOE/newvdoe/CareerSwitcher/programbackground.html*

Virginia Department of Education, Virginia Licensure Regulations for School Personnel, Effective July 1998, *www.pen.k12.va.us/VDOE/Compliance/TeacherED/nulicvr.pdf*

Notes:
The Virginia State Board of Education is the constitutional body vested with general supervision of the public school system and is authorized to establish regulations necessary to carry out the school laws, Code of Virginia (Title 22.1), and to establish criteria for teacher preparation programs in cooperation with the State Council of Higher Education.

Other Admissions Requirements:
Priority is given to applicants eligible to teach in one of the critical shortage teaching areas, including:

- Mathematics
- Foreign languages
- Sciences
- Technology education

Washington
Degree or Previous Education Required:
Route 1: Classified instructional employees with an associate's degree: associate's degree.
Route 2: Classified employees with a bachelor's degree: bachelor's degree.
Route 3: Career changers: bachelor's degree.

Grade Point Average (GPA) Required for Admission:
No state policy found.

Program Admissions Test:
All alternative teacher candidates must receive a passing score on the WEST-B basic skills test in reading, writing and mathematics.

To pass the WEST-B examinees had to answer correctly 63 percent of the multiple-choice questions on both the reading and mathematics sections. To pass the writing section, examinees had to get 62 percent of the multiple choice questions correct and get 11 of 16 points on two writing tasks. Examinees have unlimited opportunities to retake all or subsections of the test.

TeachWashington.org, The Road to Certification, *www.teachwashington.org/certification.php*

Washington State Professional Educator Standards Board, Alternative Routes, Frequently Asked Questions, *www.pesb.wa.gov/AlternativeRoutes/AlternativeRoutes.htm*

Washington State Professional Educator Standards Board, Future Washington Teachers Receive WEST-B Results, *www.pesb.wa.gov/Assessment/WEST-B/WEST-B_Cut_Score.pdf*

Washington Title II Report (2002), Certification/Licensure, Alternative Routes, *www.title2.org/title2dr/Description.asp*

Other Admissions Requirements:
All alternative teacher candidates must be of good moral character and personal fitness.

West Virginia
There are currently no alternative route programs to teacher certification in West Virginia.

Wisconsin
Degree or Previous Education Required:
Alternative teacher candidates must have a bachelor's degree in the subject area to be taught.

Grade Point Average (GPA) Required for Admission:
No state policy found.

Program Admissions Test:
No state policy found.

Notes:
Wisconsin Department of Public Instruction, Wisconsin Alternative Program for Teaching, *www.dpi.state.wi.us/dpi/dlsis/tel/wapt.html*

Other Admissions Requirements:
No state policy found.

Wyoming
Degree or Previous Education Required:

All applicants must have a bachelor's degree from a regionally accredited institution.

Northern Plains Transition to Teaching:
To be granted full admission to the program, the applicant must:

- Hold a four-year baccalaureate degree from an accredited institution.
- Have demonstrated potential for graduate study
- Have no content area deficiencies to make up and is free to enter the next available cohort without restrictions.

Grade Point Average (GPA) Required for Admission:
Portfolio Certification:
No state policy found.

Northern Plains Transition to Teaching:
In order to be granted full admission to the Northern Plains Transition to Teaching program,

the applicant must:

- Have a minimum 2.5 (on a 4.0 scale) or better undergraduate cumulative grade point average (GPA).
- Have a minimum 2.5 (on a 4.0 scale) GPA in content courses applied to teachable endorsement areas.

Program Admissions Test:
No state policy found.

Notes:
Wyoming is currently in the process of reviewing and revising program approval policy. Upon completion of this revising process, more information regarding program approval requirements will be available.

Other Admissions Requirements:
Portfolio Certification:
Wyoming's alternative certification portfolio presentation is meant to describe and verify with supporting documents how

an applicant meets the knowledge, skills and competencies required by each PTSB standards.

Northern Plains Transition to Teaching:
The Northern Plains Transition to Teaching program makes admission decisions for each applicant individually. Applicants may or may not be judged admissible, regardless of the undergraduate record or the institution submitting the credentials. Before granting admission, the appropriate faculty, NPTT program managers and the College of Graduate Studies review each application. Availability of faculty, staff, and the availability of teaching positions in various endorsement areas may limit any individual applicant's admissibility. In such cases, it may not be possible to admit all students who are otherwise qualified.

Reprinted with permission from The National Comprehensive Center for Teacher Quality. *www.tqsource.org*

LIST OF ACCREDITED INSTITUTIONS
(Dates in parentheses indicate date of next accreditation visit)

Portfolio Certification:
Alabama
Alabama A&M University **I&A** (Fall 2008)
Alabama State University **I&A** (Fall 2007)
Athens State University **I** (Spring 2007)
Auburn University **I&A** (Spring 2007)
Auburn University Montgomery **I&A** (Spring 2010)
Birmingham-Southern College **I** (Spring 2006)

Jacksonville State University **I&A** (Fall 2010)
Oakwood College **I** (Fall 2007)
Samford University **I&A** (Fall 2009)
Stillman College **I** (Fall 2008)
The University of Alabama **I&A**

(Spring 2008)

The University of Alabama in Huntsville **I&A** (Fall 2010)

The University of West Alabama **I&A** (Fall 2006)

Troy State University **I&A** (Spring 2009)

Troy State University Dothan **I&A** (Fall 2008)

Tuskegee University **I** (Spring 2008)

University of Alabama at Birmingham **I&A** (Fall 2010)

University of Montevallo **I&A** (Spring 2007)

University of North Alabama **I&A** (Accreditation with Conditions) (TBD)

University of South Alabama **I&A** (Spring 2010)

Alaska

Alaska Pacific University **I** (Provisional Accreditation) (Spring 2008)

University of Alaska Anchorage **I&A** (Spring 2010)

University of Alaska Fairbanks **I&A** (Fall 2009)

University of Alaska Southeast **I&A** (Fall 2009)

Arkansas

Arkansas State University **I&A** (Fall 2009)

Arkansas Tech University **I&A** (Spring 2012)

Harding University **I&A** (Spring 2008)

Henderson State University **I&A** (Spring 2011)

Hendrix College **I** (Fall 2010)

John Brown University **I&A** (Spring 2010)

Lyon College **I** (Spring 2009)

Ouachita Baptist University **I** (Spring 2009)

Philander Smith College **I** (Accreditation with Conditions) (TBD)

Southern Arkansas University **I&A** (Spring 2010)

University of Arkansas—Fort Smith **I** (Spring 2010)

University of Arkansas at Little Rock **I&A** (Fall 2009)

University of Arkansas at Monticello **I&A** (Fall 2008)

University of Arkansas at Pine Bluff **I&A** (Fall 2005)

University of Arkansas, Fayetteville **I&A** (Accreditation with Conditions) (Spring 2007)

University of Central Arkansas **I&A** (Fall 2010)

University of the Ozarks **I** (Fall 2009)

Williams Baptist College **I** (Fall 2005)

California

Azusa Pacific University **I&A** (Spring 2007)

California Lutheran University **I&A** (Fall 2008)

California State University Dominguez Hills **I&A** (Fall 2011)

California State University San Marcos **I&A** (Spring 2007)

California State University, Bakersfield **I&A** (Fall 2007)

California State University, East Bay **I&A** (Spring 2009)

California State University, Fresno **I&A** (Spring 2006)

California State University, Fullerton **I&A** (Fall 2007)

California State University, Long Beach **I&A** (Spring 2007)

California State University, Los Angeles **I&A** (Fall 2011)

California State University, Northridge **I&A** (Fall 2009)

California State University, San Bernardino **I&A** (Spring 2008)

California State University, Stanislaus **I&A** (Fall 2008)

Loyola Marymount University **I&A** (Spring 2010)

San Diego State University **I&A** (Fall 2009)

San Francisco State University **I&A** (Spring 2007)

San Jose State University **I&A** (Spring 2010)

Sonoma State University **I&A** (Spring 2010)

Stanford University **I&A** (Spring 2008)

University of San Diego **I&A** (Fall 2009)

University of the Pacific **I&A** (Spring 2011)

Colorado

Colorado State University **I&A** (Fall 2009)

Mesa State College **I** (Provisional Accreditation) (Fall 2006)

Metropolitan State College of Denver **I** (Fall 2006)

University of Colorado At Boulder **I&A** (Spring 2011)

University of Colorado at Colorado Springs **I&A** (Accreditation with Conditions) (Fall 2007)

University of Colorado At Denver and Health Sciences Center **I&A** (Spring 2012)

University of Northern Colorado **I&A** (Fall 2009)

Connecticut

Central Connecticut State University **I&A** (Spring 2010)
Eastern Connecticut State University **I** (Fall 2008)
Southern Connecticut State University **I&A** (Spring 2009)
The University of Hartford **I&A** (Fall 2009)
University of Connecticut **I&A** (Spring 2010)

Delaware

Delaware State University **I&A** (Spring 2010)
University of Delaware **I&A** (Fall 2010)
Wesley College **I&A** (Spring 2007)

District of Columbia

American University **I&A** (Spring 2007)
Gallaudet University **I&A** (Spring 2009)
George Washington University **I&A** (Spring 2006)
Howard University **I&A** (Spring 2009)
The Catholic University of America **I** (Fall 2006) **& A** ()
Trinity (Washington) University **I&A** (Spring 2010)
University of the District of Columbia **I** (Fall 2009)

Florida

Bethune-Cookman College **I** (Accreditation with Conditions) (Fall 2006)
Florida A&M University **I** (Fall 2007) **& A** (Accreditation with Conditions) (Fall 2006)
Florida Atlantic University **I&A** (Spring 2007)
Florida International University **I&A** (Fall 2008)
Florida Memorial University **I** (Spring 2007)
Florida State University **I&A** (Spring 2009)
Stetson University **I&A** (Spring 2007)
University of Central Florida **I&A** (Fall 2005)
University of Florida **I&A** (Spring 2010)
University of Miami **I&A** (Fall 2006)
University of North Florida **I&A** (Spring 2011)
University of South Florida **I&A** (Spring 2006)
University of West Florida **I&A** (Fall 2010)

Georgia

Albany State University **I&A** (Fall 2008)
Armstrong Atlantic State University **I&A** (Spring 2007)
Atlanta Christian College **I** (Fall 2011)
Augusta State University **I&A** (Spring 2009)
Berry College **I** (Fall 2012) **& A** (Accreditation with Conditions) (Spring 2008)
Brenau University **I&A** (Fall 2008)
Clark Atlanta University **I&A** (Fall 2008)
Clayton State University **I** (Fall 2012)
Columbus State University **I&A** (Spring 2010)

Emory University **I** (Fall 2006) **& A**
Fort Valley State University[Lp] **I&A** (Accreditation with Probation) (Spring 2006)
Georgia College and State University **I&A** (Fall 2008)
Georgia Southern University **I&A** (Spring 2006)
Georgia Southwestern State University **I&A** (Accreditation with Probation) (Spring 2007)
Georgia State University **I&A** (Spring 2006)
Kennesaw State University **I&A** (Fall 2009)
North Georgia College and State University **I&A** (Spring 2009)
Spelman College **I** (Accreditation with Conditions) (Spring 2006)
The University of Georgia **I** (Accreditation with Conditions) (Spring 2006) **& A** (Spring 2006)
University of West Georgia **I&A** (Spring 2009)
Valdosta State University **I&A** (Fall 2006)

Hawaii

University of Hawaii at Manoa **I&A** (Spring 2007)

Idaho

Boise State University **I&A** (Spring 2008)
Idaho State University **I&A** (Fall 2008)
Lewis-Clark State College **I** (Spring 2006)
Northwest Nazarene University **I&A** (Spring 2006)
University of Idaho **I&A**

(Accreditation with Conditions)
(Fall 2006)

Illinois
Augustana College **I** (Spring 2010)
Bradley University **I&A** (Fall 2006)
Chicago State University **I&A** (Fall 2010)
Concordia University **I&A** (Fall 2008)
DePaul University **I&A** (Fall 2010)
Eastern Illinois University **I&A** (Fall 2008)
Elmhurst College **I&A** (Spring 2011)
Governors State University **I&A** (Fall 2009)
Illinois State University **I&A** (Fall 2010)
Lewis University **I&A** (Fall 2006)
Loyola University Chicago **I&A** (Spring 2010)
National-Louis University **I&A** (Spring 2011)
Northeastern Illinois University **I&A** (Fall 2010)
Northern Illinois University **I&A** (Spring 2009)
Olivet Nazarene University **I&A** (Spring 2010)
Roosevelt University **I&A** (Fall 2008)
Saint Xavier University **I** (Spring 2007)
Southern Illinois University at Carbondale **I&A** (Spring 2011)
Southern Illinois University at Edwardsville **I&A** (Spring 2007)
Western Illinois University **I&A** (Spring 2010)
Wheaton College **I** (Fall 2006)

Indiana
Anderson University **I&A** (Spring 2008)
Ball State University **I&A** (Spring 2010)
Bethel College **I** (Fall 2008)
Butler University **I&A** (Fall 2011)
DePauw University **I** (Fall 2006)
Franklin College **I** (Fall 2010)
Goshen College **I** (Spring 2012)
Grace College **I** (Spring 2007)
Hanover College **I** (Spring 2006)
Huntington University **I** (Accreditation with Conditions) (Fall 2007)
Indiana State University **I&A** (Accreditation with Conditions) (Spring 2008)
Indiana University - Purdue University Fort Wayne **I&A** (Spring 2010)
Indiana University at Bloomington/Indianapolis **I&A** (Fall 2009)
Indiana University East **I** (Spring 2012)
Indiana University Kokomo **I** (Fall 2009)
Indiana University Northwest **I&A** (Spring 2012)
Indiana University South Bend **I&A** (Fall 2011)
Indiana University Southeast **I&A** (Fall 2012)
Indiana Wesleyan University **I&A** (Fall 2009)
Manchester College **I** (Fall 2011)
Marian College **I** (Fall 2012)
Oakland City University **I&A** (Spring 2010)
Purdue University **I&A** (Spring 2011)
Purdue University Calumet **I** (Fall 2008)
Saint Joseph's College **I** (Fall 2012)
Saint Mary's College **I** (Fall 2009)
Saint Mary-of-the-Woods College **I** (Fall 2008)
Taylor University **I** (Fall 2006)
Tri-State University **I** (Provisional Accreditation) (Fall 2006)
University of Evansville **I** (Spring 2008)
University of Indianapolis **I&A** (Fall 2010)
University of Saint Francis **I&A** (Spring 2010)
University of Southern Indiana **I&A** (Fall 2008)
Valparaiso University **I&A** (Accreditation with Conditions) (Spring 2007)
Wabash College **I** (Fall 2012)

Iowa
Graceland University **I&A** (Fall 2006)
Luther College **I** (Fall 2010)
Morningside College **I&A** (Spring 2007)
Northwestern College **I** (Fall 2008)
Wartburg College **I** (Spring 2008)

Kansas
Baker University **I&A** (Fall 2009)
Benedictine College **I&A** (Fall 2012)
Bethany College **I** (Accredited with Probation) (Fall 2007)
Bethel College **I** (Spring 2010)
Emporia State University **I&A** (Fall 2010)
Fort Hays State University **I&A** (Spring 2010)
Friends University **I&A** (Fall 2008)

Kansas State University **I&A** (Spring 2009)

Kansas Wesleyan University **I** (Fall 2007)

McPherson College **I** (Fall 2007)

MidAmerica Nazarene University **I&A** (Spring 2010)

Ottawa University **I** (Fall 2012)

Pittsburg State University **I&A** (Fall 2010)

Southwestern College **I&A** (Spring 2008)

Tabor College **I** (Provisional Accreditation) (Spring 2007)

University of Kansas **I&A** (Spring 2007)

University of Saint Mary **I&A** (Fall 2010)

Washburn University **I&A** (Accreditation with Conditions) (Fall 2006)

Wichita State University **I&A** (Fall 2009)

Kentucky

Asbury College **I&A** (Spring 2007)

Bellarmine University **I&A** (Accreditation with Conditions) (Fall 2006)

Berea College **I** (Spring 2011)

Eastern Kentucky University **I&A** (Fall 2009)

Kentucky State University **I** (Spring 2012)

Morehead State University **I&A** (Fall 2010)

Murray State University **I&A** (Fall 2008)

Northern Kentucky University **I&A** (Spring 2010)

Spalding University **I&A** (Fall 2010)

The University of Kentucky **I&A** (Fall 2007)

Transylvania University **I** (Spring 2007)

University of Louisville **I&A** (Fall 2008)

Western Kentucky University **I&A** (Spring 2010)

Louisiana

Dillard University **I** (Fall 2008)

Grambling State University **I&A** (Spring 2008)

Louisiana State University and A&M College **I&A** (Fall 2011)

Louisiana State University in Shreveport **I&A** (Spring 2010)

Louisiana Tech University **I&A** (Spring 2010)

McNeese State University **I&A** (Fall 2010)

Nicholls State University **I&A** (Fall 2008)

Northwestern State University of Louisiana **I&A** (Fall 2011)

Our Lady of Holy Cross College **I&A** (Spring 2009)

Southeastern Louisiana University **I&A** (Spring 2008)

Southern University and A&M College **I&A** (Spring 2009)

Southern University at New Orleans **I&A** (Fall 2007)

University of Louisiana at Lafayette **I&A** (Spring 2009)

University of Louisiana at Monroe **I&A** (Fall 2009)

University of New Orleans **I&A** (Fall 2007)

Xavier University of Louisiana **I&A** (Fall 2009)

Maine

University of Maine **I&A** (Accreditation with Conditions) (TBD)

University of Maine At Farmington **I** (Fall 2009)

University of Southern Maine **I&A** (Spring 2009)

Maryland

Bowie State University **I&A** (Spring 2010)

College of Notre Dame of Maryland **I&A** (Spring 2006)

Coppin State University **I** (Spring 2006) **& A** (Fall 2006)

Frostburg State University **I&A** (Spring 2007)

Loyola College in Maryland **I&A** (Spring 2007)

McDaniel College **I&A** (Spring 2009)

Morgan State University **I&A** (Spring 2007)

Salisbury University **I&A** (Fall 2012)

The Johns Hopkins University **I&A** (Spring 2008)

Towson University **I&A** (Fall 2007)

University of Maryland Baltimore County **I&A** (Fall 2010)

University of Maryland College Park **I&A** (Accreditation with Conditions) (Fall 2007)

University of Maryland Eastern Shore **I&A** (Fall 2008)

Villa Julie College **I** (Spring 2010)

Massachusetts

Bridgewater State College **I&A** (Spring 2007)

Fitchburg State College **I&A** (Spring 2006)
Salem State College **I&A** (Fall 2006)
University of Massachusetts Amherst **I&A** (Spring 2008)
University of Massachusetts Boston **I&A** (Spring 2008)
University of Massachusetts Lowell **I&A** (Spring 2009)
Westfield State College **I** (Fall 2007)
Wheelock College **I&A** (Fall 2007)

Michigan

Andrews University **I&A** (Fall 2011)
Calvin College **I&A** (Fall 2009)
Central Michigan University **I&A**: (Spring 2010)
Concordia University **I** (Spring 2007)
Eastern Michigan University **I&A** (Fall 2010)
Grand Valley State University **I&A** (Spring 2006)
Hope College **I** (Spring 2010)
Madonna University **I&A** (Spring 2009)
Marygrove College **I** (Accreditation with Conditions) (Spring 2006)
Northern Michigan University **I&A** (Spring 2008)
Oakland University **I&A** (Spring 2007)
Saginaw Valley State University **I&A** (Spring 2009)
Spring Arbor University **I&A** (Spring 2011)
Western Michigan University **I&A** (Fall 2006)

Minnesota

Augsburg College **I** (Spring 2011)
College of St. Benedict/St. John's University **I** (Fall 2012)
Concordia University **I&A** (Spring 2008)
Gustavus Adolphus College **I** (Spring 2006)
Hamline University **I&A** (Spring 2012)
Minnesota State University, Mankato **I&A** (Fall 2011)
Minnesota State University-Moorhead **I&A** (Spring 2008)
Saint Olaf College **I** (Spring 2009)
St. Cloud State University **I&A** (Fall 2007)
The University of Minnesota, Morris **I** (Fall 2008)
University of Minnesota, Duluth **I&A** (Fall 2009)
University of Minnesota—Twin Cities **I&A** (Fall 2012)
Winona State University **I** (Fall 2010) **& A** (Accreditation with Conditions) (Spring 2006)

Mississippi

Alcorn State University **I&A** (Fall 2006)
Delta State University **I&A** (Spring 2007)
Jackson State University **I&A** (Fall 2007)
Millsaps College **I** (Spring 2006)
Mississippi College **I&A** (Fall 2010)
Mississippi State University **I&A** (Spring 2007)
Mississippi University for Women **I&A** (Fall 2009)
Mississippi Valley State University **I&A** (Fall 2006)

The University of Mississippi **I&A** (Spring 2007)
University of Southern Mississippi **I&A** (Spring 2006)

Missouri

Central Missouri State University **I&A** (Spring 2009)
Drury University **I&A** (Fall 2012)
Evangel University **I** (Accreditation with Conditions) (Fall 2007) **& A** (Provisional Accreditation) (Fall 2007)
Fontbonne University **I&A** (Spring 2008)
Harris-Stowe State University **I** (Spring 2009)
Lincoln University **I&A** (Spring 2006)
Maryville University of Saint Louis **I&A** (Fall 2008)
Missouri Baptist University **I&A** (Spring 2010)
Missouri Southern State University **I** (Fall 2008)
Missouri State University **I&A** (Fall 2010)
Missouri Western State University **I** (Spring 2008)
Northwest Missouri State University **I&A** (Spring 2012)
Saint Louis University **I&A** (Fall 2009)
Southeast Missouri State University **I&A** (Spring 2009)
Truman State University **I&A** (Fall 2009)
University of Missouri-Columbia **I&A** (Fall 2008)
University of Missouri-Kansas City **I** (Accreditation with Conditions) (Spring 2006) **& A** (Accreditation with Probation) (Spring 2006)

University of Missouri-Saint Louis **I&A** (Fall 2010)

Montana
Montana State University—Bozeman **I&A** (Fall 2008)
Montana State University—Billings **I&A** (Spring 2009)
Montana State University—Northern **I&A** (Spring 2008)
The University of Montana—Western **I** (Fall 2008)
University of Montana—Missoula **I&A** (Spring 2012)

Nebraska
Chadron State College **I&A** (Spring 2006)
Concordia University, Nebraska **I&A** (Spring 2012)
Creighton University **I&A** (Spring 2010)
Dana College **I** (Fall 2011)
Doane College **I&A** (Spring 2012)
Hastings College **I** (Spring 2010)
Nebraska Wesleyan University **I** (Accreditation with Conditions) (TBD)
Peru State College **I&A** (Fall 2008)
Union College **I** (Fall 2009)
University of Nebraska at Kearney **I&A** (Fall 2010)
University of Nebraska at Lincoln **I&A** (Fall 2009)
University of Nebraska at Omaha **I&A** (Fall 2008)
Wayne State College **I&A** (Spring 2009)
York College **I** (Provisional Accreditation) (Spring 2007)

Nevada
University of Nevada, Las Vegas **I&A** (Spring 2010)
University of Nevada, Reno **I&A** (Fall 2011)

New Hampshire
Keene State College **I&A** (Spring 2007)
Plymouth State University **I&A** (Spring 2010)

New Jersey
Kean University **I&A** (Fall 2010)
Montclair State University **I&A** (Spring 2012)
New Jersey City University **I&A** (Spring 2012)
Rider University **I&A** (Spring 2012)
Rowan University **I&A** (Spring 2007)
Seton Hall University **I&A** (Fall 2009)
The College of New Jersey **I&A** (Fall 2008)
William Paterson University **I&A** (Spring 2012)

New Mexico
Eastern New Mexico University **I&A** (Accreditation with Conditions) (Fall 2006)
New Mexico Highlands University **I&A** (Accreditation with Conditions) (Fall 2006)
New Mexico State University **I&A** (Fall 2008)
The University of New Mexico **I&A** (Fall 2007)
Western New Mexico University **I&A** (Spring 2010)

New York
Bank Street College of Education **I&A** (Fall 2007)
Brooklyn College of the City University of New York **I&A** (Spring 2010)
Buffalo State College **I&A** (Spring 2008)
Canisius College **I&A** (Fall 2009)
College of Staten Island/CUNY **I&A** (Provisional Accreditation) (Fall 2007)
Concordia College **I** (Fall 2009)
Dowling College **I&A** (Spring 2009)
Five Towns College **I&A** (Fall 2008)
Fordham University **I&A** (Fall 2008)
Hofstra University **I&A** (Spring 2009)
Hunter College of the City University of New York **I&A** (Spring 2009)
Iona College—New Rochelle **I&A** (Spring 2008)
Lehman College-CUNY **I&A** (Spring 2007)
Manhattanville College **I&A** (Spring 2010)
Molloy College **I&A** (Fall 2009)
Mount Saint Mary College **I** (Spring 2010) **& A** (Provisional Accreditation) (Spring 2007)
New York City College of Technology **I** (Spring 2010)
New York Institute of Technology **I&A** (Fall 2010)
Niagara University **I&A** (Spring 2010)
Nyack College **I&A** (Fall 2010)
Pace University **I&A** (Fall 2009)

Queens College **I&A** (Provisional Accreditation) (Spring 2008)
Siena College **I** (Fall 2009)
St. Bonaventure University **I&A** (Fall 2008)
St. John Fisher College **I&A** (Fall 2010)
St. Thomas Aquinas College **I&A** (Fall 2008)
State University of New York at Potsdam **I&A** (Fall 2007)
State University College at Brockport **I&A** (Spring 2008)
State University College at Oneonta **I&A** (Spring 2012)
State University of New York at Fredonia **I&A** (Provisional Accreditation) (Spring 2006)
State University of New York at New Paltz **I&A** (Spring 2008)
State University of New York at Oswego **I&A** (Spring 2007)
State University of New York College at Cortland **I&A** (Spring 2009)
Stony Brook University **I&A** (Spring 2009)
Teachers College Columbia University **I&A** (Spring 2010)
The City College of New York **I&A** (Spring 2009)
The College of Saint Rose **I&A** (Spring 2009)
The Sage Colleges **I&A** (Spring 2007)
University of Rochester **I&A** (Spring 2009)

North Carolina
Appalachian State University **I&A** (Spring 2006)
Barton College **I** (Fall 2010)

Belmont Abbey College **I** (Fall 2010)
Bennett College **I** (Fall 2010)
Campbell University **I&A** (Fall 2008)
Catawba College **I&A** (Fall 2007)
Chowan College **I** (Accredited with Probation) (Spring 2007)
Duke University **I** (Fall 2010)
East Carolina University **I&A** (Spring 2006)
Elizabeth City State University **I&A** (Fall 2007)
Elon University **I&A** (Spring 2007)
Fayetteville State University **I&A** (Spring 2007)
Gardner-Webb University **I&A** (Fall 2011)
Greensboro College **I** (Spring 2008)
Guilford College **I** (Accreditation with Conditions) (Spring 2006)
High Point University **I** (Spring 2008)
Johnson C. Smith University **I** (Spring 2010)
Lees-McRae College **I** (Accreditation with Conditions) (Spring 2006)
Lenoir-Rhyne College **I&A** (Spring 2011)
Livingstone College **I** (Fall 2011)
Mars Hill College **I** (Spring 2012)
Meredith College **I&A** (Fall 2007)
Methodist College **I** (Fall 2010)
Montreat College **I** (Spring 2007)
North Carolina A & T State University **I&A** (Spring 2007)
North Carolina Central University **I&A** (Spring 2007)
North Carolina State University **I&A** (Spring 2007)

North Carolina Wesleyan College **I** (Fall 2007)
Pfeiffer University **I** (Spring 2006)
Queens University of Charlotte **I** (Spring 2008)
Saint Andrews Presbyterian College **I** (Accredited with Probation) (Spring 2007)
Saint Augustine's College **I** (Accredited with Probation) (Spring 2007)
Salem College **I&A** (Spring 2008)
Shaw University **I** (Fall 2011)
Southeastern College at Wake Forest/ Southeastern Baptist Theological Seminary **I** (Spring 2009)
The University of North Carolina at Asheville **I** (Accreditation with Conditions) (Spring 2008)
The University of North Carolina at Pembroke **I&A** (Fall 2007)
University of North Carolina at Chapel Hill **I&A** (Fall 2007)
University of North Carolina at Charlotte **I&A** (Fall 2012)
University of North Carolina at Greensboro **I&A** (Fall 2006)
University of North Carolina at Wilmington **I&A** (Spring 2006)
Wake Forest University **I&A** (Spring 2008)
Warren Wilson College **I** (Fall 2006)
Western Carolina University **I&A** (Fall 2007)
Wingate University **I&A** (Accreditation with Conditions) (Spring 2006)
Winston-Salem State University **I** (Spring 2007)

North Dakota
Dickinson State University **I** (Fall 2010)
Mayville State University **I** (Spring 2006)
Minot State University **I&A** (Accreditation with Conditions) (Fall 2006)
North Dakota State University **I&A** (Spring 2012)
University of North Dakota **I&A** (Spring 2008)
Valley City State University **I** (Fall 2008)

Ohio
Ashland University **I&A** (Fall 2009)
Baldwin-Wallace College **I&A** (Spring 2011)
Bluffton University **I&A** (Fall 2010)
Bowling Green State University **I&A** (Fall 2008)
Capital University **I** (Fall 2011)
Cleveland State University **I&A** (Fall 2009)
John Carroll University **I&A** (Fall 2011)
Kent State University **I&A** (Fall 2008)
Marietta College **I&A** (Fall 2009)
Miami University **I&A** (Spring 2009)
Mount Union College **I** (Fall 2009)
Muskingum College **I&A** (Fall 2010)
Notre Dame College of Ohio **I&A** (Provisional Accreditation) (Fall 2007)
Ohio Northern University **I** (Spring 2012)

Ohio University **I&A** (Spring 2007)
Otterbein College **I&A** (Spring 2009)
Shawnee State University **I** (Fall 2007)
The Ohio State University **I&A** (Accreditation with Conditions) (Spring 2008)
The University of Dayton **I&A** (Fall 2009)
University of Akron **I&A** (Fall 2009)
University of Cincinnati **I&A** (Fall 2011)
University of Findlay **I&A** (Fall 2011)
University of Toledo **I&A** (Spring 2009)
Wittenberg University **I&A** (Spring 2008)
Wright State University **I&A** (Fall 2008)
Youngstown State University **I&A** (Spring 2010)

Oklahoma
Cameron University **I&A** (Fall 2007)
East Central University **I&A** (Fall 2011)
Northeastern State University **I&A** (Fall 2010)
Northwestern Oklahoma State University **I** (Fall 2011) **& A** ()
Oklahoma Baptist University **I** (Fall 2008)
Oklahoma Christian University **I** (Spring 2012)
Oklahoma Panhandle State University **I** (Fall 2008)
Oklahoma State University **I&A** (Spring 2006)

Oklahoma Wesleyan University **I** (Spring 2008)
Oral Roberts University **I&A** (Fall 2006)
Southeastern Oklahoma State University **I&A** (Spring 2009)
Southern Nazarene University **I&A** (Spring 2009)
Southwestern Oklahoma State University **I&A** (Fall 2006)
The University of Oklahoma **I&A** (Spring 2011)
The University of Science and Arts of Oklahoma **I** (Fall 2008)
University of Central Oklahoma **I&A** (Spring 2008)

Oregon
Lewis & Clark College **I&A** (Spring 2010)
Oregon State University **I&A** (Spring 2008)
Portland State University **I&A** (Fall 2008)
University of Portland **I&A** (Fall 2012)
Western Oregon University **I&A** (Fall 2007)

Pennsylvania
Bloomsburg University of Pennsylvania **I&A** (Accreditation with Conditions) (Spring 2008)
California University of Pennsylvania **I&A** (Spring 2006)
Cheyney University of Pennsylvania **I&A** (Fall 2006)
Clarion University of Pennsylvania **I&A** (Spring 2010)
East Stroudsburg University **I&A** (Fall 2012)
Edinboro University of Pennsylvania **I&A** (Spring 2006)

Indiana University of Pennsylvania **I&A** (Fall 2010)

Kutztown University of Pennsylvania **I&A** (Spring 2006)

Lock Haven University of Pennsylvania **I&A** (Spring 2009)

Mansfield University **I&A** (Spring 2006)

Marywood University **I&A** (Fall 2006)

Millersville University of Pennsylvania **I&A** (Spring 2006)

Shippensburg University of Pennsylvania **I&A** (Spring 2006)

Slippery Rock University of Pennsylvania **I&A** (Spring 2008)

Temple University **I&A** (Spring 2007)

The Pennsylvania State University **I&A** (Spring 2011)

University of Scranton **I&A** (Accreditation with Probation) (Fall 2006)

West Chester University **I&A** (Spring 2006)

Puerto Rico

Universidad De Puerto Rico-Rio Piedras Campus **I&A** (Fall 2010)

Rhode Island

Rhode Island College **I** (Fall 2009) **& A** (Accreditation with Conditions) (Spring 2007)

University of Rhode Island **I&A** (Spring 2008)

South Carolina

Anderson University **I** (Fall 2006)

Benedict College **I** (Spring 2008)

Charleston Southern University **I&A** (Spring 2007)

Claflin University **I** (Fall 2011)

Clemson University **I&A** (Spring 2012)

Coastal Carolina University **I&A** (Accreditation with Conditions) (Fall 2006)

Columbia College **I&A** (Spring 2006)

Francis Marion University **I&A** (Fall 2011)

Furman University **I&A** (Spring 2006)

Lander University **I&A** (Fall 2011)

Morris College **I&A** (Fall 2010)

Newberry College **I** (Fall 2010)

North Greenville University **I** (Spring 2010)

Presbyterian College **I** (Spring 2006)

South Carolina State University **I&A** (Spring 2011)

The Citadel **I&A** (Accreditation with Conditions) (Fall 2007)

The College of Charleston **I&A** (Fall 2011)

University of South Carolina **I&A** (Fall 2008)

University of South Carolina Upstate **I&A** (Spring 2010)

University of South Carolina—Aiken **I&A** (Spring 2011)

Winthrop University **I&A** (Fall 2010)

South Dakota

Augustana College **I&A** (Accreditation with Conditions) (Spring 2008)

Black Hills State University **I&A** (Spring 2010)

Dakota State University **I&A** (Spring 2009)

Northern State University **I&A** (Spring 2006)

South Dakota State University **I&A** (Fall 2011)

University of Sioux Falls **I&A** (Spring 2009)

University of South Dakota **I&A** (Spring 2012)

Tennessee

Austin Peay State University **I&A** (Spring 2007)

Belmont University **I&A** (Spring 2007)

Carson-Newman College **I&A** (Fall 2010)

East Tennessee State University **I&A** (Fall 2012)

Freed-Hardeman University **I&A** (Fall 2011)

LeMoyne-Owen College **I** (Spring 2007)

Lipscomb University **I&A** (Spring 2011)

Middle Tennessee State University **I&A** (Fall 2007)

Milligan College **I&A** (Fall 2007)

Southern Adventist University **I** (Spring 2009)

Tennessee State University **I&A** (Spring 2008)

Tennessee Technological University **I&A** (Spring 2010)

The University of Memphis **I&A** (Spring 2008)

The University of Tennessee **I&A** (Fall 2006)

Union University **I&A** (Spring 2012)

University of Tennessee at Chattanooga **I&A** (Fall 2012)

University of Tennessee at Martin **I&A** (Accreditation with Conditions) (Fall 2006)

Vanderbilt University **I&A** (Spring 2009)

Texas

Baylor University **I** (Accreditation with Conditions) (Spring 2006) **& A** (Accreditation with Probation) (Spring 2006)

Prairie View A&M University **I&A** (Spring 2006)

Sam Houston State University **I&A** (Fall 2008)

Stephen F. Austin State University **I&A** (Spring 2007)

Texas A&M University **I&A** (Spring 2009)

Texas Tech University **I&A** (Fall 2006)

Trinity University **I&A** (Spring 2010)

University of Houston **I&A** (Spring 2007)

University of Houston-Clear Lake **I&A** (Spring 2007)

University of North Texas **I&A** (Spring 2009)

University of Texas at Arlington **I&A** (Fall 2008)

Utah

Brigham Young University **I&A** (Fall 2009)

Southern Utah University **I&A** (Spring 2008)

Utah State University **I&A** (Fall 2008)

Weber State University **I** (Fall 2012) **& A** (Accreditation with Conditions) (TBD)

Vermont

The University of Vermont **I&A** (Fall 2009)

Virginia

Eastern Mennonite University **I&A** (Fall 2012)

George Mason University **I&A** (Fall 2010)

Hampton University **I&A** (Fall 2008)

James Madison University **I&A** (Fall 2010)

Liberty University **I&A** (Spring 2008)

Longwood University **I&A** (Fall 2010)

Marymount University **I&A** (Fall 2012)

Norfolk State University **I&A** (Spring 2008)

Old Dominion University **I&A** (Spring 2011)

Radford University **I&A** (Fall 2010)

The College of William and Mary **I&A** (Spring 2010)

Virginia Commonwealth University **I&A** (Spring 2006)

Virginia Polytechnic Institute & State University **I&A** (Spring 2010)

Virginia State University **I&A** (Spring 2006)

Virginia Union University **I** (Spring 2012)

Washington

Central Washington University **I&A** (Spring 2007)

Eastern Washington University **I&A** (Spring 2008)

Gonzaga University **I&A** (Accreditation with Conditions) (Fall 2006)

Pacific Lutheran University **I&A** (Accreditation with Conditions) (TBD)

Seattle Pacific University **I&A** (Spring 2006)

Seattle University **I&A** (Accreditation with Conditions) (Fall 2007)

University of Puget Sound **I&A** (Spring 2010)

Washington State University **I&A** (Spring 2008)

Western Washington University **I&A** (Spring 2012)

Whitworth College **I&A** (Spring 2011)

West Virginia

Alderson-Broaddus College **I** (Spring 2006)

Bethany College **I** (Spring 2011)

Bluefield State College **I** (Spring 2012)

Concord University **I** (Spring 2006)

Fairmont State University **I** (Fall 2010)

Glenville State College **I** (Spring 2012)

Marshall University **I&A** (Fall 2010)

Shepherd University **I** (Fall 2009)

The University of Charleston **I** (Fall 2008)

West Liberty State College **I** (Spring 2010)

West Virginia State University **I** (Spring 2007)

West Virginia University **I&A** (Spring 2011)

West Virginia University at Parkersburg **I** (Fall 2011)

West Virginia Wesleyan College **I** (Spring 2010)

Wisconsin

Alverno College **I&A** (Spring 2012)
Cardinal Stritch University **I&A** (Accreditation with Conditions) (Fall 2007)
Edgewood College **I&A** (Spring 2010)
Marian College of Fond Du Lac **I&A** (Spring 2008)
Marquette University **I** (Accreditation with Conditions) (Fall 2006) **& A** (Accreditation with Probation) (Fall 2006)
Silver Lake College **I&A** (Fall 2009)
University of Wisconsin at River Falls **I&A** (Spring 2010)
University of Wisconsin at Whitewater **I&A** (Spring 2009)
University of Wisconsin at Oshkosh **I&A** (Spring 2009)
University of Wisconsin at Platteville **I&A** (Accreditation with Conditions) (Spring 2006)
Viterbo University **I&A** (Fall 2010)

Wyoming

The University of Wyoming **I&A** (Fall 2007)

Key to Codes:

I: Initial teacher preparation level only; includes all programs at the baccalaureate or post-baccalaureate levels that prepare candidates for the first license to teach.

A: Advanced preparation level only; includes all programs at post-baccalaureate levels for (1) the continuing education of teachers who have previously completed initial preparation or (2) the preparation of other professional school personnel.

I&A: Initial and advanced preparation levels.

Provisional Accreditation: Indicates that the unit has not met one or more of the standards. When the UAB renders this decision, the unit has accredited status, but must satisfy provisions by meeting previously unmet standard(s) within two years. If provisional accreditation is granted, the UAB will require (1) submission of documentation that addresses the unmet standard(s) within six months of the accreditation decision or (2) a focused visit on the unmet standard(s) within two years of the semester of the accreditation decision. When a decision is made by the UAB to require submission of documentation, the institution may choose to waive that option in favor of the focused visit within two years. *Applies to First Accreditation visits.*

Accreditation with Probation: Indicates that the unit does not meet one or more of the NCATE standards and has pervasive problems that limit its capacity

to offer quality programs that adequately prepare candidates. If accreditation with probation is granted, the unit must schedule an on-site visit within two years of the semester in which the probationary decision was rendered. This visit will mirror the process for first accreditation. The unit as part of this visit must address all NCATE standards in effect at the time of the probationary review. Following the on-site review, the UAB will (1) continue accreditation or (2) revoke accreditation. If accreditation is continued, the next on-site visit is scheduled for five years after the semester of the probationary visit. *Applies to Continuing Accreditation visits.*

Accreditation with Conditions: Indicates that the unit has not met one or more of the NCATE standards. When the UAB renders this decision, the unit maintains its accredited status, but must satisfy conditions by meeting the previously unmet standard(s) within two years. If accreditation with conditions is granted, the UAB will require (1) submission of documentation that addresses the unmet standard(s) within six months of the accreditation decision or (2) a focused visit on the unmet standard(s) within two years of the accreditation decision. When a decision is made by the UAB to require submission of documentation, the institution may choose to waive that option in favor of the focused visit within two years. If documentation is submitted under the terms specified in the above paragraph, the UAB may (1) continue accreditation or (2) require a focused visit within one year of the semester in which the documentation was reviewed by the UAB. After a focused visit, the UAB will (1) continue accreditation or (2) revoke accreditation. If continuing accreditation is granted, the next on-site visit is scheduled for five years following the semester in which the continuing accreditation visit occurred. This scheduling maintains the unit's original five-year accreditation cycle. *Applies to Continuing Accreditation visits.*

Lp: In accordance with reporting requirements of Title II of the Higher Education Act, this institution has been identified as "low performing" by its state. For further information regarding the state action, please contact the appropriate state agency.

Reprinted with permission from National Council for Accreditation of Teacher Education. *www.ncate.org.*

INDEX